¡Viva George!

Number Forty-nine
Jack and Doris Smothers Series in Texas History, Life, and Culture

¡Viva George!

Celebrating Washington's Birthday at the US-Mexico Border

ELAINE A. PEÑA

University of Texas Press *Austin*

Publication of this work was made possible in part by support from the J. E. Smothers, Sr., Memorial Foundation and the National Endowment for the Humanities.

Cover photo: Abrazo children embrace in the middle of the Juárez-Lincoln International Bridge, 2015. Alexandra Carriedo Villarreal and Franco Garza Carmona represent Mexico. Valeria Lucia Montemayor and John Roman Galo represent the United States. Courtesy of the Washington's Birthday Celebration Association, Laredo, Texas.

Printed in the United States of America
First edition, 2020

⊗ The paper used in this book meets the minimum requirements of ANSI/NISO Z39.48-1992 (R1997) (Permanence of Paper).

Library of Congress Cataloging-in-Publication Data
Names: Peña, Elaine A., 1979- author.
Title: ¡Viva George! celebrating Washington's birthday at the US-Mexico border / Elaine A. Peña.
Description: First edition. | Austin : University of Texas Press, 2020. | Includes bibliographical references and index.
Identifiers: LCCN 2020008799
ISBN 978-1-4773-2143-0 (cloth)
ISBN 978-1-4773-2144-7 (paperback)
ISBN 978-1-4773-2145-4 (ebook)
ISBN 978-1-4773-2146-1 (ebook other)
Subjects: LCSH: Festivals—Texas—Laredo—History. | Festivals—Mexico—Nuevo Laredo—History. | Political customs and rites—Texas—Laredo. | Political customs and rites—Mexico—Nuevo Laredo. | Festivals—Texas—Laredo—International cooperation—History. | Festivals—Mexico—Nuevo Laredo—International cooperation—History. | Ethnosociology—Mexican-American Border Region. | Laredo (Tex.)—Relations—Mexico—Nuevo Laredo.
Classification: LCC GT4811.L37 P46 2020 | DDC 394.269764/462—dc23
LC record available at https://lccn.loc.gov/2020008799

doi:10.7560/321430

For Marti Franco

Contents

Acknowledgments

I vividly remember sketching ideas for this book a couple of months before I submitted my dissertation to Northwestern University's graduate school. Thirteen years on, properly acknowledging all of the people, organizations, and institutions that helped me complete this project seems like an impossible task, but I'll try my best.

I was able to conduct research for this book with the generous support from the National Endowment for the Humanities (Summer Stipends Award, FT-60803), the Texas Red Men Foundation, George Washington University's facilitating fund, and Columbian College facilitating fund. And while I could not accept the Ford Foundation postdoctoral fellowship I was awarded for this project in 2007, knowing that I had put together a successful application buoyed me forward.

I will be forever grateful to Diana Taylor, who championed my research and stuck by me through multiple rounds of applications. I would also like to thank Mary Weismantel, Stephen Pitti, Josef Barton, Ann Braude, Phil Goff, and Paul Nugent for their patience and understanding. Colleagues at the George Washington University, the Smithsonian National Museum of American History, and the Smithsonian Latino Center have also helped me navigate and complete this project. Special thanks to the late Jim Miller, Gayle Wald, Melani McAlister, Chad Heap, Terry Murphy, Tom Guglielmo, Kip Kosek, Suleiman Osman, Libby Anker, Jamie Cohen-Cole, Dara Orenstein, Richard Longstreth, David Bjelajac, Mona Azadi, Tony López, Manuel Cuellar, Peter Kornbluh, Roland Roebuck, Steve Velasquez, and Eduardo Díaz in Washington, DC. Taking a step back with colleagues and friends at the University of Edinburgh helped me cross the finish line. Richard Baxstrom, Soledad García Ferrari, Toby Kelly, James Smith, and Paul Nugent supported my interest in global and comparative border studies. Conversations with scholars who work outside the context of the US-Mexico border motivated me at key moments: Isabella Soi (Università di Cagliari), José-Maria Muñoz, Sidy Cissokho, Hugh Lamarque, Michel Wahome, Wolfgang Zeller, Gerhard Anders, Jean-Benoit Falisse, Delwar Hussain, Aaron Kappeler, and Fraser Macdonald. A special thanks to Pete Kingsley and Dave Greyhound for reminding me about the importance of the bigger picture.

This project has also benefited from questions and comments generated at conferences and invited lectures. Particularly fruitful were presentations of my research at the Hemispheric Institute of Performance and Politics *encuentros* in Bogotá, Santiago de Chile, and Mexico City; at the second world conference of the Association of Borderlands Studies in Vienna, Austria, and Budapest, Hungary; at African Borderlands Research Network (ABORNE) meetings; and as part of the Newberry Library's Borderlands and Latina/o Studies seminar. I also appreciate the feedback I received when I was invited to discuss this project at Queen's University Belfast, Emory University, University of St. Andrews, Yale University, Arizona State University, University of Manchester, Stanford University, University of Texas at Austin, and the University of Illinois Champaign-Urbana. I am also grateful to friends and colleagues who encouraged me to move forward: Tatiana Andronova, Yvette Benavides, Phil Burnham, Geraldo Cadava, Junot Díaz, Pedro Díaz Del Río, Micaela Díaz Sánchez, Guillermo Gómez-Peña, Michelle Hayford, Matt Hedstrom, Benjamin Johnson, E. Patrick Johnson, Deborah Kanter, José Luis Ledesma Vera, Cesar Martínez Silva, Kristy Nabhan-Warren, Kevin O'Neill, Julio Pantoja, Ramón Rivera Servera, Richard Schechner, and Jennifer Scheper Hughes. I would also like to extend my sincerest gratitude to Casey Kittrell, my editor at the University of Texas Press, for his vision and his steadfastness.

My research support teams in Laredo, Nuevo Laredo, and Mexico City played the most important role on this journey. Joe Moreno and Renèe LaPerrier at the Laredo Public Library; Celina Alvarado, Nino Cardenas, Marissa Espinoza, and Arlene Perez at the Washington's Birthday Celebration Association; Margarita Araiza, Andrea Ordoñez, and Christina Davila Saucedo at the Webb County Heritage Foundation; Jeanette Hatcher at Texas A&M International University; David Lintz, director of the Red Men Museum and Library in Waco, Texas; and Miguel Conchas at the Laredo Chamber of Commerce were all invaluably generous. Raymundo Ríos Mayo and Manuel Ceballos Ramírez as well as Carlos Zúñiga Garza at Nuevo Laredo's Archivo Municipal and Veronica González in Mexico City also helped me immensely. Marti Franco, Ricarda Suneson Ortiz, and

Ronald Barnstone assisted me with logistics on both sides of the border. I would also like to acknowledge the amenability of Sally Ann Smith and Lynn Marie Campaigne, who allowed me to look at Joseph Netzer's personal papers. Phil Nohl, who provided me with film footage of Washington's Birthday Celebration bullfights in Nuevo Laredo in the 1930s and 1940s, was also notably generous.

Although I have used pseudonyms to protect my interlocuter's privacy, I would like to acknowledge the kindness of several Port of Laredo actors here using their real names. City of Laredo mayor Pete Saenz, his wife Minerva Saenz, and his daughter Monica Saenz Vigil have been instrumental to this effort and, moreover, wonderful family friends. Dr. Minita Ramírez at Texas A&M International University graciously opened doors for me in the summer of 2013. I would like to extend a very special thank you to Candy Hein for her unwavering support and generosity. Victor M. Oliveros, Gene Garza, and Gerald Schwebel reoriented me at pivotal moments. Norbert Dickman, former ambassador to Mexico Tony Garza, Gil Kerlikowske, Robert Harris, and Carl Landrum have been terrific conversation partners. Pitín Guajardo, Amado Chapa, Edgardo Bueno, José Gamez, José Tellez, Andy Ramos, and Carlos Villarreal of LULAC Council No. 12, as well as members of the International Good Neighbor Council–Laredo and the Consejo Internacional de Buena Vecindad–Nuevo Laredo—especially Triana Bazán, Lupita Zepeda, Tina Cerda, and Amelia "Chacha" Bravo—showed me how their organizations maintain cross-border relationships. Mariana Barbarena Asiain of TAMIU's Binational Center provided me with important resources early on.

Dozens of WBCA actors and honored guests, past and present, walked me through the logistics of the festivities and opened my eyes to the cooperation expertise and fierce work ethic the celebration requires: Randy and Nancy Blair, Manuel B. Bravo, Eloy Cantu, Veronica Castillon, Melissa Cantu Cigarroa, US Congressman Henry Cuellar (D-Texas Dist. 28), Ramón Garza Barrios, Pati Guajardo, Ricardo Hoyos Arizpe, John Keck, Dennis Longoria, Alberto Magnon, Jimmy Notzon, Judy Notzon, Roseanne Palacios, Eddie Villarreal, Bob Weathers, Marilyn de Llano, Alan Jackson, Glen Jackson, Roseanne Winch Potts, and Texas state senator Judith Zaffirini (D-Dist. 21). I am also sincerely grateful to Graciela "Chela" Gonzalez, my preschool teacher at Kristi Linn's Academy, and her husband Tony Gonzalez. They helped me make ends meet with accommodation in Laredo when research funds were lacking. Most importantly, they reminded me how proud they were of me every chance they got.

My people in Texas and New Mexico as well as my extended family in

Spain deserve a lot of credit. Fernando Peña Jr., Sandra, Alonzo, Ozzy, and Angie Gonzalez, and Gustavo Peña and Alicia "Bunny" Gonzalez were by my side every step of the way, as were my dearest friends: Marisela Chávez, Rita Urquijo-Ruiz, Andi García Linn, Micah Linn, Veronica Solis, jesse moreno, Crystal Don, Michael Avila, Miriam Diaz, Richard and Pam Slocum, Navor and Margaret Chávez, and Yolanda Grijalva. My parents-in-law in Madrid, Álvaro Muñoz López and María Teresa Martín Bourgon, as well as my *cuñados* and *cuñadas* Álvaro Muñoz, Elena Peña, Santiago Muñoz, Lourdes Otero, Luis Muñoz, Juan Muñoz, Cristina Torío, Pablo Muñoz, and Nieves Montes remained enthusiastic and curious even as they had to listen to me go on and on about the George Washington's Birthday Celebration for the past ten-odd years. My partner José-María Muñoz has been far away from me for many years (he has a permanent position at the University of Edinburgh, and I have a permanent position at the George Washington University), but we have managed to make it work. He, more than anyone, knows how challenging this process has been for me. Here's to a future that we can share in closer proximity.

¡Viva George!

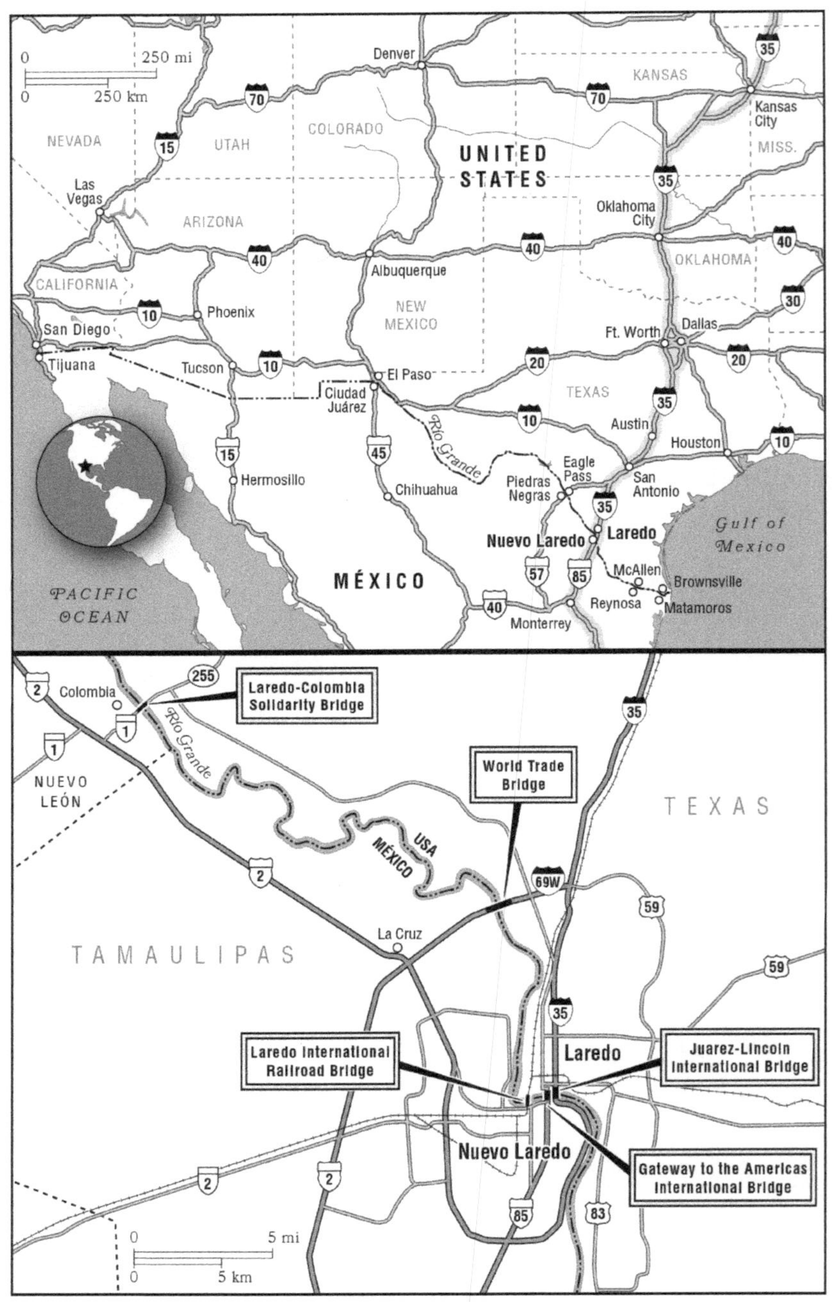

Port of Laredo–Nuevo Laredo, Tamaulipas, Mexico, and Laredo, Texas, USA. Courtesy of Elaine A. Peña.

INTRODUCTION

From Border *Capricho* to Border Scaffolding

As an academic who specializes in the study of borders, I often tell my students on the first day of class that I am a US citizen by measure of one mile. This admission gets their attention and gives them a concrete starting point from which to understand the basic juridical logic that underpins US citizenship. Born on the American side of the Rio Grande (Río Bravo), a short distance from the international boundary line that separates Nuevo Laredo, Tamaulipas (Mexico), from Laredo, Texas, USA, I explain, makes me a *jus soli* citizen—a right-of-soil citizen. *Jus sanguinis*, citizenship determined by right of blood (*sangre* in Spanish), I add, also applies to me because both my parents are US citizens. My citizenship, established by the confluence of geography, time, and chance, was one of my greatest sources of capital growing up. I did not have to think twice about using the Gateway to the Americas International Bridge to "go across" to Nuevo Laredo. Before the days of mandatory passport travel, I would cross back to Laredo with a confident and quick, accent-neutral identification: "US citizen." Raised between two countries, I learned how to deduce and decide in English, Spanish, and Spanglish. And while my cross-border social education at the Port of Laredo may differentiate me from US citizens born or naturalized elsewhere—in San Juan, in Boston, in St. Louis, in San Diego, in Honolulu, or in Dededo—we remain, as the pledge asserts, indivisible.[1]

I share part of my border biography to illuminate the ties that bind land, law, and mobility, but I have always been careful not to share too many personal details in my classes. I do not want to risk being misidentified as the professor from the border who teaches her life story. Doing so would obfuscate the larger point of my scholarship, which is to demonstrate how analyzing the microhistories of border-crossing politics and privileges (or the lack thereof) alongside broader political economic shifts can help clarify contemporary hot-button debates around immigration, security, and trade. And not just at the Port of Laredo or in a North American context but globally.

I am inclined to share some of my story here because this book explores these issues in far more depth than any academic lecture or workshop I have designed or contributed to in the past ten years. I will narrate key aspects of conducting fieldwork at "home," as it were, but also at a time when US-Mexico border environments and actors are daunted by the moral and political responsibilities that go hand-in-hand with caring for asylum-seeking families, by the ubiquity of transnational criminal organization activity, and by highly polemical plans to construct a border wall.[2]

I will begin with a quirky—and surprisingly relevant—anecdote about my mother. The story goes that she got stuck in the middle of the Washington's Birthday Celebration (WBC) parade traffic while in labor. Continuing a tradition started in 1898 by the Improved Order of Red Men (IORM)—a Baltimore-born fraternity whose members model themselves after the Sons of Liberty and the Society of Tammany—generations of Laredoans and neolaredenses (residents of Nuevo Laredo) have participated in the parade.[3] The annual procession features sleepy but well-coiffed Society of Martha Washington (SMW) debutantes being transported atop elaborately adorned flatbed trucks, Princess Pocahontas and her court on horseback, as well as public school and private business entries.[4] For over a century Port of Laredo residents have sponsored floats to communicate their mission statements in the colors of the US and Mexican flags: red, white, and blue; green, white, and red; or combinations of all. Additionally, schoolchildren from both sides of the border have a long track record of enlivening the march with meticulously choreographed routines and/or piercing bugle arrangements. Hearing my mother recount what was to be a false-alarm trip to the hospital that morning never got old; her guilt game could be charming. Only half-joking, she would complain that labor pain, *excruciating pain*, was prolonged (and this is the polite version) because Mexican acrobats and Shriner clowns driving toy-size cars had blocked the intersection.

At several points in my early life we lived near the parade route, so I developed an intimate connection with the festivities. Every birthday I can remember involved getting up extra early to watch the parade. Some years I would watch and work—sell water bottles and soda cans from an ice chest to make easy money. Most years my family would go to popular WBC events like the carnival and the Jalapeño Festival. The smell of deep-fried corndogs made me dizzy and watching contestants eat jalapeños hand-over-fist troubled me, but I looked forward to going all the same. Like hometown fairs elsewhere, the WBC festivities give people something to do. They not only guarantee fun and promise novelty but also create multiple opportunities to see and to be seen.

It wasn't until my senior year studying at Laredo's only parochial high school (which I attended on scholarship) that I became aware of how "popular" activities and the crowds they attracted differed significantly from the guest lists of the WBC festivities' more exclusive events. A class divide—informed not by American or Mexican citizenship necessarily but by over two centuries of strategic intermarriage and property acquisition—determined who could participate in and watch certain rituals. The majority of Laredoans and neolaredenses, for example, are unable to secure tickets to the SMW pageant, the Princess Pocahontas pageant, or the League of Latin American United Citizens (LULAC) Noche Mexicana gala. In contrast, several of my well-to-do classmates, including many friends who lived in Nuevo Laredo and crossed the border every day to attend school, participated in the festivities as debutantes or escorts.

I attended an elite event for the first time in 1996. Watching my best friend participate in the Princess Pocahontas pageant was overwhelming: the costumes, set design, and lighting scheme were dramatic and dazzling. I remember feeling immense joy and pride for my friend. But I also recall being secretly confused by the voice-overs and choreography that narrated Native American tribal histories. I had learned a bit about the history and culture of North American indigenous tribes in school, but those lessons did not match up with the spectacle I was watching. I did not yet have the vocabulary to explain my point of view, so I never entertained my doubts out loud; and, it seemed, neither did my peers, my teachers, nor my elders.

Those experiences inspired me to study the WBC festivities, but this book itself draws from over a decade of research conducted on both sides of the border. It follows two trajectories. The first addresses the doubts that the WBC festivities raised for me while growing up in Laredo and explores questions that have developed since I left Texas and grew into my profession. One of the many difficult tasks that I faced while conducting research was allowing myself to search for the deeper significance of the idiosyncratic, bizarre, or just plain offensive aspects of the celebration. I had to "make the familiar [less] strange and the strange familiar" to analyze borderlanders' penchant for "playing Indian," "playing colonial," and "playing Mexican" every year for over a century.[5] With that said, I have done my best to turn that uneasiness, the impulse to disparage controversial racial performances outright, into an opportunity. I challenged myself

Improved Order of Red Men members "playing Indian" as part of the Washington's Birthday Celebration International Parade, 1934. Courtesy of the Washington's Birthday Celebration Association, Laredo.

to grow as an ethnographer, as a historian, and as a geographer; to pursue labor-intensive and out-of-the box research trajectories (e.g., tracing the civil religious aspects of the celebration through the eyes of the IORM fraternity, scripting a theater play based on preliminary ideas, and even participating in a horseback ride-along with Border Patrol agents) to understand the origins, development, and broader impact of the celebration.

Unlike other studies of the WBC, this book does not attempt to offer a comprehensive history of the festival.[6] Simply put, that task is too daunting. Archival records show, for example, that the 1898 celebration of Washington's birthday was not the City of Laredo's first attempt. An earlier generation of border residents had commemorated Washington's birthday in 1870 with "five races (foot and horse) and cash prizes."[7] The truth is that I am still awestruck by the celebration's tenaciousness and resilience. The WBC festivities have grown from being a two-day event at the end of the nineteenth century to a monthlong extravaganza featuring more than thirty events that generate approximately $15 million in revenue.[8] The festivities include the above-mentioned SMW presentation and ball, Princess Pocahontas pageant, Jalapeño Festival, a youth parade, an international parade, and a Noche Mexicana gala as well as the Mr. South Texas luncheon (past honorees include George W. Bush and US Senator John Cornyn, R-Texas), and the International Bridge Ceremony. Bejeweled colonial gowns and Indian princess costumes may cost anywhere between $5,000 and $50,000. Depending on the political climate, WBC events may not take place in Nuevo Laredo. Even then, as the following chapters will show, high-profile figures from both sides of the border diligently attend the festivities to fulfill their duties, to prove a point, or to seal a deal.

As one of the WBC's longest-running traditions and the most public binational exercise, the International Bridge Ceremony will take center stage in this story.[9] State and nonstate actors based on both sides of the border have had a hand in meticulously casting and choreographing that ritual each year since its first iteration in 1898.[10] Its current configuration features US and Mexican politicians, clergy members, diplomats, law enforcement officers, and even two men portraying George Washington and Miguel Hidalgo walking toward each other on the International Bridge to embrace. More evocative still, the rite showcases the participation of two "American" children representing Laredo who are attired in eighteenth-

Miguel Hidalgo (Claudio Lerma) and George Washington (Douglas Howland) pose for the press after embracing in the middle of the Juárez-Lincoln International Bridge, 2017. Abrazo children and US Border Patrol agents sitting on the dais look on. US abrazo children: Ella Alessandra Gonzalez and William Joseph Palumbo; Mexico abrazo children: Cassandra Cabrera Zamudio and Mateo Cañamar Morales. Courtesy of Elaine A. Peña.

century colonial costumes and two "Mexican" children representing Nuevo Laredo who are dressed as a *charro* and a *china poblana*.

This book's second research trajectory pursues how those "gateway performances" do more than advance US interests and ideals. To be fair, the festivities' US-centric preferences arise from its namesake: it honors George Washington, not George Washington and Benito Juárez (or any one of Mexico's *águilas caídas* [fallen heroes]).[11] The evidence presented here, however, will show how that conclusion underestimates the ability that borderlanders have for capitalizing on their either/or environments.

Key Concepts: Border Enactment, Border Scaffolding, and the Expectation of Ritual

As a work of anthropological history, this book draws on archival research, including access to personal papers and uncatalogued documents, and fieldwork conducted intermittently between 2006 and 2017 to shed new light on the history of cooperation at the Port of Laredo and to make bold claims about US-Mexico border security, immigration, and trade issues. I propose that events staged at or across an international boundary line and which involve the repurposing of border infrastructure to occasion face-to-face contact are *border enactments*. Whether presented on a reoccurring or ad hoc basis, border enactments create opportunities for an international "audience" to discern mutual behavior, to publicly signal willingness to co-ordinate, or to subtlety indicate disillusionment. Border enactments can gather people en masse, including an international media presence tasked with documenting and circulating images, text, and soundscapes of the proceedings. The takeaway point here, and one that transcends the site-specific characteristics of the WBC festivities and the International Bridge Ceremony, is that producing border enactments can maintain as well as generate cross-border lines of communication during times of crisis.[12]

This project underlines the celebration's binational and cross-border characteristics to develop the concept of a border enactment for cross-cultural and comparative purposes. It demonstrates how port-of-entry actors can use border enactments to prove, suggest, intuit, or imagine bonds that exceed the politics of international boundary lines. Following Henri Lefebvre's critical approach to space production and his thinking about "representational spaces," this analysis not only factors in but also highlights planning efforts that occur in conjunction with festive time.[13] It takes us behind the scenes to consider the nitty-gritty details and cross-border work that go into coordinating "American" and "Mexican" rituals, events, and popular gatherings in their "proper place"—on national soil or in between two nations.

This study draws attention to three of the celebration's high-profile traditions: the International Bridge Ceremony (described above); LULAC Council No. 12's custom of honoring two Señor [or Señora] Internacional award recipients during their Noche Mexicana gala; and the SMW's long, albeit inconsistent, history of inviting a debutante from Mexico to participate in an American colonial pageant. Those events are noteworthy because their success depends on the strength of sustained bilateral communication and cross-border relationships with neolaredenses as well as with actors based across the Republic of Mexico. In practice that means private citizens and public officials from both sides of the border must plan year-round. On a volunteer basis, those actors bear the responsibility of finding ways to collaborate across different levels of government, in the best and the worst of circumstances. Some nongovernmental actors may even pay out of pocket or take vacation days to get the job done. All the same, interest in maintaining cross-border networks may not always be public-spirited or altruistic; putting in the work not only secures the celebration's future but may also protect border elites' deeply interlaced livelihoods.

Taking that argument a step further, I have developed the idea of *border scaffolding* to explain the WBC festivities' reach and impact beyond its appearance as a symbolic communication of goodwill.[14] Scaffolding (*andamiaje* in Spanish) refers to the temporary wooden or metal structures that surround a building while it is being cleaned (e.g., window washing) or while it is undergoing repair (e.g., roof replacement). The building under construction in this story is the Port of Laredo. We can think of the International Bridge Ceremony as a yearly opportunity to maintain and polish. Erected (performed) binationally every year during the month of February, the scaffolding (the WBC festivities, and the *abrazo* ritual in particular) reinforce and repair the port of entry's "gateway" reputation—an optimal place to move goods and the best place to meet and form relationships with members of North America's and Latin America's business elite.[15]

While not referring specifically to borders, anthropologist Claudio Lomnitz's views of the give-and-take elements of nationalism and nationality can help us envision how the tradition of meeting in the middle of the international bridge can double as border scaffolding. He writes:

> The shape of a territory is never perfectly attuned to the traditional habitat of a people, even in cases when such relations between a people and a ter-

> ritory can be credibly made. *Territories need to be claimed, boundaries need to be enforced, and so they are dependent not only on the national community, but also on its neighbors*. In short, neither a people nor its connections to a state and territory are stable facts. Instead, these relationships need constantly to be shaped and reshaped. (emphasis mine)[16]

Maps, treaties, and good old common sense may evince the fact that the soil underneath one's feet may belong to, or technically fall under the jurisdiction of, one nation or one union. Nevertheless, those sound assumptions are unreliable because, as Lomnitz eloquently reminds us, territory is lived.[17] Members of congress or of parliament, for example, can debate all they want, but borderlanders' ways of inhabiting space—their daily rounds, quotidian habits, interactions, and negotiations—ultimately determine what a nation becomes and how territorial affiliation plays out in practice (e.g., the difference between living in Northern Ireland or in the Republic of Ireland).

This research also underscores the broader significance of Port of Laredo actors' long-standing commitment to playing Indian, playing colonial, and playing Mexican as part of the WBC festivities. I specifically address how Laredoans and neolaredenses have consistently used border enactments to revisit, fine tune, and validate commerce-friendly images of nation and nationality. The content and management of those rituals have changed over time, of course, but as anthropologist Roy Rappaport reminds us, "Rituals composed entirely of new elements are likely to fail to become established (the test of the establishment being that they be performed again on categorically similar occasions)." In dialogue with Victor Turner, Rappaport does concede that "there is room for the rearrangement of elements, and even for discarding some elements and introducing others, but invention is limited and the sanction of previous performance is maintained."[18] In short, repetition with a meticulously crafted sense of decorum, even if enacted with indifference (as will be the case at different moments in the history of the International Bridge Ceremony), communicates stability.

Building on interdisciplinary debates centered on ritual as an object and method of study, each chapter attends to how the *expectation of ritual*—that is, the ways in which generations of families, businesses, civil society organizations, and government agencies on both sides of the border anticipate the festivities and plan accordingly year after year—has strengthened the Port of Laredo's trade and international commerce profile, grown the tourist economy, and even advanced border health initiatives.[19] Proceeding with the understanding that "play" is distinct from "ritual," the concept underlines how borderlanders thoughtfully fashion ways of playing colonial, playing Indian, and playing Mexican as part of the ritual preparation process.[20] Pivoting away from discussions of pathos, poverty, and illegality that currently dominate academic and policy conversations about US-Mexico border history, this project draws our attention to "playing" to give insight to overlooked aspects of border social life.

This book's sustained focus on infrastructure and ritual will also advance debates in the anthropology of infrastructure and develop new pathways for the study of border cooperation among state and nonstate actors.[21] Scholarship and popular analyses focused on border infrastructure—bridges, gates, fences, walls, and tunnels—have consistently alerted us to the ways in which international as well as intranational tensions are deeply enmeshed in the local and the particular.[22] Talk about fences and walls is particularly revealing. They can go big or go small when making political, ideological, or religious claims. They can signal the separation of economic and political systems (e.g., the Berlin Wall, the DMZ) while simultaneously shaping formal and informal economic networks.[23] They can pop up at a moment's notice in response to a surge of refugees, as a means to gain control of contested territory, and/or as a way to maintain nationalist fantasies of racial purity.[24] And while globalization and economic integration narratives may want to tell another story, the bottom line is that, with or without border infrastructure, we do not live in a "borderless world."[25]

Recent ethnographic research, applied architectural studies, and cross-border urban planning approaches have added nuance to those generalizations.[26] Scholars have identified border infrastructure's "tactical" and "productive" qualities: how a federal agency's use of fences can "produce specific patterns of trauma" or how walls can secure the border and offer "the very backbone of a borderland ecosystem."[27] Bridges, however, often produce a different conversation. Unlike polarizing interpretations of the role of walls and fences in modern society that position them as necessary (because they provide unparalleled security benefits) or as antiquated (because they are medieval solutions to a twenty-first-century problem), international bridges are touted as symbols of friendship, modernity, and progress. But they can also be used to divide and control. Taking on the challenge of looking beyond the physical and immediate function of border infrastructure, this book invites us to ask what else international bridges can do.[28] It will encourage us to think about international bridges not only as examples of infrastructure that facilitate movement but also as repositories of transregional memory, as platforms for negotiation, as a course of action for reconciliation, and as places to engage in festive security.[29]

Border Enactments in North America and Beyond

The US-Mexico boundary line accommodates border enactments that range from the lighthearted to the heartbreaking. Among these well-known events and traditions is the stretching of "Hands across the Bridge" between Brownsville, Texas, and Matamoros, Tamaulipas, as part of Charro Days (established in 1937).[30] In the 1950s champion horses raced on both sides of the physical border at Agua Prieta, Sonora, and Douglas, Arizona.[31] Indeed, the tone and frequency of repurposing border infrastructure and barriers changed significantly after the Hart-Cellar Immigration Act of 1965 created "impossible subjects" out of economic migrants from the Western Hemisphere.[32] US president Richard Nixon's war on drugs proclamation in 1969 further promoted the hardening of the border and perturbed border business communities.[33] This study draws on the work of US-Mexico border scholars who have painstakingly examined the contours of those shifts (for example, the historicizing of the construction of physical barriers along the border, the planning of paramilitary operations, and the management of war-on-terror politics) as well as having coined evocative terms such as "tortilla curtain" and "border games" to analyze escalation processes.[34]

Using border infrastructure as a meeting point, especially after the events of September 11, 2001, is sometimes the only way loved ones can see each other, pray together, get married, or simply attempt to hold hands. At the same time, border enactments can unabashedly play up irreverence or indulge in whimsy (the *capricho* in this chapter's subtitle)—such as playing volleyball or doing yoga across the boundary line—while making intimate political statements.[35] For example, the Paso del Norte Bridge at El Paso, Texas, and Ciudad Juárez, Chihuahua, has doubled as a stage upon which women from both sides of the border braided their hair to form one uninterrupted chain, tying themselves to one another as a symbol of discontent with the results of the 2016 US presidential election.[36] The border fence at Tecate, Baja California, and Tecate, California, has also been used as a repurposing point. In the fall of 2017 it doubled as the site of a "giant picnic" where attendees ate the same food, shared water, and listened to live music. Half of the band played on the Mexican side of the fence and the other half on US soil. The *eyes of the dreamer*—an oversized art installation straddling the international boundary line—linked the border enactment to pro-DACA (Deferred Action for Childhood Arrivals) efforts.[37]

In drawing our attention to celebratory, recreational, or subversively playful border enactments, this book is not downplaying the perverse border logics that make interacting through a fence a way of life. It seeks to broaden how we think about border security options, with a particular orientation toward nonviolent and demilitarized engagement. To that end, this research thinks with studies conducted at borders located outside of North America to make clear that the festive repurposing of border infrastructure and barriers is much more than the product of US-Mexico relations. Border enactments are a global phenomenon. And while political context will inevitably vary from place to place, we will learn how borderlanders across the globe act in similar ways at and across international boundary lines.[38] The Pan-European picnic staged near Sopron, Hungary, on August 19, 1989, for example, reminds us how border enactments can play a pivotal role in initiating social change. As Helmut Kohl, then German chancellor, noted, "The first stone [had] been knocked out of the Berlin Wall" at the picnic.[39]

We will find that border enactments staged at and beyond the Port of Laredo are much more than goodwill gestures or opportunities to consolidate and/or compartmentalize national identity. They can resolve international and cross-border tensions as well as sustain communication in spite of a volatile political landscape and charged regional histories. This book will highlight those positive developments, but it will not underplay the inconsistencies or overinflate the value of symbolic reciprocity for the sake of argument. It will not insist on notions of cultural hybridity or "contact zones" as neutral spaces of engagement.[40] Nor will it forget how uneven living standards and class disparities in South Texas and northern Tamaulipas are intimately connected to the transborder dynamics that make the WBC festivities a success.[41]

As I build on WBC-focused studies that pinpoint how the festivities impact race, ethnicity, class, citizenship, and gender dynamics at the border, I will not shy away from the fact that border enactments can also polarize.[42] This book makes time to examine quieted inconsistencies and to reflect on instances of public protest at different points in the festivities' history: for example, protestors chanting "Let them eat cake" outside the SMW colonial ball and pageant in the late 1960s or holding up posters of missing children at the International Bridge Ceremony in 2006. It will also ask us to think through how several aspects of the binational rituals under consideration prioritize differences based on language (Spanish or English), history (águilas caídas or George Washington), and patriotic customs (for instance, Zogist salute or palm placed against the heart), even when the relevance of those distinctions may vary on a day-to-day basis.

A Note on Research Methods

As mentioned earlier, I was quite familiar with WBC events from a young age—as a spectator but not as a researcher. Still, I had the gall to jump into this project. Even before defending my doctoral dissertation in 2006, I had started to sketch out my ideas with think pieces, drawings, and scripts.[43] I attended the festivities that year even though I did not have a clear plan of action. Pushing forward for the sake of pushing, I realized that I was more than ready to listen but not prepared enough to understand what I was hearing. I had read the relevant literature on the history of the celebration and had reviewed the port of entry's political and economic history. I was well versed in anthropological theory, race and ethnicity theory, transnational studies, and US-Mexico border studies, but I could not get past asking basic questions. Why commemorate George Washington's birthday at the Port of Laredo? How did Laredoans and neolaredenses come to participate in the festivities? Why do Laredo-area high school girls and boys dress up as Indian princesses and Indian chiefs while both Laredoans and neolaredenses dress up as colonial Americans? How did an embrace shared between George Washington and Miguel Hidalgo come to be part of the International Bridge Ceremony? How did these historical figures get so far away from home?

In retrospect, I spent too much time questioning the validity of the ideas behind the festivities, wondering if the ritualistic mythologizing of history could lead to any conclusion other than evidence that communities invent traditions. Eric Hobsbawm, one of the great interpreters of the notion of "invented traditions," notes that rituals—exercises that seek to impress values and norms through repetition—"are evidence." Those practices are "important symptoms and therefore indicators of problems [or solutions, as I argue] which might not be otherwise recognized, and developments which are otherwise difficult to identify and to date."[44] Reading up on dramaturgical approaches to "the importance of occasions" and critical studies of nation and nationalism helped me take a big step back.[45]

Discussions with colleagues around this time were not helpful, often producing a bit of shock and then nervous laughter, followed by a weak "good luck" or "that's interesting" (and sometimes a condescending pat on the back). Listening in different settings (at a WBC event or on a business trip) to Port of Laredo residents reflect on why they think the celebration is misunderstood helped me put my research questions into perspective. I was particularly struck by one WBC associate's standard response to the question, "Why do you celebrate George Washington's birthday in Laredo?" Answer: "Why aren't you celebrating George Washington's birthday where you live?"[46]

Thinking myopically about patriotism's "proper" geography (as if places like Boston, Philadelphia, and Washington, DC, or Mexico City, Puebla, and Guadalajara could be the only worthy generators of American history or Mexican history) was a hurdle I cleared only after figuring out why and how the IORM fraternity came to organize the WBC festivities in 1898 (explained in chapter 1).[47] Learning about the civil religious aspects of IORM members' patriotic behavior also allowed me to see playing Indian, playing colonial, and playing Mexican as something more than racist caricature or racial desire. An important lesson emerged: national narratives are designed to last but are not built to abide. Put another way by geographers David Newman and Anssi Paasi, national narratives, especially at state borders, are generated by a "relatively small number of representations of general sociospatial consciousness in their daily life and local experience, and most of these are representations set forth by the media and education."[48] That insight helped me refine my ethnographic fieldwork plan and move forward, this time with a binational focus that lent itself to seeing the Port of Laredo's annual celebration as part of a region that maintains intranational and regional ties and not just as two municipalities divided by an international line.[49]

Conducting fieldwork in Laredo and Nuevo Laredo presented a different set of challenges. Shifting between English, Spanish, and Spanglish, I interviewed current and former WBCA executive committee members, honorary board members, and staff members as well as affiliates who work for the City of Laredo, the municipality of Nuevo Laredo, and US federal law enforcement agencies. I attended WBCA planning meetings and volunteered to organize in-house photos and documents. I worked with affiliate organizations as well as title sponsors to understand their roles in the festivities and to trace how the expectation of ritual may impact their planning process.

Admittedly, I had a harder time conducting fieldwork in Nuevo Laredo because of the insecurity precipitated by the threat of drug cartel violence. I heard "Don't go," "Be careful," "They are going to mistake you for a journalist," "You are so stubborn," and other dire cautions from WBCA interlocutors, family members, and colleagues on more occasions than I would like to recall. Such warnings were not baseless, and my research in Nuevo Laredo proper was limited, but I was able to conduct interviews and do archival work thanks to the guidance and support offered by a handful of people, including the unshakeable Marti Franco. It helped that several of my interlocutors who (still) live in Nuevo Laredo but who travel to Laredo frequently very generously offered to meet me on the US side of the border. And they did so without me asking. It is also worth mentioning that I attended WBC/Consejo Internacional de Buena Vecindad–Nuevo Laredo (CIBV-NL) events in Nuevo Laredo with bridge ceremony/abrazo actors in protected vehicles and accompanied by a security detail. I discuss those research experiences in chapters 3 and 4, not to dwell on the idea of a violent borderscape but to show how borderlanders work through specific challenges.

In addition to fielding anxieties about border violence, I found that moving through and between so many worlds was demanding and just plain exhausting once the celebration came around. My research took me to different municipal and university libraries as well as to different homes and businesses on both sides of the border where I conducted interviews. But I could also count on playing pool after LULAC Council No. 12 meetings, sipping tequila and listening to Maná with different generations of parents of abrazo children, and attending nighttime events dressed in smart business attire several times a week. The hardest moments, by far, transpired when my interlocutors would ask me to reflect on my story: to explain who I was, where I grew up, who are my parents, or which schools I attended, among other topics.[50] I found answering those questions to be particularly difficult because my father, a person who had run for political office several times (unsuccessfully), was sent to federal prison in the early nineties. He was sentenced to eight years for intent to distribute cocaine and black tar heroin. I often avoided the subject because it distracted me and made me melancholy. Indeed, my standard response became, “Oh, it’s a sad story.” This was usually followed by “But who are your parents?” And I would say, calmly and with great authority, “They’ve passed.”

In those moments I thought a lot about my ethnographic training, especially the wise words of my mentor Dwight Conquergood, to find other ways to reciprocate and to go the extra mile in terms of fieldwork practice. Co-performatively witnessing the International Bridge Ceremony in three different ways—among Laredoans walking from the United States, among neolaredenses riding in a bus from Mexico, and in the center of the bridge with the volunteers (e.g., the Texas Army National Guard and IGNC-L and

CIBV-NL members) who set up a dais for the bridge ceremony speaker and other honored guests at five a.m.—was not only a real privilege but also allowed me develop the research on my own terms.

Teaching border studies courses to undergraduate and graduate students in D.C. between fieldwork visits, I was able to dig into analyses of festive border practices beyond North America. Thinking about the project with a global and comparative focus made fieldwork visits less nerve-wracking. Listening to stories people wanted to tell about themselves (or others) in relation to the International Bridge Ceremony took on another level of significance. Those conversations gave me insight into how border actors from different economic and professional backgrounds found ways to treat the festive repurposing of border infrastructure as an opportunity to make things happen. Because some aspects of what my interlocutors shared are sensitive, I use pseudonyms throughout the work, save for instances in which the events are on public record.

After more than five years into the project, I had finally found my way. Adopting a dual focus on border infrastructure and ritual gave me a reference point that adequately addressed the material and ephemeral qualities of the celebration. That framing device inspired me to ask bigger questions—to work through what is local and particular about the Port of Laredo and extrapolate how similar negotiation pathways may transpire at borders outside of North America. Of course, and as I will explain in the following chapters, cooperation was never easy, and it was never guaranteed. Antagonistic exchanges were common—a necessary part of the process—but I found that the face-to-face collaboration the bridge ceremony requires could produce a range of benefits, not only for the port of entry's power brokers but, in some instances, for the population at large.

A Note on Language

Throughout this US-Mexico border study I interweave not only Spanish but also Spanglish words and phrases. I have translated all quotes from Spanish to English and have done my best to give the most precise interpretation of Spanglish idioms.[51] This includes semistructured and informal interviews, scholarly texts, periodicals, and celebration promotional materials. I have left proper names and place names in their original language.

PART 1

PLAYING FOR POWER

CHAPTER 1

Playing Indian, Playing Colonial

Red Men Are Rustlers and Doing Grand Work in Laredo: They Will Awaken Patriotism on the Border and Make Us Realize That We Live in the United States.

"VENI, VIDI, YAQUI," *LAREDO DAILY TIMES*, FEBRUARY 22, 1898

In February 1898 thousands of people from both sides of the US-Mexico border gathered in Laredo, Texas, to celebrate George Washington's birthday. Organized and promoted by members of IORM Yaqui Tribe No. 59, the two-day event featured a reenactment of the Boston Tea Party followed by a grand pyrotechnic show, an international parade, and a meet and greet in the middle of the International Bridge.[1] The reenactment of the Boston Tea Party (1773) was a real crowd-pleaser. Onlookers were enthralled when brothers of Yaqui Tribe No. 59 "violently" overtook a "full rigged ship one hundred feet long, with masts, sails, lookout station, windlass, and cannon" docked in front of city hall. Costumed in buckskin outfits and boasting faces smeared in war paint, they crawled up on deck to engage local military personnel and municipal employees in "a fierce and realistic hand to hand struggle." Absolutely committed to their roles, both groups took turns having the upper hand. But they stayed close to the script; the "savage" Indians (IORM Yaqui Tribe No. 59 fraternity members) triumphed—they successfully captured the last sailor, pretended to scalp him, and cast his body into the crowd. Those closest to the ship were pleasantly surprised when the victors also threw boxes of candy labelled "tea" overboard (perhaps a brilliant homage to *piñata* logic). Thousands waved American flags, a choir sang "The Star-Spangled Banner," and a fireworks display capped off the celebration. The final image of the lightshow

Large birthday cake in front of city hall during Washington's Birthday Celebration, 1903. Courtesy of the Joe A. Guerra Laredo Public Library.

featured Washington's likeness adorned with a halo and the words "GOOD NIGHT." Perhaps not the founding father's first apotheosis on the U.S.–Mexico border, but definitely one of the most sensational.

More than a century later, commemorating George Washington's birthday at the Port of Laredo continues to draw thousands of spectators from both sides of the border. The content and rhythm of the festivities have changed over time, of course, but some elements of the celebration would prove to have staying power. Washington's likeness, for example, would still appear in the night sky after that inaugural year but would be adorned with different symbols. Similar to popular Wild West shows of the era (e.g., Buffalo Bill's Wild West Show and Congress of Rough Riders of the World), IORM Yaqui Tribe No. 59 members would continue to stage Indian attacks on city hall. Depicting violent encounters among Indians, cowboys, and soldiers became one of the celebration's calling cards. The difference at the Port of Laredo is that Yaqui Tribe No. 59 fraternity members played all of the parts—Indians, colonials, frontiersmen, and sometimes even themselves. Out of costume, for example, City of Laredo Mayor Amador Sánchez was playing Indian alongside his fraternity brothers.[2] When the "savage" Indians raided city hall in 1906, they took the white flag of surrender from him—an original Yaqui Tribe No. 59 member and a member of Laredo's *gente decente* (respectable folk).[3] Conversely, when the "Indians" burned a "paleface" at the stake, they were pretending to set a fellow Red Men member—possibly a naturalized US citizen born in Western Europe or Canada—on fire.

Historian Philip Deloria coined the term "playing Indian" to shed light on American colonials' boundary-setting practices, rituals, and spectacles such as the Boston Tea Party. Enacting Native American rituals, taking on the characteristics of the "noble savage" through literary texts, and exporting or trading in Native American goods helped colonials untether themselves from the past. He explains:

> Playing Indian was a performance of doubled identities—those known through visible faces or context and those suggested by inappropriate clothing. For people who linked Indian with metaphor and who found so many useful meanings encoded in Indian identity, it was not hard to imagine that both the sign of the disguise and the visible identity of the wearer could be true: *a shoemaker in Indian costume was both a shoemaker and an Indian.* These identities existed simultaneously, and they were something more than make-believe. They did not represent a "wilderness marriage" synthesis of European and Indian character. Neither were they a schizoid, back and forth confusion of alternating Indian and white identities. *White Indians were metaphors come to life[;] they allowed colonists to imagine themselves as both British citizens and legitimate Americans protecting aboriginal custom.* (emphasis mine)[4]

Deloria's study not only shows us how playing Indian served American colonials but also helps us understand how those modes of self-actualization can evolve beyond the American Revolution. In Laredo at the end of the nineteenth century, L. J. Christen in Indian costume was both the mayor and an Indian; A. M. Bruni in Indian costume was both the county treasurer and an Indian; and so on. Deloria's scholarship provides us with an excellent starting point, but the presence of an international boundary line makes a profound difference in this story; it will require us to do a triple take—to account for Indian, colonial, and Mexican identity performances—to understand how legacies of "playing" inform territorial claims to power and authority.[5]

Similar to the fate of other Mexican settlements after the Mexican-American War (1846–1848), la Villa de Laredo was split in two by the Treaty of Guadalupe Hidalgo—Laredo on one side of the Rio Grande and

Nuevo Laredo on the other.[6] The treaty introduced new and often conflicting ways of thinking about territorial affiliation, political participation, and jurisdiction.[7] But the document's fine print could not compete with la Villa de Laredo's *raison d'être*—its equidistant, trade- and transport-friendly location at the Paso de San Jacinto between San Antonio, Texas, and Monterrey, Nuevo León. La Villa de Laredo's favorable topography impelled the maintenance of laredenses' (Laredoans) long-standing linguistic, religious, and kinship ties. Military personnel and indigenous populations as well as "ordinary citizens" continued to cross and crisscross navigable points located along the Rio Grande with relative ease, but dealing with two sovereign entities certainly modified the conditions for interaction.[8] Whether based on the east or west side of that natural boundary line, laredenses eventually had to adapt their daily rounds and worship practices, confront violent land ownership conflicts, and pursue education or business opportunities on uneven footing.[9] And everyone still had to deal with a certain level of illegibility in their long-distance political relationships with officials based in each nation's capital (Mexico City and Washington, DC).

This chapter begins the task of understanding how the presence of an international boundary line shapes playing. Building on performance theorist Richard Schechner's early thinking about "environmental theater," it will emphasize how performance spaces are not just places where actors and spectators stage stories. In this analysis border infrastructures—spaces of action like the International Foot Bridge—are agential; they also have a story to tell.[10] Binational and cross-border relationships develop with the construction, maintenance, and repair of border infrastructure. To that end, it will keep WBC actors, laborers, and festivalgoers—the consumers and coproducers of identity-centric practices, rituals, and spectacles—within its frame of reference. This means that Yaqui Tribe No. 59 nonmembers, which includes soldiers, vendors, and local residents as well as day tourists who traveled to the Port of Laredo to attend the festivities, may not have donned an Indian costume. But they, too, were participating in the project of playing Indian. That mode of analysis reveals how playing not only fostered collective identity among IORM members but also sedimented historical narratives onto border soil.

This chapter will also provide key expository information to help us understand how IORM symbols and civil religious rituals, especially ones that appeal to imaginative thinking about American history, patriotic duty, and approximations of indigenous cosmologies, were not only taken seriously by the actors themselves in regard to cultivating social norms but also tethered playing to the accumulation of political power. Historian and border studies scholar Paul Nugent's research in West Africa has helped me think through the how and the why of the Red Men fraternity's reenactments, particularly how eccentric behavior can settle into a pattern. He notes in his study of the Gambia-Cassamance borderlands:

> Broadly speaking, there are two reasons why historical patterns might repeat themselves: the reproduction of a given set of structures may produce cognate responses, and/or actors may self-consciously seek to re-enact the past. . . . Settlement patterns therefore represent a good example of historical concatenation that has worked itself out over more than a century. But equally, continuities may take the form of ideational inversions. . . . To say that history does not repeat itself is true in a literal sense, but there are societies for whom the possibility of recurring patterns needs to be taken seriously, not least because contemporary actors operate in the belief that they exist.[11]

This chapter digs deep to account for how and why IORM members, many of whom fall into the gray etymological area of terms like colonizers, settlers, and patriots, methodically played Indian at a point on the map that could no longer be claimed as a frontier.[12] It adheres to their point of view, but not to glorify the fraternity's appropriation techniques or to reinforce the idea that "white Americans blissfully used Indianness to tangle with their ideological dilemmas while native people stood idly by[,] exerting no influence over the resulting Indian images."[13] Rather, it offers pertinent details that have been overlooked in previous narrations of this border phenomenon and provides a nuanced backstage analysis of intragroup thinking among IORM members to locate playing at the border in its "appropriate context."[14]

Why Is George Washington's Birthday Commemorated at the Port of Laredo?

The publication of the *Official History of the Improved Order of Red Men* in 1893 institutionalized Washington's preeminence among Red Men members at the end of the nineteenth century.[15] Advertised and distributed widely, the six-hundred-page tome is an exercise in fantasy and didacticism.[16] It also details the fraternity's history, particularly its indebtedness to the Society of Tammany. The publication also details how to approximate Native American ceremonies (such as tribal council fires) and rites of passage (such as adopting palefaces and raising chiefs).[17] The handbook's goal: to develop a unifying American spirit—a way of being in the world that makes use of indigenous cosmologies to promote collective action and shared responsibility. Unlike the debauched proceedings of its precursor, the Society of Red Men, IORM fraternity rituals were as practical as they were recreational. The brotherhood's new motto, "freedom, friendship, and charity," for example, was a nod to the utility of passing the peace pipe during tribal council fires. Sharing a calumet with your brothers facilitated a symbolic culture of belonging but also ensured that fellow Red Men members would subsidize your disability pension and pay for your funeral.

The *Official History* encourages IORM brothers to invoke the Great Spirit before every ceremony, not to proselytize but to offer a paradigm of American behavior. To be clear, Red Men did not aspire to be Indian, but they could learn how to believe like Indians to controvert their old-worldness. Acknowledging, appreciating, and enacting indigenous ways of being could be transcendent. The *Official History* mythologizes George Washington's life to evince that point. While Washington was always an important icon for IORM fraternity members, the publication made him a mediating figure in ways that were previously unpublicized. The widely circulated text foregrounds his innovative patriotic spirit—how he plotted revolution dressed in Indian garb as a member of the Sons of Liberty and as the first president-general of the Tammany Society.[18] More provocatively, it emphasizes his deep appreciation for and benevolent treatment of the Iroquois, characteristics that earned him the respect of the Great Spirit and an eternal resting place alongside Indians. How the Red Men imagined Washington in the "Indian heaven" is worth quoting at length:

> According to their [Iroquois] present belief, no white man ever reached the Indian heaven. Not having been created by the Great Spirit, no provision was made for him in the scheme of theology. He was excluded both from heaven, and from the place of punishment. But an exception was made in favor of Washington. Because of his justice and benevolence to the Indian, he stood pre-eminent about all other white men. . . . A belief was spread among them that the Great Spirit had received him into a celestial residence upon the plains of heaven, the only white man whose noble deeds had entitled him to his heavenly favor. . . . The faithful Indian, as he enters heaven, passes the enclosure. He sees and recognizes the illustrious inmate [Washington], as he walks to and fro in quiet meditation. But no word ever passes his lips. Dressed in his uniform, and in a state of perfect felicity,

> he is destined to remain through eternity in the solitary enjoyment of the celestial residence prepared for him by the Great Spirit.[19]

Envisioning Washington as the only "white man" in the Indian heaven was not an original idea. Handbook authors George W. Lindsay, Charles C. Conley, and Charles H. Litchman poached this passage word-for-word from Lewis Henry Morgan's *League of the Iroquois*, a study of six Indian nations: the Mohawks, the Onondagas, the Senecas, the Oneidas, the Cayugas, and the Tuscaroras.[20] Often recognized as a pioneering text in the field of American ethnology, *League of the Iroquois* is built from interviews, observed rituals, and circulated questionnaires. Morgan relied heavily on his native informant, Hä-sa-no-an'-da (Ely S. Parker), a Seneca Indian, to encourage "a kinder feeling towards the Indian, founded upon a truer knowledge of his civil and domestic institutions."[21] But as Deloria notes, there was more at stake than making valid scientific claims or preserving American Indian traditions vanished by genocide. Morgan's overarching intellectual pursuits were patriotic; they involved combining observation, his own ritual experiences playing Indian as a founding member of the Grand Knot of Iroquois, and drawing "liberally on literary imagination" to create a blueprint of American character based on indigenous values.[22] Morgan's project and methods were particularly appealing for groups like the IORM that "desired Indianness, not Indians."[23] His social scientific approach cut out the middleman. Red Men did not actually have to meet or engage with Native Americans to grasp their innate American character. Morgan's findings reassured them that George Washington was a worthy proxy.

The authors of the *Official History* borrowed copiously from *League of the Iroquois*, and particularly from Morgan's description of Iroquois eschatology, to validate Washington's honorary Native American status. But their reading of Washington was decidedly less critical. In Morgan's "Indian heaven" Washington is both a gatekeeper—a symbol of brotherly affection that exceeds the material world—and a mute American military leader on display for the viewing pleasure of the Iroquois. The Red Men organization focused less on notions of reverse anthropology and more on Washington's altruistic behavior. It was Washington's actions on Earth that had allowed him to achieve the impossible. He successfully transcended earthly racial, political, and religious constraints to live among Indians, the most genuine Americans, forever.

The legend of Washington inspired Red Men across rank and region. Soon after the *Official History*'s publication, Andrew H. Paton, the recently elected Great Incohonee (the highest-ranking official in the fraternity), instructed fraternity brothers to renew their allegiance to Washington—to commemorate his birthday, iconic scenes from his life, and the fast-approaching centennial of his death (1899). He spearheaded the revival through expressive play scripts, speaking engagements, and a series of official proclamations.[24] Nationally circulated IORM bulletins like the *Council Brand* announced his directives and later reported which tribes had heeded the call. There were dissenters within the fraternity whose protests were not against celebrating Washington but against having to finance that holiday in addition to "Saint Tamina's Day (May 12) and the Fourth of July."[25] Grievances notwithstanding, commemorating Washington on his natal day would become Paton's legacy.

Considering the ubiquity of the tradition of commemorating George Washington's birthday's, Paton was late to the game. Echoing the fervor of centennial celebrations, Congress had made Washington's birthday a federal holiday in 1879. And they, too, seemed to be a step behind. As early as the 1840s, societies were already using his natal day, the Fourth of July, and reenactments of the Boston Tea Party to replace "carnivalesque, revolution-tinged Indian celebrations with sanctioned holidays in which Indian play transformed the wildness of the Revolution into an obedient patriotism."[26] And, as scholar of American religious history Catherine Albanese notes in her study of the American Revolution, Washington was revered as a "living 'tribal' totem for an emerging nation-state even before his death in 1799. He was 'good for thinking,' for he helped the patriots define the good by embodying it in visible form."[27] Mandating citizens to commemorate Washington's birthday was a pragmatic and intuitive progression of America's nation-building ethos.

George Washington "Beyond the Mississippi"

Inspired, not intimidated, Paton promoted Washington's legacy with theatrical flair. In 1901 Paton published *Ceremonies for Celebration of "Washington's Birthday" and "Tamina's Day,"* an imaginative play script that includes dialogue, stage direction, interludes, poetic digressions, and stirring perorations. It is esoteric, which makes it unlikely that recently adopted "palefaces" would have caught every nuance. However, we can imagine that the script, when enacted with regalia and choreography, acquires another degree of accessibility. One of the play's recurring themes is that Washington is "dead, yet speaketh." Red Men learned that Washington could live on through dramatization. Moreover, they could incorporate his impeccable moral code into their lives through embodiment. Learning by doing. Enough so, perhaps, to eventually earn them a spot alongside him in the "Indian heaven."

Red Men members, particularly those in leadership roles, recognized that rituals (such as kindling the council fire [starting the meeting], quenching the council fire, adoption degree ceremonies, warrior's degree ceremonies, and the visitation ceremony) were more palatable with a group of warm bodies reciting and moving together as opposed to one brother reading from the page. The official ceremony booklet—a staple at every tribal council fire because it details the Red Men's calendar, their coded vocabulary, diagrams of council chambers, and the proper way to greet and exchange information—stipulated that climatic ritual moments be accompanied by singing "as music adds dignity and interest to the ceremonies." Following choreography precisely was also pivotal to maintaining propriety during ceremonies.[28]

Paton was absolutely committed to text publication and embodied practice as modes of knowledge transmission. But he also recognized the power of physically moving the brotherhood's moral code westward—an executive decision that set him apart from previous Great Incohonees. Since the fraternity's inception in the 1830s, one key growth strategy involved sending East Coast–based Red Men members westward on "mission" trips.[29] Brothers from different ranks traveled, recruited, and eventually established thousands of tribes across the United States. They tallied their miles and claimed a per diem. And when (and if) they returned, they were duly recognized and promoted. Only after 1893 did high-ranking Red Men members actually attend council meetings "beyond the Mississippi."[30] Unlike his predecessors, Paton spent much of his time enforcing protocol closer to the Great Lakes and the Gulf of Mexico. His visits coalesced the fraternity's vision outside of New England and the mid-Atlantic states.

In March 1896 Paton traveled to Houston to rekindle the "first Great Council Fire of the Great Council of Texas."[31] At this meeting Paton related the idea of celebrating Washington's natal day to the eventual founder of the Laredo Red Men tribe, Charles M. Barnes. He was at that gathering alongside other state-level Red Men members. Council minutes indicate that Barnes was already familiar with the Great Incohonee's original proclamation to celebrate Washington's birthday. Those reports also relate that he had listened to Paton personally explain the significance of the commemorative ceremony. And it turns out that Barnes and fellow Texas Red Men carried that knowledge with them on their recruiting trips.[32]

Paton could not have imagined a better interlocutor. Barnes was a recruiting machine. Between August 1896 and August 1897 he established five tribes in disparate locations across Texas. He was also in contact with potential Red Men in Corpus Christi, Floresville, Kerrville, Eagle Pass, and Uvalde.[33] Moreover, as a former newspaperman for the *San Antonio Express*, and later as author of *Combats and Conquests of Immortal Heroes: Sung in Song and Told in Story* (1910), Barnes, like Paton, was a savvy communicator who encouraged the circulation of ideas in print and through storytelling.

Barnes often promoted the fraternity's veritable American origins before his visits. In 1896, for example, he used the *Dallas Morning News* to advertise the brotherhood's prodigious qualities. He proposed: "[IORM] is one of the oldest orders in this country. . . . Its founders were the framers of the declaration of independence and the Boston tea party was composed of Red Men. Washington, the father of his country, was one of the founders of the order and, in fact, all of the leading American revolutionists were members of it also." Similar to the *Official History*, Barnes's go-to pitch was instructional. But newspapers and word-of-mouth publicity were not his, or the fraternity's, only teaching tools. Nuts-and-bolts documents (such as "adoption books," "ode cards," and *Copies of Proceedings G.C. of Texas*) also transmitted the brotherhood's overarching principles and aspirations.[34]

Upon induction, every Red Man acquired an "adoption certificate"—the price of which was routed into "supplies and rituals, etc." and "adoption" fees for every tribe.[35] Akin to a birth certificate, it not only linked the initiate to the fraternity symbolically but also served as a legally binding document during times of duress such as death or injury. Like the *Official History* and Paton's play scripts, it was didactic. Using tableaux, a popular technique among nineteenth-century societies, it created visual touchstones for new members. The images featured on that standard document gave prominence to Washington alongside Indian heroes like Tecumseh and narrated Indian customs like invoking the Great Spirit and hunting buffalo. The tableaux acknowledged the fraternity's progenitors (e.g., the Society of Red Men, 1813) and eighteenth-century figureheads like "Tamany" [*sic*]. So an initiate studying his adoption certificate at the end of the nineteenth century in Laredo, Texas, for example, would be able to trace his new family's roots back to the American Revolution.

By including images of Montezuma and Uncas, the certificate also suggested a Pan-American vision of Indian life that preceded modern Euro-American history.[36] The adoption diploma was particularly efficacious for audiences at the US-Mexico border as well as other multiethnic/multilingual areas because it made the fraternity's tenets accessible to spectators whose first language was not English and who perhaps were not familiar with US mythos. In addition, having to procure official adoption certificates and other paraphernalia from state-level Red Men officials not only moved money but also maintained lines of communication across Red Men outposts.

Barnes carried adoption certificates, a well-rehearsed version of Red Men history, Paton's call to celebrate Washington's birthday, and a deep appreciation for storytelling on his recruiting trip to Laredo in the spring of 1897. Despite the city's long history of dealing with bouts of political instability and uneven economic development, the Laredo that Barnes sought out and encountered was an ethnically, linguistically, and religiously diverse environment. Its economy thrived on international freight train transportation, cattle ranching, mining industries, and onion production.[37] Barnes routinely sought out the best progeny or "tribal children"—"young men prominent in the leading professions and pursuits of [the] city"—and Laredo proved to be a viable place for Barnes to establish Yaqui Tribe No. 59.[38]

A quick word about the name Yaqui Tribe No. 59: regionally and nationally, IORM initiates often tried to identify with an Indian tribe in their immediate geographic area. In Laredo, as in Nuevo Laredo, this would have been the Lipan Apaches. But naming practices could also be determined by a traveling recruiter, who was aware of which names had been taken and where. In Laredo Barnes adopted the Yaqui, a tribe based in the northern Mexican state of Sonora.[39]

Yaqui Tribe No. 59 was an exclusive club. There were only sixty-three members' names on the inaugural roster in a town with over thirteen thousand residents.[40] And those men were the city's most powerful citizens. Several members had arrived in Laredo after the railroad boom in the early 1880s and had since vied for political office, married well, bought property, taken control of media outlets, pledged allegiance to various societies, and fostered synergistic business relationships on both sides of the border. Original Yaqui Tribe No. 59 member S. N. Johnson bottled Coca-Cola and Budweiser; J. S. Penn edited the *Laredo Times*; A. Sanchez was part owner of a stock ranch of a hundred thousand acres in the state of Tamaulipas, Mexico; L. J. Christen was mayor; L. R. Ortiz was county sheriff; A. M. Bruni was county treasurer; A. C. Hamilton was district attorney; J. Gilligan ran the beer garden.[41] They all contributed to society in different ways. Several initiates already belonged to the Masons, the Knights of Pythias, and/or La Sociedad Mutualista "Hijos de Juárez" (the Sons of

[Benito] Juárez). And many actively worshipped and tithed as Catholics, Baptists, Methodists, Episcopalians, and Jews.[42] The one factor that unified the inaugural cohort was nationality. All were US citizens—born in places as diverse as Texas, Louisiana, New York, Tennessee, Missouri, and Ohio, or naturalized from Germany, France, Italy, and Canada.

It seems that those men did not join Yaqui Tribe No. 59 to combat boredom. They did not play Indian to simply pass the time. Rather, a shared investment in establishing America's dominion in a binational environment bonded them. Living in a geographic area that teetered between national identities—an American city dominated by Mexican rituals—inspired them to act on a common goal. According to a letter written by Joseph Netzer, one of the most prominent members of Yaqui Tribe No. 59, the inaugural cohort recognized that "it was customary in Laredo to celebrate all kinds of Mexican Celebrations such as 5 de Mayo, 16 de Sept. etc. etc. [and] No American memorials were considered seriously."[43] Curbing border residents' "mañana" attitude was also crucial.[44] Xenophobic quirks aside, the border city's built environment instantiates the ambiguities they sought to rectify. Even walking downtown heightened their sense of purpose: streets named Moctezuma, Matamoros, Hidalgo, Juárez, Iturbide, Santa María, San Bernardo, and San Agustín intersected or ran parallel to Washington, Lincoln, Farragut, Houston, Davis, and Grant, for example.[45]

City hall, which was also popularly known as Independence Hall or Independence Plaza, was an ideal place for Yaqui Tribe No. 59 members to make their views public. Erected in 1883 on Lincoln Street, the building served multiple purposes. It provided municipal office space on the first floor, but it also housed an auditorium with a stage, dressing rooms, electric lights, and seating for several hundred on the second level.[46] Outside, city-authorized vendors sold their goods daily as well as during theatrical productions put on by traveling troupes. Because of their political ties, Yaqui Tribe No. 59 members had unrestricted access to the building. Moreover, city hall was located a half block from their wigwam—the place where they would meet every Friday to hold tribal council fires, raise chiefs, adopt palefaces, and host state-level officials.[47]

There were many gatherings at the wigwam and an intense rehearsal period at city hall before the first celebration in February 1898.[48] Organizing a night of burlesque, a parade, a moment of recognition with their neolaredense counterparts in the middle of the International Bridge, a reenactment of the Boston Tea Party, and a dazzling pyrotechnic display around that space was labor intensive. To prepare, the Red Men split up into committees to oversee "transportation, advertising, accommodations, finance, parade, exhibition, music, and military."[49] They assigned parts, learned lines, designed costumes, and commissioned a one-hundred-foot-long colonial-era ship. C. G. Brewster, chairman of the "military" committee, persuaded officials at Fort McIntosh to have army men parade past city hall. Two months later those same soldiers would go on to fight in the Spanish-American War. As a city council member, Brewster also introduced the motion to hang an official portrait of Washington in the "colonial chamber" of city hall before the festivities.[50] Newspapermen like J. S. Penn generated buzz. Municipal workers decorated the city on the clock. Transportation committee members made deals with the Texas-Mexican railroad company to draw in spectators from both sides of the border.

The parade, the reenactment of the Boston Tea Party, and Washington's pyrotechnic apotheosis were sensational displays of American identity. They commanded the attention of thousands of spectators. But it was an intimate, standing-room-only event that tells us the most about how IORM members' civil religious practices informed their Americanization techniques. Held on the second floor of city hall, the gathering took pleasure in improvisation and broke a lot of rules. Past sachem Charles Pierce portrayed "Washington Red Eagle." Other brothers played "Western Union Uncus, the terror of the Southwest," "Hot-Booze, Man Afraid of Fire Water," "Squally Pete, the Onion Eater," and "Long-Fire-Tom-Tom."[51] Their Indian stage names suggest that Yaqui Tribe No. 59 members attempted to draw border residents into their world by combining local references (onion eater and terror of the Southwest) and generic prejudicial tropes (hot-booze). They joked at the expense of individuals whom they emulated but who would never be admitted into their club. And while absolutely perverse, Laredo's Red Men had fun making fun, all in the name of making their fraternal rituals palatable for an international audience.

That evening, aptly called "One Night with the Red Men" because they did not offer a repeat performance, showcased elements of the brotherhood's secret adoption ceremony. The initiation rite began with "the paleface, John Timid" voicing his intention to join the fraternity. In a classic but highly imaginative turn of events, IORM members not only rejected his petition but also tried to blow him up on a keg of gunpowder, made him ride a buffalo, burned and tortured him at the stake, gave him a ride on a chariot, and "scalped" him until he lost consciousness. But as this performance is also an object lesson in American grit, John Timid survives and eventually accepts his place in the Yaqui No. 59 wigwam.

Although staged to induce laughter with Wild West show antics, his hero's journey culminated solemnly. At the end of the ritual, he received "final instructions, [and] was given *the grip* [which was] also the sign of recognition" (emphasis mine). That gesture was not the most noteworthy moment of the evening, but it intimates that IORM ceremonies involved more than parody. State-level official S. T. Howard, that night also known as "Hail-Stones-In-His-Stomach," later noted:

> Upon reflection—The ceremonies are truly beautiful, they do not compose the sum total of all there is in our beloved Order. Its teachings are not confined nor limited to the signs, passwords and grips.
>
> The objects and teachings are but partially, aye, poorly illustrated by the ceremonies of the degrees. There is something back of them, under them and over them that is the essence, the power, the strength and the beauty of the order of the IORM.[52]

The "something back of them, under them and over them" Howard notes is the unifying potential of ritual. The embellishments—costumes, improvised script, musical selections, and silly names—were meant to charm and potentially recruit border businessmen.

At the same time, merrymaking made IORM "objects and teachings" and tableaux vivant of the "buffalo dance" and the "rain dance" appealing to a binational audience. And at its most entertaining, collectively reveling in American mythos could bind spectators together in an ambiguous space, in an either/or border environment. But the quiet moments counted, too. The "signs, passwords and grips" were transformative and reassuring, especially for border residents in the know. Those codes were the building blocks of what they considered model Indian behavior as described in Morgan's *League of the Iroquois* and prescribed in the *Official History*. On the US-Mexico border they were also Americanization techniques.

Yaqui Tribe No. 59 members not only became more genuinely American after exchanging these codes but also more purposefully American. IORM members could imagine that their secret rituals were more than Native American minstrel performances, that their interpretative labor could make an impact beyond the walls of the wigwam. And they would not have been wrong. Municipal documents, reviews, newspaper accounts, photos, and the commemorative program all indicate that public events—the parade, the reenactment, and the pyrotechnic display—were a smashing success.

In that respect, it is tempting to conclude that celebrating Washington's birthday—reenacting epic moments in American history, offering a night of Native American–inspired entertainment, and encouraging thousands of border residents to wave American flags—reflected "civil religion in the strictest sense of the term . . . [where] national life is apotheosized, national values are religionized, national heroes are divinized, national history is experienced as a Heilsgeschichte, as a redemptive history."[53] Onlookers could appear to be as invested in coalescing a shared sense of national identity as were the Red Men. But it was the preparatory rituals, rehearsals, and performances like "One Night with the Red Men" that were deeply enmeshed in idiosyncratic IORM principles. Non-IORM audience members (and even affiliated participants) may not have gleaned the consciousness-forming significance of dressing in Indian garb while pretending to burn a "paleface" at the stake. And while they advanced the organization's broader patriotic aspirations, those nuances may not have consolidated a sense of national identity as much as they introduced border residents to the esoteric rituals of powerful local fraternity members.

Onward

This chapter has outlined how IORM fraternity brothers pursued a specific goal at the US-Mexico border: to unequivocally claim Laredo, Texas, for America. It has traced how the fraternity's ideas, at once civil religious and patriotic, made their way to the border and has demonstrated how Yaqui Tribe No. 59 members' appropriation and practice of Native American rituals served as a differentiation strategy—a spectacular show of patriotism aimed to authenticate their Americanness and to claim political legitimacy.

At the Port of Laredo, Red Men members used the "power of high theater" offensively and defensively to stimulate cross-border business opportunities and to counter the popularity of Mexican holidays such as Cinco de Mayo (May 5) and el Dieciséis de Septiembre (September 16) that dominated borderlanders' secular festive time.[54] But we have learned that there is much more depth to that fairly obvious conclusion. Worshipping, not just celebrating, George Washington was part of a strategic decision taken by IORM members to "Awaken Patriotism on the Border and Make Us Realize That We Live in the United States."[55]

This chapter's focus on IORM members' civil religious sensibilities-cum-Americanization techniques should not suggest that border residents and festivalgoers from the surrounding area were a blank slate, a mass of bodies lacking agency. Non-IORM members generally took part as paid workers, attendees, and perhaps as entrepreneurs. Their involvement did not require envisioning a shared feeling of nation as much as it involved witnessing IORM members' vision unfold. As "environmental" spectators, however, they too contributed to the project of Americanizing the soil underneath their feet.[56]

Staging, participation, and spectatorship details illuminate key aspects of the celebration's reasons for being as well as its reasons for persisting. The next chapter continues that mode of analysis, but it shifts our focus toward controversial articulations of Mexican national identity. Staging Mexico-centric events on US soil, while commercially sound, revealed deeply engrained ideas about patriotism's proper geography.

CHAPTER 2

Playing Mexican

The Noche Mexicana, originating here where people know what a Mexican fiesta really is, and carried out with the help of people to the manner born, is the newest of our innovations, and perhaps of all the features given here pleased our visitors best, for it is the exotic, the novel, that attracts, and while it is all an old story to our home people, it is absolutely new to most of those from a distance, and to the Mexican from the interior, it could not but please as it was a bit of his own country on our soil.

"BEING NEIGHBORLY," *LAREDO TIMES*, FEBRUARY 24, 1925

In 1925 Matias de Llano, a Mexican citizen, a skilled bilingual businessman, and acting president of the recently chartered WBCA, introduced the celebration of a "Noche Mexicana" into the port of entry's repertoire. He chose Laredo's San Agustín Plaza, located two blocks away from the Port of Laredo's International Foot Bridge, as the place to showcase Mexican history and culture. Not only a new addition to the WBC program but also presented "for the first time outside of Mexico," the Noche Mexicano showed that de Llano was well aware of the need to exceed expectations.[1] He aimed to produce a version of Noche Mexicana that would attract a record number of festivalgoers and out-dazzle events of years past.

The odds, however, were stacked against him. Previous celebrations had boasted an "electrically illustrated automobile pageant of artistically decorated floats bearing George Washington and Martha Washington, 13 young ladies representing the colonies, and their guest, 'Miss Mexico.'"[2] Moreover, the annual "Indian" attack on city hall had been uprooted and upgraded. That event now unfolded in front of an international audience (spectators watching from both sides of the border) as a full-scale battle between Indians and "settlers" at the International Foot Bridge.

Businesses big and small showcased their wares with flair as part of the Washington's Birthday Celebration International Parade, 1924. Courtesy of the Joe A. Guerra Laredo Public Library.

Repurposing border infrastructure to stage the attack reinvigorated how WBC boosters communicated power and claimed authority. In previous years a Yaqui Tribe No. 59 member portraying George Washington would cross the Rio Grande (presented as the Delaware River) while giving orders to his men in Spanish.[3] The airspace over the bridge had also served as a reference point for daredevil pilots writing out "Welcome to Laredo" and for pyrotechnicians delineating a "portrait of George Washington in flame."[4]

WBCA president Matias de Llano rose to the occasion. He directed scenery builders to inundate San Agustín Plaza with water and set gondolas afloat to evoke the feeling of visiting Xochimilco, Mexico City's iconic floating gardens. A wonderful idea in theory presented a nightmare in practice. Laborers had to work tirelessly for months to transform 5,733 square meters of plaza space (think slightly bigger than the White House, a tenth the size of the Zócalo in Mexico City, or a quarter the area of Moscow's Red Square).[5] In the days leading up to the celebration, young men and women portraying charros and china poblanas rehearsed "national dances of Mexico, music of Mexico, [and] songs of Mexico" amidst the construction of wooden platforms, rocky cliffs, and a miniature volcano. The plaza's illumination plan, which de Llano designed to entrance the masses after sundown, created its own set of technical difficulties. Ambitious—teetering on potentially dangerous—the scheme required the exact placement of "tri-colored incandescent lights, frosted globes and shielded globes" between "thatched huts," arched bridges, and the plaza's exterior walkways. Lights also lined interior walking paths for "outline purposes, even down to the 'water's edge.'"[6]

Noche Mexicana plans drew intense scrutiny from members of Laredo's business community for being too expensive.[7] To be fair, indulging de Llano's elaborate lighting scheme and financing the construction of one-time-use scenery, not to mention supplying the water required to create artificial lakes in a semiarid climate, were not the most cost-efficient ways to grow the celebration. De Llano's WBCA colleagues, many of whom were skeptical that the project would be completed on time, made it known that they could not offer the project their "whole-hearted support."[8] Fortunately for de Llano, he was a well-regarded border figure renowned for his bilingual business acumen and his charming resemblance to Hollywood star Adolphe Menjou. Moreover, as the owner of the Mexican Products Co.—a leading exporter of Mexican baskets and pottery in the United States—de Llano nurtured a vast business network well into the interior of Mexico. And many of those business associates were expected to attend Noche Mexicana to have fun, no doubt, but also to take advantage of favorable train rates and special shopping rebates offered exclusively during the festivities.[9]

The underlying point to stress here is that mounting controversy was not linked exclusively to cost concerns. Noche Mexicana's success (or failure) could impinge on Yaqui Tribe No. 59 members' original vision for the celebration and their ongoing commitment to protecting patriotism's proper geography; that is, to commemorate the lives of US heroes as well as epic moments in US history to remind residents of Laredo that the soil underneath their feet was indeed American. Recall from chapter 1 that IORM fraternity members were not shy about expressing what they wanted the festivities to achieve. The morning of the Boston Tea Party/attack on city hall in 1898, the *Laredo Daily Times*, edited by Red Men member J. S. Penn, printed a headline that played on the popular Latin phrase *veni, vidi, vici* (I came, I saw, I conquered): "Veni, Vidi, Yaqui" (I came, I saw, I yaquied[?]).[10] The tropes and symbols put on display as part of Noche Mexicana would not only undermine America's right to that stretch of borderland but also compromise the brotherhood's most intimate civil religious truths. Moreover, and perhaps even more troubling, as this chapter's epigraph intimates, is the idea that taking part in Noche Mexicana would come naturally to border residents, would be enjoyed by American tourists seeking to experience "Old Mexico," and would be appreciated by Mexican business actors with deep pockets. In other words, playing Mexican in Laredo would come easily, be fun, and generate profit.

De Llano was able to manifest his vision on time despite the backstage chatter. Unlike the colonial pageant and members-only wigwam gatherings, Noche Mexicana was free and open to the public. It attracted record crowds, received excellent press, and even inspired members of the Associated Advertising Clubs of the World to consider staging a Noche Mexicana as part of their annual meeting later that year.[11]

Noche Mexicana's success was undeniable, but it was also short-lived. De Llano's executive decision to thrust Mexico into the WBC spotlight—to showcase Mexico's humanity, culture, and business potential—laid bare deep-seated ideas about patriotism's proper place in a border setting. The behind-the-scenes backlash against Noche Mexicana was so strong, in fact, that it was not featured in the WBCA program the next year. It would take a decade for the event to headline the celebration again.[12] But before jumping into Noche Mexicana's backstory, we should familiarize ourselves with how the *idea* of Mexico was rotated in and out of public circulation by border elites before de Llano took the reins as WBCA president.

Mexico in Doses

Old-guard Yaqui Tribe No. 59 members had never rejected the idea of including Mexico in the festivities. Benefiting from Laredo district attorney and fellow Red Men member John Valls's close relationship with Mexican president Porfirio Díaz, for example, the fraternity happily accepted Díaz's offer to have a Mexican military band perform during the festivities in 1905.[13] Inviting Mexican school groups to participate in the parade and providing a performance space for Nuevo Laredo's municipal band had also become standard practice.[14] But Red Men members actively monitored the location and scope of celebration events. Designating a "Nuevo Laredo Day" in 1911, which included bullfights, cockfights, and roping contests (all prohibited by law in the United States), for example, made sense. It quietly reified national boundaries while also capitalizing on the port of entry's bicultural selling points.[15]

It is also important to consider that the Red Men were not the only actors working to make their values public and influential at the Port of Laredo; a number of organizations, civil as well as religious, were active even before Charles M. Barnes made his way to Laredo in 1897.[16] A key difference is that clubs, societies, and congregations often chose projects based on the resources on hand. Recall from the last chapter that Yaqui Tribe No. 59 members mounted the festivities using municipal funds and resources (city hall). This is a case in which "power served pomp, not pomp power," as anthropologist Clifford Geertz would put it.[17] Members of La Sociedad Mutualista "Hijos de Juárez," on the other hand, had to petition to make specific modifications to Laredo's built environment and fundraise privately. Like the Red Men, the Hijos de Juárez's sociopolitical aspirations were imbued with civil religious discourse. They solicited donations to create a park in honor of the "Gran Indio de Ixtlán, el Gran Reformador Lic. Benito Juárez" and organized annual *veladas literarias* (literary evenings) to commemorate his birthday in March.[18] Working toward different goals and at a different pace, groups like the Club Internacional were able to organize El Primer Congreso Mexicanista (first Mexican congress) in Laredo in 1911.[19]

Laredo city council members, many of whom were founding Yaqui Tribe No. 59 members, may not have been entirely receptive to Mexico-centric events but they did not necessarily contest those organizations' efforts when they had the power to do so. In 1914, for example, city council members approved a motion (with preconditions) to erect a monument at Independence Plaza in Laredo to honor the memory of Miguel Hidalgo y Costilla and to commemorate the centennial of Mexico's independence.[20] Ambivalent support for those projects reaffirms what border scholars around the world have often found to be the case: that articulating and emplacing national identity via statues, parks, or gatherings near an international boundary line can bring to the surface underlying tensions around identity, belonging, authority, and power.[21]

Playing Indian and Playing Colonial during the Mexican Revolution

Unlike Mexico-centric political gatherings, literary events, and petitions to modify Laredo's built environment that had unfolded earlier in the twentieth century, Noche Mexicana was a high-production-value "cultural performance" staged on American soil as part of the WBC. This made the event a threat, particularly to celebration boosters who had grown accustomed to maintaining curatorial control over the festivities. Anthropologist David Guss's work on nationalism in Venezuela is helpful here because it clarifies how "cultural performances," which he interprets as "sites of social action where identities and relations are continually being reconfigured," can upend the balance of power and challenge established hierarchies. Critically engaging Mikhail Bakhtin's work on popular festive forms, Guss proposes that cultural performances can be "instruments of social control." He explains, "Often this process is imperceptible, with the event appearing as a mere affirmation of the relations that already exist. At other moments, however, *groups will use a festive form to shift the way in which history is told, to rethink the boundaries of community*" (emphasis mine).[22] Yaqui Tribe No. 59 members had done just that from year one of the celebration. And even when confronted with additional responsibilities and unexpected setbacks during the Mexican Revolution and World War I, their fervor for claiming Laredo for America did not wane.

The Red Men's decision in 1912 to move their annual "Indian" attack from Laredo's city hall to the International Foot Bridge (from the City of Laredo's power center to the Port of Laredo's power center) as part of the festivities is revealing. Seventeen months into the Mexican Revolution, Yaqui Tribe No. 59 members staged the raid on a small river island located underneath the bridge. Further refocusing Laredoans' and neolaredenses' attention to the international boundary line, they converted one part of that ait, technically located in a space that could be claimed by either the United States or Mexico, into a "peaceful" pioneer settlement.

Crowds on both sides of the riverbank jockeyed for a nice view of the action that February morning. US soldiers stationed at Fort McIntosh stood at attention dressed as cowboys along the east (U.S.) bank of the river. In this reenactment of "the hardships and misfortunes suffered by the early pioneers," the Indians (Yaqui Tribe No. 59 members), who were hiding in the dense chaparral on one side of the ait, attacked the settlers (also Red Men members) and emerged victorious.[23] They kept their adrenaline going by opting to climb a fifty-foot rope ladder hanging from the International Foot Bridge. Once atop the bridge, they were able to stand on the same plane as official delegations from Laredo and Nuevo Laredo who were waiting on their respective sides of the bridge.[24] Robert McComb, the mayor of Laredo and an original Yaqui Tribe No. 59 member, presented the key to the city to Pocahontas. Portrayed by Mrs. J. A. Applewhite that year, Pocahontas stood alone and apart from border officials but with an excellent vantage point in the middle of the bridge.[25] Once Mrs. Applewhite accepted the key to the city, members of the Laredo delegation were then able to make their way to the middle of the bridge to formally welcome municipal representatives from Nuevo Laredo to the celebration.

Let us now zoom out to examine how that location change pronounced America's authority and asserted Red Men members' natural right to power. "Indians" battle "pioneers" on a tract of land that is literally located

Early in the celebration's history the same woman would often portray Pocahontas several years in a row. Mrs. J. A. Applewhite played the part in 1909, 1910, 1912, 1913, and 1916. Estelle Palacios, featured here, received the key to the city as Pocahontas from 1927–1929. Courtesy of the Webb County Heritage Foundation, Laredo.

between two countries. An "Indian" princess watches the battle from above and is never in danger. Crowds of people watch the action from a safe distance. One of the groups authorized to protect that land—the Mexican army—is nowhere to be found. The other group with the power to exert force in that situation—the US army—does not intervene; they feign unfamiliarity with the environment (how to get to the ait) and get stuck on the sidelines. In contrast, the "Indians" (Yaqui Tribe No. 59 members) are able to defeat the settler-colonists because they do possess a deep understanding of the land. Their "native" knowledge of the natural landscape and their expertise as the day-to-day managers of that built environment as municipal officials underwrite their rightful claim to authority. Distinct from staging an attack at city hall on American soil, Red Men members' "colonizing myths" acquired additional relevance when they unfolded across an international boundary line and with the attention of Mexican officials.[26]

Now take a moment to consider that year's location change as an example of Yaqui Tribe No. 59 members' festive repurposing of border infrastructure during a marked time of instability. The mock attack/bridge ceremony in 1912 confirmed that the celebration could (and would) proceed in spite of the Mexican Revolution.[27] Staging the action below, above, and in proximity to the International Foot Bridge created an opportunity to idealize *their* version of history and to show an international audience where the boundaries of their American community lay.

The location change produced what performance theorist Joseph Roach would call a "vortice of behavior": a site of memory driven by architectural or technological innovation and maintained by ludic forms of self-expression. Drawing on the work of French historian Pierre Nora and French literary theorist Roland Barthes, Roach explains that the function of a vortice of behavior is to canalize specified needs, desires, and habits in order to reproduce them. Those places have "the gravitational pull of social necessity [that] brings audiences together and produces performers (candidates for surrogation) from their midst."[28] As part of the Treaty of Guadalupe Hidalgo's material legacy, the International Foot Bridge pulled audiences from both sides of the border into the story. That site of performance pulled Mexican citizens in but kept Mexico in its place.[29]

At the same time, spectators standing in two different countries could watch Pocahontas receive the key to the city. They all had front-row seats to a symbolic transfer of power that painted "Indians" as foregone border authority figures. Choices of casting and staging, particularly having delegations meeting in the middle of the bridge (but only after Pocahontas accepted the key to the city), punctuates that point. The symbolism also made clear that the international boundary line dividing Mexico and the United States could be enforced if need be.[30] Staging the attack at the border proper demonstrated that Laredo, Texas, could be the eye in the center of the storm—a place where binational ties could remain intact despite political upheaval across the river.

Making the best of those US-centric spectacles made economic sense for neolaredenses. As the editors of *La Crónica* suggested during the WBC festivities in 1910, "Laboremos, pues, porque sea este el festival que nos sirva de anucio para traer capital e industrias permanentes a esta region" (Let us all contribute to make this festival an advertisement that attracts capital and permanent industry to this region).[31] And during the early years of the revolution, that logic held.[32] Mexican officials continued to respond to WBC planning memos in spite of the escalation of violence that followed Gen. Victoriano Huerta's coup against President Francisco Madero. In what Geertz would call an act of "appropriate politesse,"[33] Nuevo Laredo Commandant A. Garza Galán even published a letter of support for the festivities in 1913.[34] A delegation from Nuevo Laredo did participate in the bridge ceremony that year, but its members did not walk over to join the festivities. Neolaredenses would not participate formally in the celebration again until 1921, when the "Nuevo Laredo Washington Birthday Committee" organized bullfights, *jamaicas* (Mexican street fairs), and concerts in Nuevo Laredo and arranged for guest passes so that Mexican citizens could attend the events in Laredo.[35]

It is important to note that when the revolution took physical hold of Nuevo Laredo toward the end of 1913 and coordinating the bridge ceremony seemed too risky a prospect, Red Men members openly discussed the idea of canceling the WBC festivities. Yaqui Tribe No. 59 members organized a series of public meetings in Laredo to discuss whether to move ahead with the celebration after a brutal battle between Huertista and Constitutionalist forces ravaged Nuevo Laredo on January 1, 1914. A general consensus among Laredo's business elite suggested that Mexico's revolution was Mexico's business. One attendee sounded off: "Gentlemen, we are not celebrating the birthday anniversary of any Mexican patriot; we are not responsible for Mexico's troubles and we are not depending on whether the rebels or federals win in Mexico—we are Americans preparing to commemorate the birthday anniversary of a grand American patriot, soldier and statesman, George Washington." The vote eventually favored arranging the festivities, but with one provision: the WBC celebration that year would be more "elaborate" and last longer—six days instead of three.[36]

Throughout the Mexican Revolution and World War I, celebration boosters searched for ways to manage border space, set national boundaries, and protect the Port of Laredo's economic interests. Red Men members organized baseball games in Laredo in the hope that tourists willing and able to travel from the interior of Mexico would make the trip.[37] They advertised more generous cash prizes for competitions, like ten dollars for the most typical Indian and fifty for the best allegorical float. They added events in Laredo to give American tourists proxy access to Mexico, including a moving picture session at the Royal Theater featuring footage of the battle that took place in Nuevo Laredo on January 1, 1914.[38] They also pounced on any opportunity to promote the festivities. In 1915, for example, a group of twenty-five Kickapoo Indians traveled to Laredo from Coahuila, Mexico, to "do some peddling and sell Indian trinkets and curios." Putting a WBC spin on their trip, a newspaper article mentioned that the Kickapoo "expect to remain in [*sic*] the section of the two Laredos until after the Washington celebration, hence visitors to Laredo will be afforded an opportunity to see a real band of Red Men while taking in the celebration."[39]

In lieu of bullfights and cockfights in Nuevo Laredo, Red Men members arranged for "Aztec dancers, Spanish dancers, and 'Tapatio' dancers from Guadalajara, Mexico," to enliven the *jamaica*.[40] Those small-scale events were always popular, but became more so when tensions were high because they could deliver on fantasies linked with travel to "Old Mexico." Advertisements teased, "Winsome señoritas" could pinch you, take you captive, and fine you dressed as a guard, a policeman, or a judge. Here is where every hombre makes it his business to fall a victim to these fair ones."[41] A reminder, if one is needed, of the far-from-innocuous ways in which chasing patriotic ideals and tourism revenue are gendered affairs.[42]

Noche Mexicana Means Business

Noche Mexicana may not have made its WBC debut until 1925, but the event was years in the making.[43] The creation of the WBCA in 1923 and the vital role de Llano played in securing the International Bridge's long-term profitability during that period helped bring Noche Mexicana to fruition. Furthermore, featuring Mexico in a prominent way during the

WBC was made possible because of turmoil within the IORM organization. The fraternity had scaled down the festivities out of respect for American brothers serving in Europe during World War I, but even then it lacked the membership and the resources to handle festival logistics. Still, Red Men aspired to make the WBC festivities competitive with Mardi Gras.[44]

Yaqui Tribe No. 59 workhorse Joseph Netzer, whose ties to the IORM spanned four decades, desperately tried to get in front of the hard times he knew were coming. After years of putting in requests to city officials, he finally convinced newly instated Laredo Chamber of Commerce (LCC) board members to come to the fraternity's aid in late December 1918.[45] The majority, which included a few old-guard Red Men members, had unequivocally opposed several requests to assume planning responsibilities, citing their "inability and unwillingness to support every single civil and military activity in the city."[46] But they could not deny the economic benefits that commemorating Washington's birthday brought to the city. Stalling for as long as possible, board members finally agreed in 1921 that a "permanent organization should be perfected." Still, they held off on voting until more research on the implications of planning a large-scale celebration could be conducted.[47] Fortunately for Netzer, he did have one very powerful ally on the board: Matias de Llano. Not because they were friendly, but because de Llano had consistently championed the idea of establishing a permanent WBC organization.[48]

De Llano's support could go a long way. His language skills and international business acumen made him the chamber's most valuable member. He not only worked well with colleagues in Nuevo Laredo but also developed relationships with Mexican chambers of commerce on behalf of Laredo and, crucially, in service to the port's trade interests. He was able to neutralize the tensions that arose in 1918 when Laredo-based chamber members proposed that their neolaredense counterparts "were not familiar with the active workings of the Chamber of Commerce" and should thus organize a separate "Mexican-American branch" so that they could discuss pertinent issues "in their language."[49] At this time, Nuevo Laredo did not yet have a *cámara* (chamber) of their own. That would not happen until 1921.[50] Appointing de Llano chairman of the Mexican American branch, Laredo chamber members envisioned a team of colleagues from Nuevo Laredo working separately but focused exclusively on sharing port-of-entry promotional information with Mexican chambers of commerce (e.g., Victoria, Mexico City, Guadalajara, Mérida, and Torreón).[51]

The LCC's recommendation to formally charter the WBCA in 1923 opened up new leadership possibilities for de Llano, who was still a Mexican citizen at the time. He eventually became a US citizen in 1926, the year after he staged Noche Mexicana for the first time as part of the WBC festivities.[52] His future in the organization, including the prospect of becoming WBCA president, was tied to his work on two high-stakes border infrastructure projects. First and foremost, he helped expedite the reconstruction of the International Bridge at the Port of Laredo after a massive fire destroyed the structure in April 1920.[53] He also played a vital role in securing the City of Laredo's Meridian Highway bid, a multiyear process that coincided with the establishment of the WBCA.

Winning the Meridian Highway bid remains one of the Port of Laredo's most important twentieth-century business deals. The International Meridian Highway Association's design and pavement plans teased that the road could be extended to run from North Dakota (and Canada) to [Laredo] Texas (and Mexico), thus making it "North America's Main Street."[54] Having the Meridian Highway extend southward from Laredo to Monterrey, Nuevo León, would increase the port's trade revenue prospects beyond rail to include automobiles. The stakes were high, and border business elites proceeded accordingly.

In a powerful example of the WBC's border scaffolding potential, Laredo Bridge Company board members scheduled the dedication of the newly reconstructed International Bridge to coincide with the WBC festivities in 1922. They pressed LCC members to "invite the Governor of Texas, *and stage* [the ceremony] *as an international trade relation*, or commercial relations affair" (emphasis mine).[55] Chairman de Llano invited powerful Mexican elites such as Governor O. López de Lara of the State of Tamaulipas. He formed a separate subcommittee to invite representatives from the Texas State Highway Commission, the International Meridian Highway Association, and the Department of Communications and Public Works of Mexico City.

Laredo chamber members also sought guidance from the president of the Texas Chamber of Commerce. President Cullinan advised that the bridge should be promoted as an important step toward the construction of an international highway because that was what Meridian Highway decision-makers based in Mexico were looking for. He also suggested that "local names be eliminated" from promotional materials to make it "an international highway."[56] Maximizing his advice, chamber members hosted an International Chambers of Commerce committee meeting in Laredo around the time of the celebration.[57]

The day of the bridge inauguration ceremony, and with all of the right decision-makers on site, port boosters took another bold step to try to seal the Meridian deal. They announced that everyone would be able to take advantage of paso libre during the festivities. Offering free bridge-crossing privileges to Mexican nationals flew in the face of the Emergency Quota Act of 1921 and several other early twentieth-century amendments to US immigration law.[58] But it sent a powerful message to Meridian Highway officials who were in the process of deciding which Texas-Tamaulipas border town would emerge triumphant. Tying the bridge inauguration ceremony to the festivities demonstrated that Port of Laredo actors could work together and play by their own rules if need be. Being able to merge their resources and authority with style, via the festivities, signaled that they had the social infrastructure in place to continue developing the Port of Laredo's international profile.[59]

Their efforts were well received, the bridge was operational, and chamber members were ready to start the laborious task of establishing the WBCA, but the Meridian Highway deal had not yet been secured. De Llano, who was keeping a close eye on cooperation efforts between the Mexican government and other Texas/Tamaulipas trade posts, kept his colleagues focused on the goal. He bluntly advised them to "wake up and take up a constructive program to offset the diversion of business" through other routes.[60] A competing route through Matamoros/Brownsville, for example, could communicate Mexico City and Veracruz—Mexico's number one port of entry—with US markets. A highway through Laredo would not bring Veracruz into the fold.

Anticipating that the final decision would be made at the Mexican Confederation of Chambers of Commerce convention scheduled to take place in Monterrey, Nuevo León, in early April 1923, chamber members petitioned to become the "first American Chamber of Commerce to be elected outside the Republic of Mexico."[61] Working with board members of the recently chartered WBCA (February 2, 1923), they put together one last pitch for the bid.[62] A promotional packet circulated in the United States and in Mexico ahead of that meeting. It included a stenographic report of the 1922 WBC bridge ceremony/inauguration program. The addresses given by Governors Pat Neff (Texas) and de Lara (Tamaulipas) featured prominently, "having one page printed in English, and one opposite in Spanish."[63]

Border business elites would continue to use the WBC festivities as border scaffolding to advance Meridian Highway construction plans after winning the bid. Ahead of the Meridian Highway's anointment as US Highway 81 on October 11, 1926, for example, the City of Laredo hosted a Meridian Highway convention during the WBC festivities.[64] Canadian delegates boarded special trains in North Dakota to attend the event. The governors of the Dakotas, Nebraska, Oklahoma, and Texas did the same from their respective train depots.[65] Still headed by Matias de Llano, the WBCA organized a "Frontier Days" pageant that year. Staged at "Liberty Park" and in honor of the 150th anniversary of American Independence, the special event featured "Indians, cowboys, soldiers, Red Cross workers and . . . the familiarly known covered wagon and pack mule of early days."[66] A small-scale scenic production of Noche Mexicana was included as part of Frontier Days but was not publicized.

Playing Mexican

Seen from afar and without knowledge of Matias de Llano's background or the border business projects that preceded his tenure as WBCA president, the staging of Noche Mexicana in Laredo could be interpreted as a fun example of border blending. But that is the view from afar. Introducing Noche Mexicana into the WBC's repertoire and staging it in Laredo was not a covert political act; it was an overt business move that made sense on both sides of the border. Noche Mexicana may have encouraged people to "play Mexican" on US soil—that is, to take part in and potentially buy into highly stylized and sensualized displays of Mexican culture—but it was not meant to sway spectators one way or the other when it came to national identity or territorial affiliation. The bottom line was clear to de Llano and many others. But as the epigraph that introduces this chapter suggests, Noche Mexicana incited too much uncertainty around patriotism's proper place.

It is worth taking a look at an extended excerpt from a letter to the editor of *Laredo Times* titled "Being Neighborly," mentioned at the beginning of the chapter.

> Then the Red Men, the originators of the celebration here, brought in their sachems and sagamores, their Princess Pocahontas and her devoted followers willing to attack the pale-faces in order to capture the key to the city, and this also was original. The Noche Mexicana, *originating here where people know what a Mexican fiesta really is*, and carried out with the help of *people to the manner born*, is the newest of our innovations, and perhaps of all the features given here pleased our visitors best, for it is the exotic, the novel, that attracts, and while it is all an old story to our home people, *it is absolutely new to most of those from a distance, and to the Mexican from the interior,*

"A Happy Crowd." Matias de Llano with Washington's Birthday Celebration revelers at the Cadillac Bar in Nuevo Laredo, Tamaulipas, Mexico, 1937. Courtesy of Marilyn de Llano.

> *it could not but please as it was a bit of his own country on our soil.* (emphasis mine)[67]

Published the day after the celebration ended in 1925, the letter makes a compelling case for making Noche Mexicana a permanent part of the WBC festivities. It tactfully praises the Red Men organization's imaginativeness. Or, put another way, it reassures Yaqui Tribe No. 59 members that they will always be known as the WBC's creators, the inventors, or "wizards," as historian Mauricio Tenorio-Trillo would put it.[68] At the same time, it suggests that the Red Men's festive techniques (i.e., attacking city hall), while still crowd-pleasers, had become predictable.

The letter also raises biocentric ideas about citizenship and ethnicity. It underlines how the inclination to stage Mexico on the US side of the border may be innate, that it may come naturally to border residents with Mexican heritage and therefore should not be resisted. Moreover, festivalgoers traveling from the interior of Mexico, particularly businessmen, would find special satisfaction in encountering that familiar feeling on foreign soil. But perhaps most alarming of all is the idea that Noche Mexicana's favorability proved that the WBC festivities could (and really should) be able to profit from national narratives that did not draw their inspiration from American colonial history. The message was finessed but clear; it was time to upgrade the celebration program and to trade out some border scaffolding materials. But moving ahead with those changes would require sourcing new building materials. And therein lies the problem. Yaqui Tribe No. 59 members, many of whom were still alive and kicking, could only see the tradition of commemorating George Washington's birthday as a *replacement of, not a complement to,* the celebration of Mexican identity in the United States.

They dreaded the possibility that Noche Mexicana would encourage borderlanders to bear witness and buy into curated depictions of Mexican culture, history, and values.[69] This is what I refer to as "playing Mexican." My use of the term builds on Deloria's concept of playing Indian but differs in important ways. Recall that Deloria describes playing Indian as a process in which Americans could "invoke a range of identities—aborigine, colonist, patriot, citizen—all of which emerged from the categories Indian and Briton. In the process they created a new identity—American—that was both aboriginal and European and yet also neither."[70] As mentioned in the last chapter, Yaqui Tribe No. 59 members did not play Indian to negotiate the dual qualities of their American identity. Their ways of playing Indian were far removed, temporally and politically, from the complexities of actualizing one's identity in early modern American society. Border-based Red Men gravitated toward the civil religious elements of playing Indian and focused their efforts on teaching residents-cum-citizens as well as neighbors-cum-consumers how being American could, and perhaps, *should* feel. Playing Indian for an international audience as part of the WBC was as much an opportunity to display control over border space as it was a "metaphor come to life."[71]

Like playing Indian, playing Mexican thrives on poaching and eliding indigenous peoples' histories, cultural practices, and modes of knowledge transmission.[72] But playing Mexican could never vacillate between two core categories (i.e., Indian or Anglo). As generations of scholars have shown, Mexico's conceptions of race and ethnicity are unequivocally distinct from US racial politics because they are informed by different legal principles (Mexican law was not premised on the "one-drop rule") and they carry the weight of Spanish colonial or *casta* intermarriage schemes. Those distinctions assume another layer of complexity in a border environment, which often encourages "either/or" identification, depending on the state of immigration enforcement, for example, or "always both" affiliations shaped by "sister city" tropes and positive talk about interdependent border economies.[73]

Performance theorist Manuel Cuellar's analysis of the Mexican government's first postrevolution staging of Noche Mexicana can help us sort through the site-specific underpinnings of those points. Held at Chapultepec Park in Mexico City in 1921, the event attracted a crowd of two hundred thousand—an amalgam of people from different class backgrounds and with varying language abilities.[74] As Cuellar notes, that year's Noche Mexicana was much more than a fiesta; it was an opportunity to foster cohesiveness and a sense of sociability among Mexican citizens—racially, ethnically, and economically heterogenous groups of people who had been divided by the revolution.[75]

Staging Noche Mexicana for the first time after the Mexican Revolution in a storied, open space like Chapultepec and tying the event to Mexico's Independence Day were strategic choices. Orchestrating a festive occasion that generates specific ideas about nation and national identity (for example, that Mexico is diverse but unified) and that circulates those ideas as accepted knowledge through embodied performance (that is, we all share the capacity to move forward with the certainty that Mexico is diverse but unified) exemplifies what Cuellar and Angela Marino call "fiesta epistemology." In conversation with performance theorists Diana Taylor and Leda Martins, and thinking hemispherically (not just about Mexico), Marino and Cuellar argue that "fiesta performance shapes time and space and the body itself carries and transmits knowledge."[76] Noche Mexicana architects drew on fiesta epistemology to inspire spectators, however diverse, to recognize themselves corporeally as Mexican citizens.[77]

Mauricio Tenorio-Trillo's magisterial study of Mexico's participation in the World's Fair sheds light on parallel aspects of those strategies. He discusses how José Vasconcelos—the Mexican minister of education who is best known for his theories about *la raza cósmica* (the cosmic race) and who self-identified as a "Mexican Ulysses"—led Mexico's participation in the World's Fair hosted by Rio de Janeiro in 1922. Tenorio-Trillo notes that Vasconcelos disagreed with the government's decision to send a statue of Cuauhtémoc, the last Aztec emperor, to Brazil. He objected not only because that gesture had become customary during Porfirio Díaz's regime but because doing so would reproduce "the image of an Indian hero of a nation that was, he thought, fundamentally Hispanic." If Mexico were to convincingly communicate its commitment to modernity, Cuauhtémoc's monument should remain in its place—along the Paseo de la Reforma in Mexico City. Unapologetically displeased when he presented the statute in Rio de Janeiro, Vasconcelos proclaimed that "it was time for Latin America to achieve its second Independence—'an independence in civilization, an emancipation of the spirit.'" But this was his personal preference based on his ideal version of Mexico as a place that should outgrow its reliance on an indigenous past and move forward with full knowledge of its superior racial makeup.[78]

In Mexico City after the revolution, spectators were encouraged to play Mexican in an attempt to reconcile a nation that had been torn apart by a decade of bloodshed. In sharp contrast, the WBC version of Noche Mexicana did not endeavor to generate a sense of social cohesion or foster goodwill. It was designed to attract as many spectators as possible, Mexican citizens or otherwise. Showcasing Mexican symbols like the charro and the china poblana alongside installations inspired by nature such as the volcanoes Popocatépetl and Iztaccíhuatl and national landmarks like Xochimilco offered a celebration boost, not an identity fix.

Playing at the Border

It is worth pausing here to consider journalist Fernando Piñon's memoir *Searching for America in the Streets of Laredo* before we move on to the second part of the book. Piñon recalls feeling uneasy while interviewing Mexican president Luis Echeverría Álvarez (1970–1976). President Echeverría's thoughts about the contradictions embedded in a *criollo* (Creole) government, particularly the idea that *campesinos* (farmers or country folk) "can do nothing and the political system can do nothing until they kill the *charro*," left Piñon speechless. "Unable to respond [in that moment]," he explains:

> I just thought about the *charro*, the Mexican folkloric symbol that is the ideological equivalent of the American cowboy, a character created and forged during Mexico's colonial period when the *hacienda* dominated the social, political, and economic life of the country. . . . The *charro* culture, then, is negative and self-defeating; yet, it is precisely these weaknesses that are glorified and are kept alive through countless songs and ballads that romanticize the image and are especially appealing to the *mestizo* mindset.[79]

Piñon's acerbic analysis of the figure of the charro resonates deeply with questions and themes explored in this book. How do we reckon with deeply racialized colonial legacies? Is a confrontation necessary to move forward? Is it even possible to kill off an idea, a symbol, and/or a collective way of knowing that lives on, and sometimes happily so, through popular

Noche Mexicana dancer, 1939. "Dancing a Revoltijo Mexicano—that is, a potpourri of Mexican dances—Miss Lela Peña of Nuevo Laredo concentrates on her footwork." Courtesy of the Washington's Birthday Celebration Association, Laredo.

expressive forms? Piñon's view of the bigger picture raises more questions than answers, but it can help us maneuver through the gratuitousness of playing with a fuller appreciation of the power expressive modes of knowledge transmission can have over our present.

To be clear, my objective here is not to point out all of the things that playing traditions enacted as part of WBC ceremonies grossly misrepresent but to draw attention to the goals that celebration coordinators set out to achieve. In this light, Noche Mexicana in Laredo marked a turning point in the history of the WBC and introduced its value as border scaffolding. The event's initial success in 1925, subsequent rejection, and eventual institutionalization a decade later would continue to shape cross-border business and networking strategies for years to come.

Showcasing Mexican culture on US soil as part of the US-centric tradition of commemorating Washington's birthday at the border produced two

Originally part of an intricate waterway system that carried goods and people across Tenochtitlán (present-day Mexico City), Xochimilco, known today for its canals and floating gardens, is one of Mexico's most iconic tourist sites. This "Los dos Laredos" Washington's Birthday Celebration parade float was designed by members of Martin High School's Pan-American group, c. 1950. Courtesy of the Washington's Birthday Celebration Association, Laredo.

noteworthy effects. First, it validated the Port of Laredo's trade-friendly "gateway" reputation. Second, it paved the way for the creation of Pan-American and internationally themed events such as the Border Olympics (also spearheaded by de Llano) as well as the international broadcast of the WBC International Bridge Ceremony across "27 Mexican stations and the N.B.C. system in the United States" in the 1930s.[80] Moreover, and as the next chapter will show, embracing Mexico, albeit festively, could prove beneficial for a broad range of border actors as opposed to a select group of border elites.

PART 2

PLAYING UNDER DURESS

CHAPTER 3

Hurricane Alice and the International Bridge Closure Crisis

Allí mismo se decidió que el paso por el nuevo puente durante las próximas 48 horas será gratuito para los peatones. (It was decided right then and there that pedestrians would be able to cross the bridge free of charge for 48 hours.)
"GESTO DE HERMANDAD DE FUNCIONARIOS DE AMBOS LAREDOS," *LA PRENSA*, FEBRUARY 22, 1957

On February 22, 1957, representatives from Mexico and the United States met in the middle of the International Bridge at Nuevo Laredo, Tamaulipas, and Laredo, Texas. Hundreds of spectators looked on as Dr. Héctor González Lugo, the municipal president of Nuevo Laredo, and Laredo mayor José "Pepe" Martin Jr. walked toward each other from their respective ends of the bridge to share an abrazo. The governors of four Mexican states—Durango, Coahuila, Tamaulipas, and San Luis Potosí—as well as the governor of Texas were also in attendance. Their objective that morning was twofold: to commemorate Washington's birthday, as residents of Laredo had done annually since 1898, and to inaugurate the newly reconstructed bridge, which had been completely destroyed during a flood in the summer of 1954. After two and half years of relying on a wooden pontoon bridge and a low-water bridge to get across the Rio Grande, the occasion brought a deep sense of relief to daily border crossers, high praise to bridge reconstruction officials, and good press to visiting politicians. Moreover, as the primary fixed link to the Pan-American Highway and as the busiest trade port of entry at the US-Mexico border, the bridge's inauguration ceremony's celebratory feeling surely reverberated far beyond that stretch of the border.

Meeting face-to-face is not a goodwill gesture that is exclusive to the Port of Laredo or an inauguration technique that is particular to the US-

Mexico border, but that year's ritual is noteworthy for several reasons.[1] Beyond coinciding with Laredoans' long-standing tradition of commemorating Washington's birthday, what is most striking about that bridge inauguration ceremony is that it was a redo. Bridge co-owners—Mexico's federal government and the City of Laredo—had attempted to open it in early December 1956. Right-to-toll disagreements (specifically, US-based border actors' expressed desire to raise tolls once the bridge was operational) prompted Mexican officials to keep their end of the completed structure closed for two months. The failure to open the bridge exemplified a distrust at the border that could not be easily resolved. That year's WBC, with its long-standing tradition of meeting in the middle of the international bridge, provided a way out of the crisis. Unlike diplomacy, force, or economic sanctions, the ritual that year invited a deeper level of participation across the border among ordinary people and political elites. The festivities not only successfully restored physical communication between the two Laredos, but they also made stakeholders out of border residents who fell outside the purview of official bridge business.

One of the bridge inauguration ceremony's idiosyncrasies was that participants, invited guests, and the public at large could take advantage of paso libre crossing privileges. Oriented toward Mexican citizens (not Mexican laborers exclusively), paso libre allowed thousands of people to cross the International Bridge free of charge and without documentation during the festivities. As was discussed in the last chapter, offering a free pass to mark momentous occasions (e.g., the Port of Laredo bridge inauguration ceremony in 1922) or to encourage travel between two countries is not unique. At and beyond the Port of Laredo, a certain level of leniency or bending of the rules for the sake of the greater economic good was common during that period. US-Mexico customs authorities strategically expedited cross-border traffic based on the daily volume at a particular port of entry rather than applying the letter of the law.[2] Even immigration enforcement officials had to "dry out wetbacks" during the Bracero Program (1942–1965) to meet US agribusiness demand for labor.[3] What differentiates the granting of paso libre in 1957 is the fact that border officials purposefully linked the bridge crisis strategy to the festivities. More compellingly, authorities managed to sustain the ad hoc policy for twenty years.

This chapter will show that paso libre was a targeted and enduring response to the bridge closure crisis that arose in the aftermath of a natural disaster. The expectation of ritual linked to the long-standing tradition of commemorating Washington's birthday played a vital role in helping border power brokers not only move past the impasse but also protect the port's economic interests. Drawing on the work of performance scholars like Shannon Jackson who have identified that "habitus and tactical and practical consciousness constitute an interspatial collection of environmental practices [that are] recalled, used, and adapted as an agent moves through familiar space [as well as] during 'critical situations' or 'times of crisis,'" this chapter sheds light on intracity and cross-border negotiation strategies that rallied bridge reconstruction efforts and highlights the backstage political maneuvers that justified an open border policy.[4]

The Crisis

Nothing points out an international boundary line's power to unite and differentiate quite like a natural disaster. Toward the end of June 1954, Hurricane Alice wreaked havoc in northern Tamaulipas and South Texas. Nonstop rainfall was particularly devastating for Laredoans and neolaredenses who lived near the Rio Grande and its confluent creeks. Rising above sixty feet, floodwater took dozens of lives; displaced thousands of people; destroyed residences, businesses, and schools; brought down gas and power lines; and damaged the water treatment plant.[5] Government officials and public utility companies on both sides of the border had tried to get ahead of the flood by evacuating residents and installing "mobile power substations."[6] But there was little anyone could do to protect the International Bridge, which was submerged under twenty feet of water for more than thirty-six hours. Anxious onlookers could only speculate about its future. A sudden drop in water levels confirmed the worst—both the International Bridge and the railway crossing bridge were gone. Assessing the damage in a riveting play-by-play account, civil engineers determined that a "log jam," which included a "raft of bridge ties and rails from a railroad bridge which had washed out at Eagle Pass," forced a buildup of debris and water pressure against the upstream side of the bridge.[7] The lifelines of the two cities since their construction—and even more vital after the completion of the Pan-American Highway from Nuevo Laredo to Mexico City in 1935—the bridges and their restoration became the focal point of the crisis.[8]

Both sides reacted quickly. The US Army Corps of Engineers built a temporary rubber-pontoon bridge within three days. The City of Laredo and the newly created Laredo Bridge System (LBS), which had acquired the US end of the bridge in 1946, replaced the rubber structure with a wooden pontoon structure soon after.[9] Wanting to ensure the transport of "automobile parts for assembly in Mexico, frozen foods, butane, and gasoline,"

"Pictorial Aspect of Disaster." Post–Hurricane Alice International Bridge wreckage, 1954. Courtesy of the Joe A. Guerra Laredo Public Library.

the Junta Federal de Mejoras Materiales (JFMM)—the federal agency responsible for Mexico's half of the bridge since 1924—proposed the construction of a low-water bridge made of steel to accommodate heavy trucks.[10] Laredo mayor José "Pepe" Martin Jr.—a widely influential and controversial political boss who put the "*patrón*" in "patron democracy"—received letters of support and telegrams from concerned business owners and high-profile elected officials.[11]

Lyndon B. Johnson, for example (at that time the Senate minority leader), offered "all aid that is possible for emergency relief and rehabilitation both to the citizens of Texas and of Mexico."[12] US Congressman Lloyd M. Bentsen (representing Texas's 15th district) and his successor, Joe M. Kilgore (then a Texas state representative from Hidalgo County) expressed their concern for the victims but also seized the opportunity to voice their support for dam construction.[13] Politicking aside, military personnel, federal-level agencies (e.g., Secretaría de Recursos Hidráulicos), nonprofit organizations (e.g., Cruz Roja Mexicana), local authorities, and business elite reached across the border to help flood victims without too much fuss or intrigue.[14] Reflecting on the fiftieth anniversary of the disaster, neolaredense Norma Fernández recalled that what she remembered most was not being able to understand the English-speaking US soldiers who provided dinner for her and other evacuees at a mobile military kitchen set up in Tamaulipas.[15] Response protocols and well-wishers may have initially provided or promised cross-border emergency relief, but rebuilding efforts demonstrated that those living in the United States or living in Mexico did eventually experience a difference.

Having the wooden pontoon and low-water bridges in place alleviated some of the pressure, but they did not diminish the urgency of the situation.[16] More than compromising the day-to-day rhythm of family activities or laborers' daily rounds, making do with provisional structures stunted cross-border shopping and slowed import/export traffic. And that was a crisis. Consider that in the early 1940s the port of Laredo was processing more than 80 percent of all exports and over 65 percent of all imports moving from the United States across Mexican border districts. In 1950 border crossings, tourist crossings, and rail freight generated $3,248,870 in duties at Laredo Customs Service.[17] Between July 1, 1954, and June 30, 1955, Laredo processed over $4.5 million in import trade from Mexico, close to $3 million ahead of the port at Brownsville/Matamoros.[18] It was absolutely necessary to protect that advantage.[19] Moreover, it was important to maintain the loyalty of Mexican consumers who crossed the border at Nuevo Laredo—not at Matamoros or Piedras Negras, for example—to buy items in bulk.[20] From shop floors and storage warehouses on the border, to truck rigs, rail cars, and single-engine planes en route, to production lines in the interior of both countries, doing without border infrastructure affected profit potential across several fronts.[21]

Eager to resolve the situation, JFMM officials, LBS trustees, and an International Bridge Reconstruction Committee, which included three representatives from Nuevo Laredo and three from Laredo, gathered to talk reconstruction.[22] In less than a year, they had studied various bridge design options, prepared plans and specifications in "both metric and English units," secured permission from both governments to provide duty-free working spaces near the river, and pitched the project to Mexican and American contractors.[23] Awarded the contract in August 1955, Concretos S.A. of Monterrey, Mexico, worked closely with Secretaría de Comunicaciones y Obras Públicas (SCOP) personnel in Mexico City as well as with the City of Laredo's consultants and engineering advisors based in San Antonio to decide on the prestressed concrete superstructure design. Only too aware of the international character of the project, consultants agreed that "United States cement would be used for the facia girders in piers and abutments," while Mexican cement, which was significantly darker in color, "would be used for interior girders and slabs."[24]

Even with extraordinary coordination demands—translating plans across languages and units of measurement, conferring with appropriate government agencies, dealing with additional debilitating rises in water levels, and negotiating unexpected costs—construction efforts moved forward through the spring of 1956 without too many delays.[25] It helped, for example, that Mayor Martin lobbied for Mexican "noncommercial vehicles including inter-city buses and taxi cabs, pickup trucks not used for hire," and so forth, to be exempted from Texas license provisions.[26] Optimistic that the bridge would be ready to inaugurate by August 1956, SCOP engineer Jorge García Obregón communicated to the press that four hundred laborers were working three shifts, night and day, to get the job done.[27]

LBS trustees unwittingly jeopardized that timeline at their monthly meeting in June 1956. Three of their colleagues with the LCC proposed that the opening of the new bridge was a "very appropriate occasion" to increase toll fare for vehicles. They argued that an additional charge of ten cents per vehicle could serve two purposes: it "could be used for matching Federal funds in the plans for slum clearance, blighted area abolition, Urban Renewal work," and it could be used to cover LCC advertising and promotion expenses such as "road markers, road maps and other means to increase the tourist flow through the Port of Laredo."[28] LBS trustees only offered to give the matter "serious consideration" but the damage had been done.[29] The mere suggestion of raising the toll fare unilaterally undermined the equilibrium that had been cultivated with conscientious decisions about concrete placement and duty-free working spaces. Laredo officials took steps to restore goodwill, but bridge completion was delayed through the fall. In mid-September they offered to share an abrazo at a *garita* (guardhouse at the end of the wooden pontoon bridge) in Nuevo

Laredo to celebrate Mexican Independence.[30] More brazen attempts to drive momentum and apply political pressure followed but proved ineffective.[31] Even the actual completion of the structure in mid-December failed to open the bridge to the public.

Mexican members of the International Bridge Reconstruction Committee explained that JFMM officials based in Mexico City advised them not to "deliver" their side of the bridge because construction costs had not been paid in full. Also, the lighting scheme on the Mexican end of the structure was not on par with the one installed on the US side in terms of voltage and appearance.[32] More than a disagreement about pending payments or finishing touches, those statements exemplified neolaredenses' gateway consciousness, a self-awareness of the city's reputation as "Primer Puerto Fronterizo de México" (Mexico's principal border port). Speaking of the need to renovate checkpoints at the International Bridge and along the highway leading to Mexico City, Mexican customs brokers emphasized the construction efforts' symbolic importance—their capacity to communicate "la potencialidad económica de nuestra Patria" (our country's economic potential).[33] As such, they continued, "debemos presentar la cara limpia, porque del exterior una persona [*sic*] se juzga el interior y las naciones son como las personas" (We should take care to present the best version of ourselves because people judge a person based on appearance and nations are like people).[34] Not just a pretext for delay, guaranteeing the aesthetic integrity and the structural soundness of the Mexican side of the bridge communicated competency.

The flood of 1954 made it necessary to revisit previous right-to-toll discussions. It is worth noting that JFMM officials and LBS trustees had outlined their distinct approaches a decade earlier during the transition from private to municipal ownership of the US side of the bridge. Throughout those discussions, Mexican officials wanted to balance and to scale back what they saw as highly capricious practices of giving out free bridge passes. In August 1947, for example, Alfonzo Flores, then the chief JFMM official in Nuevo Laredo, and Enrique Romo Ruiz, head engineer of Nuevo Laredo's water and light plant, voiced their opposition to the LBS's policy of selling discounted ticket books to people who "could afford" to pay a crossing fee. They also expressed concern with the high number of free passes in circulation, suggesting instead "all passes [be] cancelled except for [those given to] school children."

Flores and Romo proceeded to test the waters by asking what would happen if Mexico City obligated them to cancel all free passes. LBS trustees responded that they would reciprocate by cancelling all free passes previously recommended by the JFMM. But they would reserve the right to extend free passes to anyone on either side of the border whom they felt "should be extended this courtesy." From the trustees' point of view, offering US and Mexican government officials free passage (and sometimes their family members or perhaps associates from other bridge companies) was an "inexpensive manner of showing the bridge System's appreciation for such cooperation." Surrendering the right to facilitate travel between the two cities was unconscionable; it would tip the scales against them for years to come.

JFMM officials and LBS trustees continued debating those issues informally at the Laredo National Bank offices and at the Cadillac Bar in Nuevo Laredo. While those discussions did not yield a clear win for either side, they did teach a valuable lesson: out-of-office gatherings could bring differences in bridge management to the fore without tension. Indeed, LBS trustees noted early on that face-to-face time could potentially ensure "future pleasant relations with our neighboring City and should be of value in the handling of traffic problems on the bridge."[35]

Restoring confidence and "pleasant" working relationships after Hurricane Alice, not only between JFMM officials and LBS trustees but also among the general population and prized Mexican consumers, may have felt like an impossible task in light of the fact that the structure was completed but not open for business. The two-month-long bridge closure put Mayor Pepe Martin Jr., head of the reconstruction committee, in a particularly difficult position.[36] Maintaining patrón-level political control rested on his ability to control employment opportunities, to procure votes from barrio residents, to distribute city funds selectively, and to keep local merchants happy with "low inventory taxes."[37] Delivering efficient cross-border flow was an integral part of his machine's success. Also, being able to nod to the steady presence of Mexican nationals in Laredo either as shoppers, stand-in voters, or low-paid and zero-benefit workers drew attention away from citywide corruption and misuse of funds. Indeed, when pressed why traffic violation revenues did not increase alongside the city's ever-noticeable traffic problems, Mayor Martin would mention that "many traffic tickets were given to Mexican nationals shopping in Laredo, and that they would not pay their fines."[38] While Martin and his Independent Club supporters wielded enormous power in Laredo and in Washington, DC, their brand of local influence could not sway JFMM officials in Mexico City.

Crisis Resolution

The International Bridge remained idle for more than two months. With each passing day, debates about toll increases and revenue distribution became more labyrinthine. JFMM officials did not agree with the terms set by the LBS, which would cap their earnings potential at 18 percent. Laredo authorities argued that the 82/18 percent allocation was justified because their overhead costs (for instance, the number of employees on the US side) were higher. Intentional or not, delaying the bridge inauguration became the ultimate negotiating chip for Mexican authorities. As owners of 40 percent of the structure, the Mexican government was well within its rights to close its side of the bridge to traffic until both parties could agree on the terms of operation. Without a clear endpoint in sight, merchants, customs brokers, and import/export business associations based in Nuevo Laredo requested a *zona libre* (free zone) policy to offset losses.[39] Talk of recuperating construction costs and then making bridge crossing toll-free was also on the table in both cities.[40]

Considering that bridge revenue made up approximately 25 percent of the city of Laredo's annual budget, LBS trustees were unable to give serious consideration to those propositions.[41] Yet the burden of restoring international goodwill and public confidence fell primarily on their shoulders. Unable to continue negotiating with diminished political capital, LBS trustees solicited support from the LCC, community organizations, and federal agencies.[42] Reflecting the interests of banks, utilities, insurance providers, and retailers, the LCC was deeply invested in resolving the situation and not just because they had a hand in creating the crisis. The International Bridge was the focal point of their advertising materials; it exemplified Laredo's business-friendly Pan-American character and gateway qualities.[43] The chamber depended on the bridge's quantifiable and unquantifiable value to attract tourists and entrepreneurs—both of which kept Laredo's population, their shared customer base, dynamic and healthy. To that end, they began working on a solution that explicitly addressed pending right-to-toll concerns.

Building on previous years' unsuccessful efforts to work out a "plan where Mexican people could visit Laredo during the WBC without formality," chamber members requested that Walter W. Orebaugh, the American consul in Nuevo Laredo, and Allan C. Skinner, director of Immigration and Naturalization Service (INS) in Laredo, arrange for a temporary open-border policy.[44] Referred to colloquially as paso libre, it would legally permit thousands of Mexican citizens to cross the International Bridge free of charge and without documents for ninety-six hours during the WBC festivities that year (February 21–24, 1957). Restrictive immigration legislation and broad-scale border enforcement initiatives like Operation Wetback in 1954 had limited the range of what was permissible. But as mentioned earlier, expediting border-crossing procedures was not uncommon during that period. What differentiated and neutralized this paso libre proposal was that it was oriented toward Mexican citizens at large, not to Mexican laborers specifically. Even then, securing support for the initiative required impressive intranational and cross-border coordination skills.

Speaking with Laredoans who were old enough to experience and/or take advantage of paso libre, I began to understand how LCC members could have wielded so much influence. One longtime Laredo resident explained that the LCC, particularly in the 1950s, had a lot of power and "more control than politicians or government officials because they did not have to worry about elections and securing votes. They did not have elections to keep them from pushing." Moreover, he added, getting ahead, asking the bank for a loan, for example, could easily turn into the banker suggesting you join the chamber. He described the experience as a "forceful joining."

The fact that Director Skinner and Ángel Cano del Castillo, Mexican consul in Laredo from 1956–1960, were in the process of issuing new crossing cards and opening a new visa center in Nuevo Laredo played in paso libre's favor.[45] Most decisive was the American consul and the INS director's joint authority to issue a 212(d)4: a waiver of passport and visa.[46] While officially the work of the INS after changes imposed by the McCarren-Walter Act in 1952, the waiver could also be issued by the staff at the consulate in Nuevo Laredo, which had chosen to "retain issuing authority" and continued to "issue Cards on a limited scale" in light of the port's appeal to persons outside of "recognized categories" (e.g., business elites from Monterrey and Mexico City).[47] In addition to coordinating efforts between the INS and the State Department, chamber members also had to pool their resources to confirm support from customs agents in charge of processing bridge revenue. They pushed for a "keep our fingers crossed" approach with Laredo Health Department officials whose job it was to stop infectious diseases from crossing the border.

Dealing with the bureaucratic and logistical complications of opening an international bridge was cumbersome but ultimately worthwhile. Unlike previous attempts to force the hand of Mexican officials, extending free and clear bridge-crossing privileges to Mexican nationals intimated that LBS trustees and other key players had grasped what was at the heart of the bridge closure crisis. Namely, that pursuing unilateral policies (such as raising toll fares) begets unilateral action (such as bridge closure). Laredo officials' ability to rally the support of federal-level officials like Chief Skinner and Consul Orebaugh to solve the bridge closure crisis was also reassuring because it extended accountability beyond city hall.

After months of struggling to find the right language to restore trust, the LCC's proposal—a free-pass policy using the International Bridge Ceremony as a platform, even if on a temporary basis—was a powerful enough "social occasion" to set bridge inauguration plans into motion.[48] Representatives signed a "maintenance and operation" contract at Laredo's city hall on February 18, 1957, and repeated the act at the JFMM offices in Nuevo Laredo on February 20.[49] Focusing specifically on toll issues, it stipulated that bridge-crossing fees would match preflood rates. More importantly, neither of the bridge's owners could raise rates over a ten-year period. It was possible, however, to lower the price at any time and/or declare paso libre.[50] Representatives from Laredo and Nuevo Laredo opened the bridge and launched paso libre one minute after midnight on February 21, the first day of the WBC, and they inaugurated it formally as part of the festivities' annual International Bridge Ceremony the next day.

Joining the paso libre initiative to bridge inauguration plans and to the WBC was largely improvised but not coincidental. As discussed in the last chapter, not more than a generation earlier port actors had offered free bridge-crossing privileges to court Meridian Highway stakeholders. Paso libre privileges were made known to the general public in 1957 but not without outlining ground rules. J. E. Trout, an INS inspector in Laredo, advised: "Border permit cards for the Washington's Birthday Celebration will be issued to American citizens only who are entitled to them, these cards being good for three days—February 21, 22, and 23. In other words, there will be no change in the regulations, but a sufficient force of men will be detailed for passport work to insure everyone being waited on. *The rumor that the port will be wide open during the celebration and that there will be no restrictions has no foundation*" (emphasis in original).[51]

While the political context is substantially different, a clear through line links the WBC festivities in 1922 and 1957. In both years border elites used the International Bridge Ceremony and a free-pass scheme to protect the port's economic interests. Comparable cooperation dynamics within and between municipal offices and the executive boards of civil society organizations are also worth noting. Elected officials and key board members shared very close ties. Chester C. Wine, vice president of the Central

Power and Light Company, was president of both the WBCA and the LCC in 1957. Longtime chamber member A. E. Guajardo Sr. served as WBCA president in 1956. With practical knowledge of and access to the two organizations, Wine and his contemporaries were able to make a compelling case for paso libre. Similar to de Llano decades earlier, they were aware that the bridge ceremony was an ideal platform for the initiative because it guaranteed an international audience, including powerful guests from the interior of both countries.

The custom of inviting high-ranking political officials to the festivities fueled inauguration plans. Erving Goffman's work on behavior in public places is instructive here: specifically his thinking about social occasions that involve "focused interaction," the "kind of interaction that occurs when persons gather close together and openly cooperate to sustain a single focus of attention, typically by taking turns to talk."[52] Since the WBC's inception, representatives from both sides of the border had consistently fulfilled the expectation of meeting in the middle of the International Bridge during the celebration, regardless of the political climate. Planned weeks in advance and carefully choreographed to communicate a sense of social equilibrium, the "eye-to-eye ecological huddle" that Goffman describes was not the work of that moment; it was not spontaneous. That border enactment (face-to-face engagement practiced at and across an international boundary line) ensured a reoccurring opportunity to "monitor one another's mutual perceivings."[53] In-the-know, select classes of border actors recognized the ritual's potential to create "a shared definition of the situation . . . a 'working consensus,' involving a degree of mutual considerateness, sympathy, and a muting of opinion differences."[54] Through decades of practice, that mode of engagement generated an unspoken yet binding commitment to interact—to show up, present oneself in person, even if it involved going through the motions. Encouraged by the expectation of ritual and justified by the economic stakes embedded in International Bridge co-ownership, the bridge ceremony was not only a symbolic gesture but also a barometer used to measure commitment, resolve the crisis, and plan for the future.

WBC organizers' long-standing tradition of requesting that Mexican schoolchildren participate in the festivities was also integral to paso libre's success that year. Having Mexican authorities lead "2500 colorfully dressed Mexican school children" across the bridge to participate "in Field Exercises, calisthenics, Mexican regional dances in costume, patriotic ensembles, and mass singing of American and Mexican anthems and patriotic hymns to [George] Washington" at Liberty Park in Laredo in 1929, for example, not only drew large crowds of parents and proud family members but also promoted attendance across generations.[55] Chamber members emphasized the important role that Mexican school-age children had consistently played in the festivities. They chided US customs officials into compliance by suggesting that not opening the bridge to the general public, and denying children no less, could potentially signal malicious incompetence. Did they really want to prevent children from enjoying the fun? Would they not be able to handle the volume of border crossers?

Chamber members were also able to draw on the WBC's well-established reputation for supporting Pan-American and "good neighbor" issues to bring paso libre to fruition.[56] WBCA/LCC leadership built on earlier efforts to promote Washington as the "Father of the Good Neighbor Policy." Pre-flood WBCA promotional materials boasted:

> The well-informed give Laredo credit for having originated and fostered the Good Neighbor Policy more than 50 years ago—30 years before it was widely publicized as a national policy. Through the Washington's Birthday Celebration and other close contacts with the people of the Southern Republic, the people of Laredo have striven constantly to implement and supplement this policy and are proud of their contribution to the development of the splendid relations which exist now between the two countries.[57]

Multiple US-Mexico border scholars have rightly suggested that "Good Neighbor" rhetoric frequently promised more than it delivered.[58] But Port of Laredo actors' handling of the International Bridge closure crisis and their negotiation of a solution featuring paso libre offer a provocative counterpoint.

To be clear, this analysis does not deny WBC festivities were often top-down affairs that benefited landed and trade-oriented border actors. Yet, as David Guss reminds us, while "festive forms have often been dismissed as mere instruments of social control . . . as safety valves through which the ruling class could dissipate revolutionary energy and thus maintain the status quo" or, conversely, as catalysts and vehicles for rebellion, "the idea of cultural production (as opposed to simple reproduction) is not contingent on the permanent overturning of the social order, for oppositional practices may take many other forms as well."[59] Up until LCC members implemented paso libre, the courtesies extended to WBC bridge ceremony participants did not reach a popular audience. Festival organizers had selectively provided free and clear crossing privileges to high-ranking political officials and to high-value participants like Mexican military bands and school groups. For generations those border elites used the celebration to define and protect class standing through selective participation.

Paso libre's underlying criterion, which mandated bridge privileges to any and all Mexican citizens, poor or rich, young or old, did not jeopardize their status quo. On the contrary, in opening the bridge for business, paso libre benefited longtime WBC planners and participants whose livelihoods were tied to International Bridge traffic. Deliberate and not necessarily altruistic, paso libre's democratizing logic was compelling enough to move bridge inauguration plans forward. In this regard, the backstage labor of LCC associates and WBCA members, in particular, is different from instances in which "social networks step in when material infrastructures fail to deliver."[60] Offering paso libre to the masses was a decision that willed border infrastructure to overdeliver.

Envisioning thousands of potential consumers descending on Laredo's downtown retail district during the festivities had an appeal that was difficult to resist.[61] In the same vein, the US State Department's willingness to extend an "open house" waiver was tied to the WBC's built-in "goodwill" qualities.[62] In light of Nuevo Laredo–based US consular staff's lack of success with "International Educational Exchange Programs," specifically the failure of newspaper advertisements, film screenings, and scholarship opportunities to mold favorable public opinion toward the United States in Nuevo Laredo, the festivities offered a highly evocative and efficacious alternative.[63]

Paso Libre Endures

Paso libre was publicized as a spontaneous goodwill gesture. But that was not the case. Accounting for the symbiotic relationship shared by infrastructure and ritual in a border environment, this chapter has demonstrated that port-of-entry actors purposefully built on the *expectation of ritual* that is linked to Washington's birthday and mined International Bridge co-ownership conventions to offer a free bridge-pass option. Instituting paso libre mitigated the sting of toll-fare disagreements, alleviated the humiliation of having to restage an inaugural bridge ceremony, and revitalized cross-border trade and spending. We can attribute paso libre's efficaciousness to four principles: first, it was a targeted response to international bridge co-ownership tensions related to right-to-toll disagreements; second, it distributed accountability among international, federal, municipal, and civil society groups; third, it invited broad-based participation; and, finally, it produced a wide range of benefits, not only for in-the-know stakeholders but also for a diverse set of border actors.

This chapter has also shown that although compelling on its own, paso libre would not have necessarily produced a favorable outcome if pitched as a stand-alone policy. Tying the circumvention of US federal immigration policy to a quaint cross-border ritual was crucial to its success. Faced with a crisis that could not be solved with diplomacy, military force, sanctions, or monetary incentives—a situation fueled by misgivings and made all the more complicated by issues of scale and ownership—bridge stakeholders had to seek out all available resources.

Building on their working knowledge of binational festival coordination, port actors recognized the International Bridge Ceremony as an ideal vehicle for paso libre. Border elites' decision to festively repurpose border infrastructure in this situation—that is, to use the bridge ritual as a pretext and a platform to repair binational and cross-border relationships—encapsulates the idea of border scaffolding. Drawing on interviews, ethnographic insights, and access to uncatalogued documents, the next chapter will illuminate how paso libre endured well after the International Bridge closure crisis was resolved.

CHAPTER 4

Paso Libre

February, May, and September

Laredo immigration chief Allan C. Skinner had a big problem on his hands. The year was 1963 and Skinner was in charge of overseeing bridge traffic during the WBC. And that included managing paso libre. As we learned in the last chapter, Director Skinner helped champion paso libre to mend commerce-paralyzing tensions between the co-owners of the Port of Laredo International Bridge—the Mexican federal agency Secretaría de Comunicaciones y Transportes and the City of Laredo—after Hurricane Alice destroyed the structure in July 1954.[1] Made possible by the American consul in Nuevo Laredo and the INS director's joint authority to issue a 212(d)4 waiver of passport, and protected as an "open house" event by the US State Department, paso libre persisted well into the 1970s amidst escalating anti-immigration rhetoric and nativist politics depicted as the "browning of America."

The fact that paso libre (1957–1976) overlapped with the Bracero Program for over a decade amid ongoing "commuter situation" discussions certainly complicated Director Skinner's task.[2] As did the fact that Nuevo Laredo's population had taken to consistently doubling and even tripling every February in anticipation of the International Bridge Ceremony—the ritual that tethered paso libre to the WBC festivities. In 1962, for example, Director Skinner "estimated that northbound crossings for the first 24-hour period of the four-day visa waiver period had totaled 50,000 persons."[3] Consider that Nuevo Laredo reported a population of 92,627 in 1960.[4] This means mass groups of people totaling more than half of that Mexican border city's regular population crossed the Gateway to the Americas Bridge toward the United States during the first day of the festivities. Many of those actors had traveled from the interior of Mexico days in advance.[5] Nuevo Laredo effectively became a "staging area," a commercial landscape that generates bursts of economic activity linked to food, lodging, transportation, and communication, well in advance of the celebration.[6] And during the WBC festivities, neolaredenses and Laredoans alike, particularly merchants near the bridge, benefited from the mass influx of pedestrian/consumer traffic.[7]

In 1963 Director Skinner could claim over thirty years of experience in federal government, including eight years as director of the INS in Laredo.[8] He was well aware of paso libre's broader impact—not only for the US and Mexican governments but also for border residents at large. Simultaneously, as a private citizen Skinner was an enthusiastic and committed member of the International Good Neighbor Council–Laredo (IGNC-L), a cooperative group dedicated to strengthening binational and transregional business relationships across the US-Mexico border.[9]

Skinner's ardent support for paso libre as a federal officer and a private citizen may seem incongruous, but it was common then and remains so today. And not just in a US context. As anthropologist Brenda Chalfin has shown with her analysis of the work of customs agents in West Africa, "The border shows itself to be a site of expansive functionality."[10] In other words, border-based officials like Skinner may work on behalf of the state but they can also make decisions or pursue plans of action based on local factors or personal interests that diverge from the state's articulated interests. What differentiates Skinner from fellow immigration and customs officials working along the US-Mexico border during that period is that paso libre made way for thousands of border crossers at a time, not on an individual basis.

In a surprising turn of events, Director Skinner, in conversation with colleagues in Nuevo Laredo, authorized paso libre beyond the WBC. In the early 1960s, for example, they extended free bridge-crossing privileges during the Cinco de Mayo holiday in May as well as Mexican Independence festivities in September.[11] In other words, paso libre was not linked exclusively to the WBC or to single-mindedly advancing US claims to power at the border. Offering paso libre in February, May, and September bolstered economic activity without undermining national identity.

Granting paso libre in conjunction with American *and* Mexican holidays may have leveled the playing field (momentarily) and benefited a wider swath of border residents (in the long-term), but the burgeoning tradition was certainly problematic in other ways. Government officials, civic leaders, and businesspeople on the ground, including Director

Paso libre turnstile traffic, c. 1962. From 1957–1976 Mexican nationals were able to cross the Gateway to the Americas International Bridge during the festivities without having to show documentation or pay toll fare. Courtesy of the Joe A. Guerra Laredo Public Library.

Skinner, were well aware that "doing" and "showing" border control had never been more crucial.[12] Preparing for Cinco de Mayo "pedestrian traffic" in 1963, Chief Skinner asked LBS trustees for additional manpower to "help the Government officials from the Port Building *who were to decide who qualified for crossing* on the 'free port' permit and who would have to be returned back into Mexico" (emphasis mine).[13] While staffing the bridge with ancillary municipal law enforcement personnel was a strategy that had been used in the past, this situation was different.[14] In this case, extra personnel were not there to welcome people; they were called in to keep the bridge's walkways back to Nuevo Laredo clear for individuals who had been denied entry. INS officers like Skinner had to decide, and quickly, who to turn away.

Take a moment to envision what that decision process may have involved. How could Skinner and his colleagues know, just by looking, who was fit to enter and who was not? Picture thousands of people crossing the bridge after the abrazo ceremony. And be sure to factor in that each and every individual, thanks to the 212(d)4 waiver, had legal permission to do so. On what basis did Skinner and his colleagues select the people who would not gain entry? What criteria did bridge officers use to determine who was dangerous and in what sense? This mode of managing mass pedestrian bridge traffic invokes timely questions about profiling logics that unjustly bind immigration control to border security.

Indeed, several US-Mexico migration and border studies scholars have addressed immigration control's reliance on racial profiling logics, specifically the phenotypic biases that present themselves at the moment of crossing.[15] For example, having fair skin and light eyes, regardless of gender, more often than not works in one's favor when crossing the border. This chapter draws on those insights but brings different aspects of selection and crossing processes to the fore. Uncatalogued papers and municipal records suggest, for instance, that Skinner's team may not have targeted dark-skinned, working-class Mexicans but were very likely looking out for people crossing with multiple bags: first because they may have planned to relocate permanently; or second, they may have been engaged in smuggling activities. Clothing style and a certain look could also be the basis on which to identify potential drug smugglers. Indeed, line 9 of poet Allen Ginsberg's "Howl" can help us envision the fuller spectrum of border crossers during that era, including those "who got busted in their public beards returning through Laredo with a belt of marijuana for New York."[16]

This chapter breaks new ground on several fronts and, as such, has many moving parts. It examines the minutiae of the WBC bridge ritual (e.g., choreography and protocol), including unexpected gains made in the realm of identity politics. It also draws our attention to enduring components of the festivities' social infrastructure. Here I use this term to describe the cross-border initiatives and joint-labor activities shared by civil society organizations such as the WBCA, the IGNC-L, and LULAC.

Laying out archival and ethnographic evidence collected on both sides of the border will also demonstrate how free bridge privileges combined with the "expectation of ritual"—being able to count on the celebration taking place and being able to plan accordingly—enhanced the WBC festivities' border scaffolding attributes. Previous chapters have shown that port-of-entry boosters used the WBC International Bridge Ceremony to lubricate relationships with Meridian Highway decision makers and stakeholders in the 1920s, for example, and to assuage border infrastructure and right-to-toll disagreements after Hurricane Alice in 1954. This chapter will explain how the bridge ritual generated specific gains within the tourist economy, public health initiatives, and informal cross-border labor circuits through the 1960s and 1970s.

As indicated above, this analysis will draw our attention to immigration enforcement logistics and planning choices, many of which were improvised to protect the Port of Laredo's trade and business-friendly "gateway" profile. It does so not to reaffirm the idea that twentieth-century US immigration policy is wildly contradictory (a well-known fact) but to offer a glimpse of what safe and orderly migration that complements, and even protects, cross-border economic prosperity could look like.

Blink and You'll Miss It

Unraveling the puzzle that is paso libre took me a long time. I negotiated access to uncatalogued documents and then spent several months pouring over them. I also made dozens of home visits to look at and discuss personal papers, meetings that oftentimes lasted entire mornings or afternoons. Joining WBCA, IGNC-L, LULAC, and Consejo Internacional de Buena Vecindad–Nuevo Laredo (CIBV-NL) planning meetings and attending events in Laredo and Nuevo Laredo to connect with second- and third-generation WBC participants helped me see how the bridge ritual links the past and the present and how paso libre intervened in that continuum. I traveled to Washington, DC, with the WBCA's executive board members and with cultural ambassadors such as the four abrazo children, Martha Washington, and Princess Pocahontas to attend the annual "Laredo Day" party that takes place on the Hill every year, a trip that illuminated the festivities' intranational reach. Similarly, I found myself joining LULAC members on a private jet flight from Laredo to San Antonio to formally invite Texas state senator Wendy Davis (D-Dist. 19) to participate in Noche Mexicana as a Señora Internacional. Most helpfully, I co-performatively witnessed the abrazo ritual in three ways: by approaching the bridge from the Nuevo Laredo side in 2014 and approaching from the Laredo side in 2017; and by helping WBCA/IGNC-L/CIBV-NL associates and Texas National Guard volunteers roll out the red carpet and set up media stands at five a.m. in 2015. This level of participation not only clarified just how labor-intensive sustaining a binational tradition can be, but also helped me envision how caravans of people could have crossed the bridge peacefully during the era of paso libre.

While the majority of the evidence presented in this study is archival, conducting fieldwork and thinking across time corporeally helped me make sense of incomplete or redacted diaries. After all, not all knowledge is written down. Embodied practices, traditions, ceremonies, and rituals also produce and transmit knowledge. Spending days moving between archival research and ethnographic research, I found myself thinking about the ties that bind performance and performance studies to history and historical studies. Diana Taylor's work on the subject would often come to mind. This passage is worth quoting at length.

> All societies have archival materials, whether they are ornate temples or simple marks on a piece of wood. History-as-discipline, which relies on scripted archival sources, often has no way of dealing with these various pasts. What documents would ground their inquiry? If historical studies cannot legitimate the repertoire of embodied practices, how do historians approach the undocumented "event"? Perhaps this is where performance studies, as a post-disciplinary methodology, comes in—illuminating that disciplinary blind spot that history cannot reach on its own. But we would need to imagine performance studies being able to offer another aspect of history, one grounded in the repertoire as well as the archive, focused on embodied practices that distill meaning from past events, store them, and find embodied modalities to express them in the here-and-now, yet with an eye to the future.[17]

Taylor's point productively challenges us to think more carefully about how we construe an "event" and in more expansive ways about what constitutes a "source." Being able to trace various modes of knowledge production became indispensable when I was struggling to piece paso libre together.

Admittedly, many of my interlocutors were happy to recall paso libre, but conversations were often nebulous and wistful. As one can imagine, talking about paso libre, especially for individuals and families who used the tradition to cross the border permanently, remains a sensitive and elusive subject. For some Laredoans, especially those living or working near the bridge at the time, paso libre triggered memories of having to turn away "people with nothing" who were going from door to door asking for assistance. At the same time, several interviewees poked fun at my questions, snidely reminding me that Mexican military troops used to march into Laredo "carrying bayonets."[18] Two megajokesters, Laredo Public Library Special Collections all-star Joe Moreno and LULAC Council No. 12 warhorse Pitín Guajardo, giddily made me aware of a 1969 Peter Ustinov film called *Viva Max!*, which satirizes paso libre.[19]

With persistence and patience, I was able to interview Laredoans and neolaredenses who were old enough to recall paso libre's first years. But even then, many were not very sure how it started and did not venture to guess. Specific details about the days of paso libre were usually offered in conjunction with personal memories linked to the interviewee's participa-

Mexican military members have crossed the border to participate in the Washington's Birthday Celebration festivities since the celebration's inception. This image shows Mexican soldiers walking in formation alongside the general population, c. 1962. Courtesy of the Joe A. Guerra Laredo Public Library.

tion in the festivities. I learned from former mayor of Laredo Betty Flores, for example, that in the late 1950s girl scouts played "hostess" at Martin High School, offering water and sandwiches to Mexican parade participants. Sara Díaz Trujillo, a retired teacher who lives in Nuevo Laredo, acknowledged over coffee that she was too young to remember anything specific about paso libre's heyday beyond crossing the bridge to watch the parade. A while into our conversation, however, she suddenly recalled noticing when some of her family members stopped attending the festivities. "Maybe that is when it [paso libre] ended," she guessed.[20]

Semistructured interviews as well as informal conversations could bring back both positive and negative memories associated with the festivities and with cross-border class dynamics more generally. I had the pleasure of interviewing Richard Delgado, a former WBCA president, and his wife, Michelle, a former public school teacher, at their kitchen table in one of Laredo's most affluent neighborhoods. Similar to other interviewees (WBCA executives or not), Mr. Delgado had not given very much thought about why or how he started participating in the festivities. "I've been involved in WBC since I can remember, maybe as a five- or six-year-old. . . . I went to forty-one Mr. South Texas luncheons in a row, *in a row*" (his emphasis). His mother's family, he explained, had helped establish the SMW with Father Dan Lanning in 1939. In other words, for him, participating and taking a leadership role in the festivities was very much a birthright and an expectation.

Just as Mr. Delgado was getting into his family's backstory, the phone rang. A one-time Texas gubernatorial hopeful was on the line. "Should I take it or not?" he asked mischievously. "If you want sir," I responded. And then he answered the phone: "Top of the day, man [chuckling]. Oh, are you on the treadmill? Uh huh, uh for the 4th of July?" The tone of his voice changed then, and he began to grumble: "*Chingaoo* [expletive], how do you let those guys stop the bus? With the, full of children . . . that hatred is coming out, that hatred is coming out. Uh, horrible. . . . Motherfuckers!" Mr. Delgado then paused his conversation to ask me if it would be all right if he continued the call: "How much time do you have?" "As much time as you have," I responded. Ever attentive, his wife kept me company and sugared me up with coffee and pan dulce while her husband chatted in another room. I mention this unexpected break in the interview not to indulge in indiscretion but to highlight how immigration issues, specifically detention and deportation procedures in the Laredo area, can raise concern in the everyday lives of well-to-do border actors. Awareness is not a choice at the border: action is.[21]

We eventually continued the interview and covered a lot of ground over the course of three hours. I was particularly struck when Mr. Delgado's face lit up after recalling that he had serendipitously run into a long-lost friend—a buddy he had made one summer in Saltillo during his childhood—as an adult. He described how happy it made him when he saw his friend walk by in the parade.[22] "I didn't really expect to see him again," he explained. For him, that was a paso libre moment.

Not everyone had such a moving personal connection to paso libre, but it was quite common to hear that, intergenerationally and across class lines, people could bond over remembering how the festivities made them feel. Hearing the sound of bugles announcing the arrival of Mexican marching bands in the early morning hours of parade day, for example, came up again and again. Whether the buglers ultimately annoyed or delighted did not matter; the shared experience could be recalled both individually and among family members, groups of friends, and/or coworkers.[23] Other aspects of remembering, not just spectatorship but also limitations placed on participation, could be just as powerful and even contentious.

Sitting in a spacious living room in Laredo with a nice view of a swimming pool, I was able to speak at length with Hortencia Vásquez Guerra, a woman born in Nuevo Laredo who formally immigrated to the United States in 1969, and her close friend Julia Tomlinson, who had moved to Laredo in the 1950s. Hortencia described how she and her family would cross the bridge every year: "We never missed one *paseo* [parade] because my mother loved el paseo and we would come to see the *bandas* [bands] and yeah."[24] "When I was older," she continued, "*and they would carry my books*, I would come with the boyfriends to el paseo, *el 22*, and of course the carnival. We would always go to the carnival, get on all of the rides, you know really participate" (her emphasis). In that way, Hortencia's experience resonates with so many of the stories I heard that illuminated the ease with which neolaredenses and Laredoans enjoyed the festivities.

What set Hortencia apart, however, is that her parents attended public, nonticketed events like the parade and the carnival, which free bridge-crossing privileges were intended to facilitate, as well as attending more exclusive functions. She recalled that her parents would "come to Noche Mexicana. *Sometimes* they would go to, uhh . . . the Washington's Birthday, the presentation, the debutante's ball, the Society, *sometimes* they would go . . . especially if they knew someone that was being presented. But I never went, I never went" (her emphasis). And how is it that your parents attended those events, I asked? "Because of friends, they had a lot of friends that their daughters would be presented. I remember one daughter . . . ," she continued. She then added as an aside, "Remember there is always someone from Nuevo Laredo being presented, and most of the time I had lots of cousins from Nuevo Laredo that were presented. And, umm, I remember the big, the dress . . ."

At this point, Julia spoke up, and this is where the conversation opened up in ways that illuminate how free bridge-crossing privileges operated parallel to and even separately from the celebration's highly classed dimensions. Her interjection also summoned the specter of IORM Yaqui Tribe No. 59 members and their Americanization techniques.

> But I [Julia] think, I would interject that in the fifties, I think you saw a lot more integration of the people from Nuevo Laredo being presented and acting within the procession. But before that, I don't think it was that way. It was more the *gringos* [Anglos] were really the ones that were the beginning of the Washington's Celebration. And at one time you didn't see this idea of marrying a Latin girl and intervening and, and, and having them being presented at that time. At that time, it wasn't right to do that, it wasn't that way. I'm just telling you.

Hortencia nodded and added, "Yes, because my point is already the sixties . . . so I'm talking the sixties." Julia continued, "And if you look at the actual date of the Martha Washington organization, started, you would not see too many Mexican names, because they were not there. And it wasn't, you know . . . ," she trailed off.

Retaking the floor, Hortencia, audibly impassioned, added, "Because the whole purpose of the Washington's Birthday was to make Laredo America because we were so Mexican. We would celebrate only the 16th [September 16] so the Order of the Red Men wanted to celebrate, what else? George Washington. . . . They wanted to make Laredo, Texas, American and what is more American than George Washington?" "Okay, well maybe that might have been that way," Julia countered, "but I think actually, it was, if we were saying, the man who really brought that area of the Latin people from Nuevo Laredo and all of the festivities that were going, that part really had to do with Matias de Llano. ["Oh yes," Hortencia agreed.] That was really the crossing point. It's our turn, you know, our turn to celebrate."[25]

Searching for the How

On both sides of the border, many of the people with whom I worked could often agree on one point: opening the bridge did not seem like a big deal because it "happened all of the time."[26] That statement often caught me off guard. In fact, paso libre not only coincided with and outlasted the Bracero Program but also weathered landmark immigration policy changes (most notably the 1965 Hart-Cellar Immigration Act).[27] Moreover, paso libre ended in 1976, well within the purview of "low-intensity conflict doctrine" maneuvering and overt efforts to militarize the US-Mexico border.[28] Cumulatively, hundreds of thousands of people crossed the border at Nuevo Laredo during the festivities. This understanding between US and Mexican authorities required ongoing communication and cooperation across different administrations. What could keep that arrangement going for almost twenty years?

The short answer is business. The economic benefits that Laredo and Nuevo Laredo obtained from paso libre are many. But the intensity of those advantages varies from one side of the border to the other.[29] Recall from the last chapter that 25 percent of bridge toll fare is funneled directly to the City of Laredo's general fund, while Nuevo Laredo's share is determined first by the Mexican federal government and then the State of Tamaulipas.[30] The one thing that residents on both sides of the border gained from the paso libre was a substantial increase in tourism revenue, which was felt most intensely near the Gateway to the Americas International Bridge—then the port's only physical conduit for commercial and noncommercial vehicular traffic.[31]

Revenue boosts were certainly a strong incentive to keep coordinating paso libre. But even then, how could the very visible circumvention of US federal immigration law every year for almost two decades have stayed out of the history books, border studies scholarships, and border policy discussions? This elision is all the more striking when we take account of the fact that two million unauthorized Mexican immigrants were expelled from the United States between 1968 and 1973.[32] Moreover, the festivities were definitely not kept a secret; the Voice of America and the US Information Agency broadcast the International Bridge Ceremony across Latin America for most of paso libre's duration.[33]

Ever the skeptic, I scoured local and regional publications for details.[34] I found front-page announcements of paso libre in English- and Spanish-language newspapers as well as what I came to call "blink and you'll miss them" notices—page-five news items no bigger than a thumbprint.[35] The message stayed consistent from place to place, year to year, whether for Washington's birthday or Cinco de Mayo: "Por acuerdo de las autoridades migratorias estadounidenses, los días 22, 23, 24 y 25 de febrero, se concederá paso libre a los ciudadanos mexicanos que deseen visitar Laredo, Texas al celebrarse las Fiestas del Natalicio de Jorge Washington."[36] Or "Visitors from the south of the border desiring to go more than 25 miles from the border will require further US Immigration documentation."[37]

It is important to point out that port officials on both sides of the border were never shy about voicing their support for paso libre. On February 16, 1972, for example, Lic. José I. Salinas, the chief of immigration in Nuevo Laredo, clarified that "there had been false reports that many Mexicans would not be permitted to cross to the US side." His statements published in English on the front page of the *Laredo Times* and in Spanish in *El Tiempo de Laredo* assured readers: "THIS IS totally untrue" (emphasis in original).[38] Immigration and customs officers on bridge duty those days would not turn anyone away during the celebration. After the festivities, however, border crossers would have to show their "Form 13." His comments may have reassured bridge crossers headed toward the United States, but it is important to point out that paso libre always worked both ways. Indeed, statistics tracing the flow of American tourists across the border into Mexico at the Port of Laredo showed a 30 percent increase between 1971 and 1972.[39]

Interviewing former immigration and customs officers who had worked during (or who had heard stories from colleagues about) paso libre revealed further avenues I could explore to think about and analyze the tradition. The detail in the newspaper about not going more than twenty-five miles beyond Laredo, for example, was a technical point that was important to make public—even though it was common knowledge, especially among law enforcement agents on the ground, that limiting travel was very hard, if not impossible, to enforce. Permanent interior checkpoints as we know them today had not been built. There was even a book describing border crossing during that time, I was told. It is called *My Border Patrol Diary* and was authored by Dale Squint. I am a patient reader, but this text was challenging. And not only because the entire thing was printed in all caps. Nevertheless, there are some intelligible sections, like this one, which mentions paso libre explicitly.

> THEY USED TO HAVE 'OPEN PORT' DOWN HERE IN LAREDO WHEN I FIRST CAME HERE [November 1970], TO CELEBRATE THE WASHINGTON BIRTHDAY EXTRAVAGANZA. WE HAD TO HAVE A CHECK POINT ON EVERY HIGHWAY OUT OF HERE. THE TOWN WOULD LOAD UP WITH ILLEGAL ALIENS AND THEN IT WOULD TAKE THE BORDER PATROL A YEAR TO GET THEM ARRESTED AND SENT BACK SOUTH. . . . THEN HERE COMES ANOTHER 'OPEN PORT.' . . . FINALLY SOMEONE WITH ENOUGH GUTS SAID 'NO MORE' AND THAT IS THE WAY IT IS NOW. COURSE THE BUSINESSMEN IN LAREDO WERE CRYING BE-CAUSE THE 'OPEN PORT' SITUATION STOPPED, BUT I BELIEVE THEY LEARNED TO LIVE WITH IT.[40]

In addition to alerting me to Squint's diary, Border Patrol agents made it known to me that not everyone in uniform was on board with the open-port tradition because, as Squint suggests, it made everyone work harder.[41] But, as can be imagined, my interlocutors were reticent about discussing how agents actually managed that Sisyphean task.

The more I familiarized myself with paso libre's backstage logics, the more finding photographic evidence to try to grasp the intensity and impact of the tradition became imperative. I eventually located images in plastic bins and cardboard boxes mixed up with memos, receipts, thank-you letters, and scrapbooks. The earliest photos that I came across con-

Thousands of people took advantage of paso libre every February during the Washington's Birthday Celebrations from 1957 until 1976. This image from 1973 captures the scope of northward movement after the International Bridge Ceremony. Courtesy of the Washington's Birthday Celebration Association, Laredo.

firmed that paso libre drew a steady crowd of bridge crossers from its inception. In the early 1960s, for example, the flow of people was continuous but there was space between the moving bodies. On the other hand, I could liken photographs taken in the mid-1970s to cinema stills of the famous "parting of the Red Sea" scene in Cecil B. DeMille's *The Ten Commandments* (1956). Border crossers stand shoulder-to-shoulder, maneuvering heel-to-toe across the bridge. Those images can easily overwhelm but make no mistake: the bridge ritual itself was not disorderly. In fact, it was carefully choreographed and strategically cast.

Behind the Scenes: Schedules and Diagrams

Early on in my process of figuring out the paso libre puzzle, I mistakenly assumed that WBCA, IGNC-L, and chamber of commerce members (in Laredo and Nuevo Laredo), in cooperation with a close circle of municipal and federal officials on both sides of the border, took care of the minutiae of the International Bridge Ceremony. But that was not exactly the case. Since the organization's inception in 1956, IGNC-L members, including Director Skinner, played an integral role in cultivating the festivities' binational reach. They worked behind the scenes with colleagues in Monterrey, Nuevo León, to make that happen, and they attended the celebration faithfully, but they did not handle bridge ceremony logistics.[42] The actual planning and execution of the bridge ritual over the course of paso libre fell under the auspices of the City of Laredo Health Department.[43]

Laredo public health engineer José L. González began his tenure as chair of the International Bridge Ceremony committee in 1960.[44] He and his public health colleagues worked year-round with their counterparts in Nuevo Laredo to ensure that all bridge ceremony actors knew where to stand during the ritual, when to move, and who to hug.[45] They oversaw backstage logistics, including inviting special guests from Mexico and the United States, making sure that the rank of each invited guest correlated with the rank of the person they were asked to embrace, working with Mexican customs officers to halt vehicular bridge traffic the day of the ceremony, stage-managing VIP guests without ruffling feathers, and in some cases translating speeches from English to Spanish.[46]

Bridge ceremony coordinators managed those expectations from year to year with a detailed schedule of events and a diagram charting the precise starting location of abrazo ritual actors in relation to the international boundary line. The 1974 diagram shows us that the Mexican *guardia de pabellón* (color guard) and the US color guard flanked the ritual on either side of the bridge. In all, eight sets of abrazo participants faced each other standing twenty feet from the international boundary line, each in his or her respective countries. The identity of those actors could change from year to year based on elections and/or administration changes, but the elected and appointed posts they spoke on behalf of did not.

The two children representing the United States and two children representing Mexico would exchange the first embrace, followed by the mayor of the City of Laredo and Nuevo Laredo's presidente municipal. Protocol dictated that those officeholders, as the official hosts of the celebration, exchanged the next embrace.[47] The order of the following sets of abrazos could vary, but if it could be helped, it rarely ever did. The action continued with the Webb County judge and the head of the JFMM (recall the integral role JFMM officials played in resolving the International Bridge closure crisis discussed in chapter 3). They were followed by the US consul in Nuevo Laredo and the Mexican consul in Laredo; the governor of Texas and the governor of Tamaulipas; the INS chief in Laredo and the Jefe de Inmigración in Nuevo Laredo; the chief of Customs in Laredo and the Jefe de Aduana in Nuevo Laredo; and the US and Mexican ranking military commanders. The diagram also designated the location of a rostrum (*tribuna de discursos*), which straddled the international boundary line.

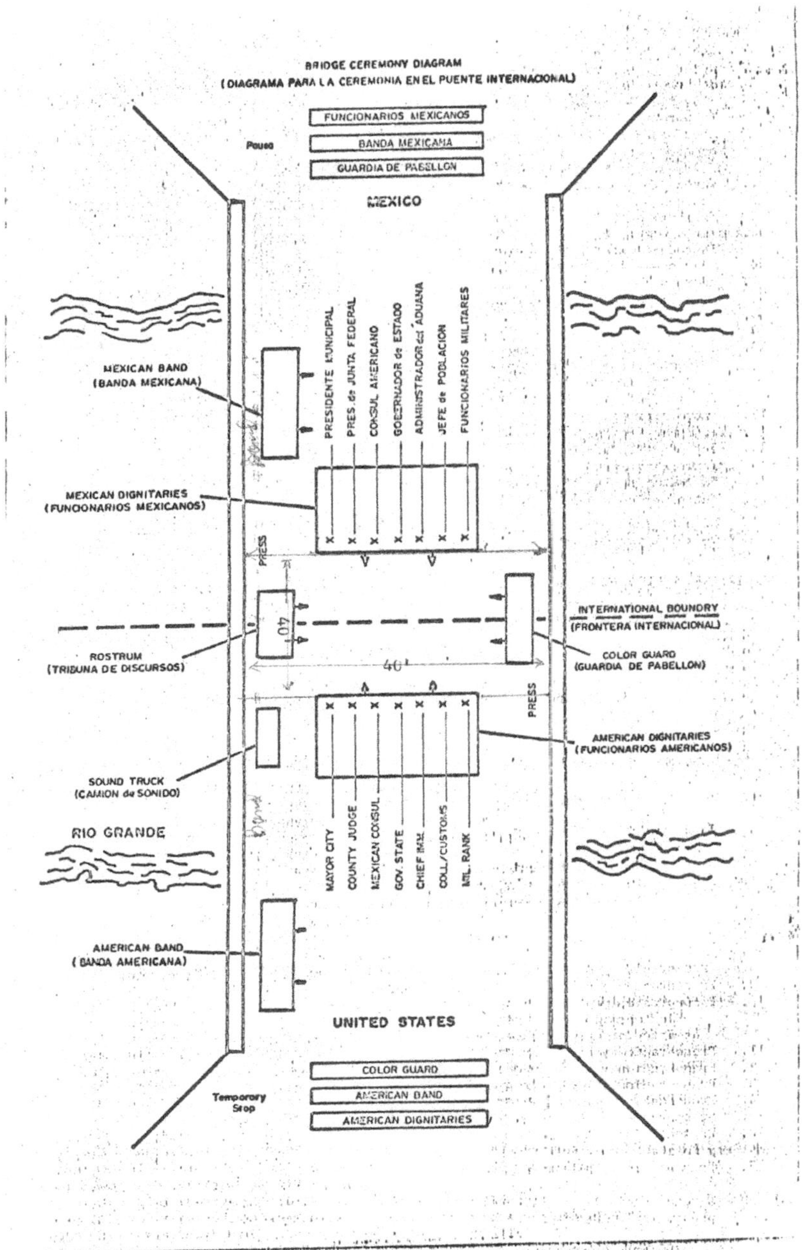

International Bridge Ceremony diagram, 1974. Courtesy of the Joe A. Guerra Laredo Public Library.

In comparing diagrams from 1974 and 1978, I found two differences. First and foremost, the ceremony's start time changed after paso libre ended in 1976. During the era of free bridge-crossing privileges, American and Mexican dignitaries would line up on their respective sides of the bridge at 9:40 a.m., after Gateway to the Americas International Bridge traffic was halted (temporarily) at 9:15. In 1978 coordinators stopped vehicular traffic at the Juárez-Lincoln International Bridge at 7:45 a.m., and the dignitaries were expected to be in their places by 8:40. The time change highlights the additional time and labor that accrued onto the event after its location change from a pedestrian bridge to a nonpedestrian bridge. Once paso libre ended, immigration officials on both sides of the border had to verify that people wanting to step on to the bridge that morning had the right credentials. Moreover, they had to verify the citizenship or visa status of all participants, even VIP guests like the governors of Mexican states. After 1976 exchanging an embrace in the middle of the bridge did not guarantee that you would be able to join the party in the United States.

The second difference involves the manner in which Americans and those Mexican dignitaries who had the right papers physically joined the festivities in Laredo after the ritual. In 1978, as was tradition, both countries' dignitaries were transported via small buses from the Juárez-Lincoln Bridge to the parade review stand. During paso libre, American and Mexican dignitaries would walk side-by-side from the Gateway Bridge to the review stand (approximately eight blocks).

A crucial detail here is that being chauffeured to a destination point with a select group of people instead of walking all together, as depicted by photos of paso libre taken in the mid-1970s in which thousands of people followed the lead of Mexican and American abrazo delegation members, communicates two very different messages. Walking in the city, as Michel de Certeau reminds us, is a "pedestrian speech act" and thus has a "triple 'enunciative' function":

> it is a process of *appropriation* of the topographical system on the part of the pedestrian (just as the speaker appropriates and takes on the language); it is a spatial acting-out of the place (just as the speech act is an acoustic acting-out of language); and it implies *relations* among differentiated populations, that is among pragmatic "contracts" in the form of movements (just as verbal enunciation is an "allocution," "posits another opposite" the speaker and puts contracts between interlocutors into action).[48]

Aerial view of the Washington's Birthday Celebration International Parade, c. 1950. Previously the parade review stand had been located in front of Laredo's first post office. Courtesy of the Webb County Heritage Foundation, Laredo.

De Certeau's last point, that walking implies "relations among differentiated populations," speaks to paso libre's broader significance as an act of correspondence. Above and beyond its idiosyncratic place in US-Mexico borderlands history, we can intuit how paso libre, and specifically the act of walking without fear across an international bridge, may have fostered a sense of freedom among participants.

Children to the Front

A factor that links 1974 and 1978—and that continues to sustain the ritual even during periods of instability or moments of crisis—is the participation of children.[49] WBCA mainstay and longtime IGNC-L member Velia Uribe can be credited as the person who added the abrazo children to the International Bridge Ceremony in 1969—seven years before paso libre was discontinued (1976).[50] Spending time with her niece, Candy Hein, and having the privilege of being able to look through personal scrapbooks, I learned that Uribe, working closely with José L. González, introduced the idea to include children in the ceremony. Showing me a photo taken in the mid-1960s, Hein explained that her aunt got the abrazo children's costume idea from her cousin in Nuevo Laredo, who had staged a photo of two boys, one dressed as a charro and the other as a cowboy, holding hands in the middle of the Gateway to the Americas International Bridge. Ms. Uribe modified that idea to complement the WBC festivities. The cowboy became a mini–George Washington, if you will, and he was joined by a little girl also dressed in early American colonial garb. A little girl dressed in a china poblana dress joined the charro to represent Mexico. Making four children the protagonists of the border enactment simultaneously created good press photos and neutralized negative coverage of paso libre as an illegal border-crossing spectacle.[51]

Children dressed to represent Mexico and the United States tied the festivities' reliance on disparate histories, timelines, occasions, and protagonists (e.g., Washington, Pocahontas, Noche Mexicana) together in ways that were not possible before. Before 1969 politicians dressed in "political uniform" (business formal attire) would walk toward each other on the bridge. National symbols such as flags adorned the scene, but those bridge ceremony actors did not dress to embody the nations they were representing. The abrazo children's participation marks but one aspect of the ritual, but it quickly took on a metonymic function.

Bringing in Claudio Lomnitz's analysis of late Porfirian Mexico—and his reading of an interview with Porfirio Díaz published in a US magazine—can help us understand how casting, wardrobing, and choreographing children generates much more than a display of international goodwill. Lomnitz borrows Mikhail Bakhtin's idea of chronotypes, which he interprets as "the spatiotemporal matrices that are the base condition of all narratives and linguistic acts." Spatiotemporal matrices, he explains, "are key elements of ideology, and in them a *single image* [Díaz's portrait featured in the interview in Lomnitz's case, and the children's abrazo in ours] *can stand iconically for a set of posited connections between time and place.* Movement in space can be figured as movement in time, and vice versa" (emphasis mine).[52]

Children meeting in the middle of the bridge enacts the concept of a chronotype. Their embrace "stands iconically for a set of posited connections between time and place" (i.e., the border as a place where the best versions of colonial America and postcolonial Mexico meet). And while George, Martha, Pocahontas, a charro, a china poblana, and Miguel Hidalgo never coincided or crossed paths in real life, the children's abrazo invites them to coexist during the festivities as personifications of national iden-

Óscar Bruni and Marco Uribe, c. 1965. This photograph of Velia Uribe's nephews meeting in the center of the Gateway to the Americas International Bridge inspired her to add the abrazo children to the ritual in 1969. Courtesy of Candelaria "Candy" Hein.

tity. After 1969 the International Bridge Ceremony was no longer defined by who was in office at any given time but by a highly curated and largely unchanging vision of the history conveyed in miniature. A past identified by celebration boosters as profitably authentic.

Year-Round Planning and Communication

Keeping everyone on task the day of the ritual was challenging, and it was not necessarily due to the involvement of children. Indeed, multiple conversations with Víctor Oliveros, an engineer who worked alongside González at the health department, reminded me that details laid out on paper and the actual execution of them do not always align. That sentiment rang true in 2015 when I helped set up the bridge ceremony. The American IGNC-L volunteer in charge of rolling out the red carpet that marks the location of the international boundary line, the place where abrazos are exchanged, counted out ten steps into the United States before setting it down. He explained, "We will have jurisdiction just in case anything happens."[53] While good to know, that detail does not change the ceremony's projected sentiment of goodwill and trust. The ritual looks the same. Then and now, coordinators' underlying goal is to ensure, through advance preparation, that the ritual communicates continuity and stability, even if that risks the event coming off as being too predictable or redundant. Even then, giving into "redundancy," to use anthropologist Stanley Tambiah's phrasing—the "unvarying recurrences" noted by seasoned bridge ceremony actors—allows the ritual to do more.[54]

Conveying stability through redundancy, even as open-bridge crowds could be seen "getting too close," required actively maintaining cross-border relationships and maintaining open lines of communication year-round.[55] My participation in the ceremony, the interviews I conducted, and the archival research I completed clarified how attending bridge ceremony planning meetings on both sides of the border, drawing up the guest list, and extending invitations could deepen relationships. Longtime coordinators and volunteers knew what to expect, whom to expect, and most importantly, what had to be done. The plan remained constant. So, over time, meetings and chats with familiar faces could easily double as opportunities to collaborate on extra-celebration projects.[56] Under the guidance of Mr. González, for example, laying the groundwork for the abrazo ceremony also advanced public health border initiatives.

González explained the benefits of cultivating cross-border lines of communication in a speech he delivered at a public health convention in Santa Fe, New Mexico, in 1969.[57] I stumbled on a copy of the speech, aptly titled "The Left Arm of Public Health," early on in the research process. Its suggestiveness inspired me to develop further my ideas about border scaffolding.

> Because of our border location this sister city of Nuevo Laredo bears an important factor and role in our public health programs. Suffice to say that truly as sister cities that we are, the bond of friendship and understanding that disease and its prevention brings, is cemented very closely in the functions of both health departments, and our lines of communication and cooperation have no barriers. I invite any and all to visit us for positive proof of this statement. The health programming in Nuevo Laredo, as ours, is discussed mutually and with a genuine interest in the benefits of the people. . . . In 1955, we began in Laredo the first of a series of cooperative programs—a food-handler educational program conducted jointly by our health department and that of Nuevo Laredo. This has developed into other programs [in] the work of the US-Mexico border environmental control project.[58]

Semi-structured interviews helped me understand how cross-border bridge ceremony coordination went hand-in-hand with cross-border program development. In addition to gifting me a copy of *The People Who Did! Fifteen Years of Progress in Disease Control, Laredo, Texas, 1954–1968*, which describes Laredo and Nuevo Laredo's role in developing the first comprehensive community disease control demonstration program, Victor Oliveros talked me through the specific instances in which bridge choreography lent itself to the Port of Laredo's public health goals. Oliveros explained, for example, that working with the *jefe de aduanas* (chief of Customs in Nuevo Laredo), a regular bridge ceremony participant, helped expedite the transport of vials used to collect *muestras de esputo* (sputum samples) when testing for tuberculosis. Depending on the urgency of the situation, water-installation materials used in border *colonias* could be deemed tax exempt. The point, he reminded me, was not that working on the ceremony solved all border health problems.[59] But the face time accrued during the planning process made it easier to collect data that helped develop communicable disease prevention programs. The ease with which bridge ceremony coordinators and participants communicated after years of working together also came in handy when dealing with unexpected problems or complications. He, or any of his bridge ceremony colleagues in Nuevo Laredo, for that matter, could pick up the phone any day of the year and call to ask for advice or help.

Additional Benefits of Careful Choreography and Strategic Casting

Strategic casting and adhering to strict rules of protocol are key to the International Bridge Ceremony's success and are important pieces of the paso libre puzzle. Unlike coordinating the ritual's choreography, which unfolds in the same place and on a predetermined date, casting the actors is much more difficult because big personalities invite big drama. One WBCA member described that pre-abrazo ceremony preparation often involved attending meetings in Laredo and Nuevo Laredo to see who was on the invitee list that year. The political landscape of that given year (the parties in power and the networking benefits certain personalities could bring to the festivities) determined the guest list. As soon as team members had a sense of who should receive an invitation, they tried to secure the governors' attendance. "That was always the first task," one WBCA member emphasized. "The governor of Texas will not agree to participate if the governor of Tamaulipas has declined the invitation," or vice versa.[60] Then came the work of drafting invitations to US and Mexican members of Congress, the general of the Mexican army in Nuevo Laredo, and the president of the United States. I interrupted him at that point to ask why they invited the president if it was unlikely that he would be able to attend. "We [the WBCA] are officially representing the United States during the bridge ceremony, so the commander in chief should be notified and welcomed," he explained. And to maintain balance, he added, protocol demands that they invite the president of the Republic of Mexico. "We do it that way because it has to be done that way."[61]

Step two of the process involves hand delivering the invitations to dignitaries and honorees based in Mexico and the United States—a standard practice over several generations. In the 1950s, for example, WBCA members, many of whom were also customs brokers and IGNC-L members, would fly to Mexico City or take a group bus trip to Ciudad Victoria, Monterrey, and Saltillo.[62] Similarly, in the 1980s, WBCA executive board members, Laredo's mayor, and state representatives would travel to Austin every other year to personally invite the governor of Texas to the festivities. The abrazo children would also travel and make an appearance in full costume. When asked about Nuevo Laredo officials' participation, a former WBCA president clarified that "they would not always go, but they were always invited."[63]

Another longtime WBCA member explained the process in a similar way. But he emphasized different elements. For him, maintaining balance was crucial because people, especially important figures, tend to get upset if they have to embrace someone who they believe is of lesser importance. An extreme example of this would be the governor of Tamaulipas having to embrace a Texas state senator. And if invited guests do not have a good time, if their presence is overlooked at an event, they will walk away with a bad impression of Laredo. If that were to happen, that invitee would be less likely to support initiatives that benefit port business. A slight—real, perceived, or accidental—would mean that "relations would be approached with reluctance."

Ensuring that WBC guests have the best experience possible requires access to municipal resources, the majority support of port businesses, and protocol training. One WBCA associate summoned his experience courting power players in the 1960s and 1970s. The association would take advantage of the fact that the Texas legislature would adjourn at noon on Thursday—the day before the start of the festivities. An oil company would oversee the transportation of congressmen from Houston, for example, to Austin and then on to Laredo. At the airport in Laredo, ten to fifteen vehicles, which were driven by WBCA members or their employees, would take the guests to the Hamilton Hotel (the best hotel in Laredo at the time). A WBCA volunteer would be assigned to each guest and would escort them to events so everyone could mingle in the same room. Indeed, several interviewees could clearly recall what their job was and how they felt doing it. International banker and longtime bridge ceremony volunteer Gerald Schwebel, for example, said he was "awestruck" his senior year in high school when he was entrusted with being Texas governor Preston Smith's "personal gofer."[64]

That level of attention made it easy for guests to want to accept their invitation year after year. As was the staging of lavish events in Nuevo Laredo, like re-creating Xochimilco at the Hacienda Hotel as part of the festivities in 1974. In another example, participants likely enjoyed the Salute to George Washington *charreada* (a rodeo with displays of horsemanship, roping, etc.) that Lic. Gilberto Cazares, head of the Mexican immigration service in Nuevo Laredo, produced on the Mexican side of the border in 1970.[65] It is also worth noting that LULAC Council No. 12 began to stage extravagant versions of Noche Mexicana in Laredo around the same time, fiestas generously sponsored by don Francisco Javier Sauza (of Sauza tequila). That event consistently attracted high-profile revelers from both sides of the border for the next two decades.[66]

Multiple WBC actors recalled that paying transportation and housing costs out of pocket or using their own personnel to get established elites or even politicians "on the ascent" to participate in the festivities was seen as a good business investment.[67] Selection committee members had to have intimate knowledge of who was being groomed for leadership positions. One of my interlocutors explained, "They weren't the big fish then, but they would be someday."[68] And getting to know them before they rose to power made it easier to pitch projects or ideas down the road.

His explanation resonated with the narratives of interviewees who reflected on the process after paso libre's termination. Several people recalled discussions to build a full-fledged university in Laredo in the early 1990s. They asked themselves whether "they wanted to have the last university of the old century or the first university of the new century." Accounts of how this was achieved varied depending on who I asked. A few people mentioned that important conversations took place at the SMW ball (on the edge of the dance floor). Others suggested that Lt. Gov. Bob Bullock's participation in the festivities as the Mr. South Texas honoree in 1993 "made things happen." Some of my interlocutors explained the process in detail. Others dwelled on heated debates about the name of the university. If the university were to have taken the name Texas A&M University at Laredo, as had been suggested by some powerful decision makers, the corresponding acronym would have been TAMAL. And that would "denigrate the school and tarnish the A&M reputation" because TAMAL would remind people of the tamale (a Mesoamerican dish prepared with steamed corn husks). In 1995 the 74th Texas Legislature approved the four-year status of Texas A&M International University (TAMIU), not TAMAL, and the city celebrated the inauguration of the university's three-hundred-acre campus located along Bob Bullock Loop (Texas State Highway Loop 20, named in honor of the man who helped make it happen).[69]

Margarita Tourism and a Maid Trade

Precise choreography and strategic casting are key elements of the border scaffolding work carried out during the era of paso libre; they could mend fences that year and shape future politicking strategies. And, more importantly, they shielded paso libre from scrutiny, which stimulated economic

“Laredo Is Up.” Laredo Chamber of Commerce promotional advertisement, c. 1965. Courtesy of the Laredo Chamber of Commerce.

activity on both sides of the border. Market Square in downtown Nuevo Laredo, for example, consistently attracted "margarita tourism," but customer numbers grew exponentially during the festivities. As one SMW member I interviewed put it, "The events were held in Laredo, but everyone wanted to party in Nuevo Laredo."[70] The use of the word "party" here signals a variety of things—from drinking and dancing to sex escapades. Indeed, as intimated in earlier chapters, celebration boosters advertised the festivities as an opportunity to travel to Nuevo Laredo and as a way to get a taste of border life.

Nuevo Laredo–bound festival participants also wanted to shop—for souvenirs and tchotchkes as well as more refined Mexican curios, including handcrafted textiles, glassware, pottery, and baskets. Marti Franco, owner of Marti's, an upscale jewelry, textile, and art shop/gallery located a few blocks from the Gateway to the Americas Bridge, told me on several occasions how important the sales in February were for her business. "We made our money for the whole year," she told me in slow, perfectly accented English.[71] Born in Turkey but raised in Mexico City, Marti moved to Nuevo Laredo in the early 1950s and opened her first store in 1954. A discerning nonagenarian, she oversaw operations at Marti's until 2009, when sales-paralyzing drug cartel violence forced her to move the business north of the border to San Antonio. When I asked her what she remembered most about the era of free bridge-crossing privileges, she mentioned "*toda la gente esperando*" (all of the people waiting to cross the border).[72] She also recalled that WBC honorees and special guests, particularly high-ranking state officials, would stop by her store with or without paso libre.

Caravans of pedestrians-cum-consumers not only spread the wealth but also kindled short- and long-term labor opportunities. For example, San Agustín Plaza (recall this is the place where Matias de Llano staged Noche Mexicana in 1925) doubled as a recruiting point for domestic workers. One Laredoan I interviewed, Raquel Gutiérrez, caught me completely off guard when she casually mentioned, "We would get all the maids . . . *las sirvientas* [during paso libre]." She explained:

> I remember in the seventies when I had a little child and, you know, I was working full time. And, oooh, let's see how many come and lots of people would come. And during the paso libre [they would] stay here until December and then they would leave . . . and then come back in February. . . . So all January we would be without. But of course they would leave in December to spend Christmas with their family and then come back in February.

But how did it work, I asked?

> We would put ads in the paper. I would put ads across the river. I would put ads. *Busco* [seeking], you know, *señora cuide niños* [childcare], *limpie casa* [housecleaning], *ayude con el trabajo del hogar* [help with housework]. I would put the ad in the paper and put my number. And they would call, "*Ay señora*, I'm looking for a job," and then I would ask, "Where are you?" "Well I am at Plaza San Agustín," you know, where they would go. And I would go and interview them and then I would bring them. A lot of people did that.

Was it necessary to put an ad in the paper? I asked. Or would it be enough just to go to the plaza? "Both things, I think, both things," she responded.[73]

Intrigued by Raquel's admission that she had placed ads for a *sirvienta*, I set out to find examples.[74] At the *archivos municipales* (municipal archives) in Nuevo Laredo and at the Benson Library at the University of Texas at Austin, I found Spanish-language newspapers whose classified ad sections consistently carried solicitations for live-in domestic workers and sometimes featured ads for work opportunities in the interior of the United States. During the years of paso libre, however, the number of ads placed in January and February multiplied. And they all basically followed the same format: "SOLICITO Sirvienta. Trabajo general de casa. Debe quedarse. Llame 72X-XXXX" (Maid Wanted. General housekeeping. Be prepared to stay. Call 72X-XXXX).[75]

The maid trade that developed during paso libre was not a border-centric phenomenon that drew widespread attention.[76] In the instances that border security was reinforced during the WBC festivities, smugglers were targeted, not domestic workers. The maid trade was certainly not unique to Laredo, but the fact that it operated systematically for close to two decades differentiates it from transborder labor dynamics at other ports of entry.[77] Domestic workers who would cross into Laredo during paso libre were not in possession of a Form 13 crossing document, a card issued at the immigration office in Nuevo Laredo. So it became customary for those laborers to stay in Laredo until the end of December or early January, at which time they would travel back to Nuevo Laredo to spend time with their families before returning in February to work, sometimes in the same house or else for different employers. That cycle could continue only as long as paso libre lasted.[78]

The End of Paso Libre

Hundreds of laborers—domestic workers as well as two-to-three-day job workers like plumbers, carpenters, and welders—animated WBC-oriented border-crossing patterns.[79] The termination of paso libre in 1977 took those options out of the equation and effectively created a new, albeit smaller, class of impossible subjects who chose to stay in the United States permanently. Similar to the way that my interlocutors were hard-pressed to locate with precision the beginning of paso libre, they refrained from pinpointing why the tradition ended. I heard several theories during my time in the field. One former customs official explained that colleagues at other ports of entry in South Texas (e.g., Brownsville-Matamoros) had long since wondered why they could not offer paso libre as part of their annual Charro Days celebration.[80] Persistent inquiries and mounting complaints about the unevenness of an arrangement that funneled pedestrian traffic to the Laredo crossing put an end to the practice. Several people suggested that border immigration had become such a hot topic nationally that paso libre could not continue. Mr. Delgado, for example, showed me an article and large photo of paso libre featured on the front page of the *Los Angeles Times* to reinforce his point.[81] Reflecting on her experience with the maid trade, Mrs. Gutiérrez wondered out loud, "Maybe that's why they stopped it?"[82]

The completion of a second international bridge at the Port of Laredo definitely played a key role in paso libre's discontinuation. From synchronizing construction schedules and determining costs to anticipating the devaluation of the Mexican peso to conducting last-minute archeological surveys and worrying about drug smuggling, second bridge planning efforts took decades.[83] In contrast, the actual construction process was relatively swift, but it also faced enormous challenges.[84] Weeks before the inauguration, Paul Garza, the lead engineer on the project (also a prominent LULAC Council No. 12 member), captured the project's expectations and setbacks when he noted, "Back in 1963 we envisioned the second International Bridge would be completed in time for travelers to use it who were going to the 1968 World Olympics in Mexico City."[85]

The long-awaited inauguration of the Juárez-Lincoln International Bridge on November 26, 1976, a wider structure that could handle commercial truck traffic more comfortably and that would link up directly to US Interstate 35, became the official reason why port authorities could not offer paso libre in 1977.[86] The WBCA decided to change the location of the abrazo ceremony from the Gateway to the Americas International Bridge to the Juárez-Lincoln International Bridge to celebrate the achievement and to build excitement around the festivities. But the new bridge was not pedestrian friendly; its purpose was to fast-track trailer trucks, not people.[87] That detail raised an indisputable point: it would not be safe to let thousands of people cross the bridge because they would walk straight into oncoming I-35 automobile traffic.[88] Offering paso libre became a public safety issue. Put another way, no one person, group, or agency decided to discontinue the tradition. Once celebration boosters decided to move the abrazo ritual to the new bridge, the end of paso libre was a done deal.[89]

The change of location did not modify ritual choreography, but it did open up a window of opportunity in terms of participation and inclusion. 1977 marked the first time LULAC Council No. 12 members presented Señor Internacional awards as part of their Noche Mexicana gala. Conceived with the intention of celebrating the "blending of two great cultures" in Laredo, the award honors two individuals: a representative from Latin America and another from the United States. An honoree must be an "internationally known outstanding personality who has distinguished himself through his achievements, recognition, involvement in business interests, and his inspirational leadership and counsel in the development of his community and country."[90] One of my interlocutors shared that the Señor Internacional award was created in response to the Mr. South Texas award (established in 1952), which he described as being for "*puros gringos*" (only for Anglo-Americans). Council members were tired of being underestimated, of being perceived as a WBC group that "could not organize a proper event" or "give out a formal award." He added that many of the council's projects were actually very successful, even if kernel ideas were initially "*puro* Mickey Mouse" (Spanglish for cartoon dreams) or "*puro guato*" (over the top, fantastical) most of the time.[91]

LULAC members agreed that the first Señor Internacional honorees—don Francisco Javier Sauza of Sauza Tequila and Dr. José Silva of Silva Mind Control—should share an embrace during the International Bridge Ceremony. It made perfect sense because Sauza, a friend of the celebration, represented Latin America and Silva represented the United States. They pitched the idea to WBCA leaders before the festivities but were unable to get Sauza and Silva on the program. General thoughts about that rejection, among LULAC members at least, assumed that the WBCA leadership did not want "to share power." And they were correct. One influential member I interviewed was quick to emphasize that declining their request was not so much about racism really: it was about maintaining full control of the ceremony. Undeterred, LULAC members approached that year's International Bridge Ceremony master of ceremonies, Reynaldo Garza, who was the federal judge for the US District Court for the Southern District of Texas (and the first Mexican American to be appointed to a US federal court), at the preceremony breakfast.[92] Judge Garza agreed to "slip in" the names of the honorees. Sauza and Silva's names were literally written on small pieces of paper and read by Judge Garza on the bridge. Executed with finesse as not to disrupt bridge ritual choreography, that moment of improvisation expanded the International Bridge Ceremony in important ways and for years to come. Thereafter, VIP participants would include celebrities like actor Mario Moreno "Cantinflas" (1979) and musician Freddy Fender (1981), not just big-name politicians. Moreover, that script modification enhanced the LULAC organization's profile and Latina/o activism efforts during a pivotal moment in the development of US multiculturalist politics.

The Tale of the "Undelivered Bridge"

I vividly remember feeling frustrated by the many question marks surrounding paso libre, particularly when I knew that it was linked to the bridge reconstruction process after Hurricane Alice but not knowing why exactly. I decided to look closely at the process of acquiring permission to construct an international bridge, not just between the United States and Mexico but also between the United States and Canada. That is when I came upon what I like to call "the tale of the undelivered bridge at Laredo." The story of Mexico refusing to deliver its side of the bridge in December 1956 had made its way into discussions in the US Senate in 1959. As the Committee on Foreign Relations debated future international bridge construction projects, the topic touched on the US State Department's prerogative to cede "privileges of international diplomacy to Texas." Sen. Ralph Yarborough (D-Texas) cautioned: "When the Laredo Bridge was finished, the Mexican Government just closed it up."[93] This was the first time Mexico came into focus for me as a motive force in the paso libre story.

Once I had figured out enough about the when, the how, and the why, I asked some of my interlocutors, particularly those who had lived it, what they thought about paso libre. Not whether it was a good idea or a bad idea, but what they thought of it as a practice. Understandably, my abstract question was often interpreted as a request to reflect on the possibility and feasibility of free bridge-crossing privileges in the here and now. More often than not, my conversation partners offered one of these three responses: things changed after 9/11; we are living in a different time; and paso libre is a thing of the past.

Open-bridge privileges at the Port of Laredo may have been suspended indefinitely after 1976, but there is one point worth reiterating before we move forward. Making border infrastructure an object of study—its co-ownership and management dynamics as well as instances of creative re-purposing—can help us learn from the past in more precise ways. That possibility came into focus when I interviewed a retired CBP commissioner at his office in Washington, DC. He noted that Mexico's decision to keep its half of the bridge closed in 1956 was a "forcing function," which he defined as a "tactical and strategic option that [is] exercised to produce the best outcome." He recalled Operation Camarena to illustrate his point. That operation was named for DEA agent Enrique Camarena Salazar, who was abducted in Guadalajara, Mexico, on February 7, 1985. Wanting to make a statement about Mexican officials' slow response to the murder and their "inability or unwillingness to find his murderers," US Customs Service Commissioner William Von Rabb "closed the bridges." He did not really close the bridges, my interlocutor clarified, but he "definitely mandated that every car, every person, every truck be inspected, thereby slowing down cross-border trade to almost a standstill."[94]

The former commissioner's thoughts on the power dynamics behind bridge closures helped me put paso libre into perspective. The practice mainly endured to serve the port's commercial interests, not to encourage immigration for immigration's sake. So, even if the days of free bridge-crossing privileges are behind us, understanding how paso libre came about in the first place and how it endured is worthwhile. The phenomenon itself may be anomalous but the lessons it can teach us are more relevant than ever. Namely, the consequences of proposing unilateral action, especially when border infrastructure is in play, are real and far-reaching. Also, rehearsing cross-border coordination and communication, even under festive pretenses, can prove useful during times of crisis.

CHAPTER 5

Us, Them, and Festive Security

Around ten p.m. on Friday, February 19, 2010, los Zetas, one of northern Mexico's most powerful drug cartels, engaged Mexican federal officers in a grenade and gunfire attack underneath the Juárez-Lincoln International Bridge in Nuevo Laredo.[1] A bilateral team comprised of federal and municipal actors with different jurisdictions and objectives gathered in a secure location to assess the damage. Although many people in the room that evening were accustomed to meeting on a monthly basis as part of post-9/11 border security protocol, the fact that the WBC festivities were in full swing raised the stakes.[2] Hundreds of people were already camping out blocks away from the site of the firefight to claim the best seats for the grand parade the next morning. In addition to assessing risk and safety issues, those officials had to factor in the abrazo ritual. (Could they ensure the children's safety?) One Nuevo Laredo official in the room that evening ominously recalled, "Ya mero se canceló" ([The abrazo ceremony] was almost cancelled).[3]

After a long night of discussion, City of Laredo officials ultimately had the final say and concluded around four a.m. that the bridge ceremony should go on as scheduled.[4] This was not surprising. Recall from the last chapter that the red carpet marking the international boundary line, the point on the bridge where abrazos are exchanged, is laid down ten steps toward Laredo to make sure that the United States can claim jurisdiction over any incident that might occur. Even then, the decision to move forward with the ritual was binationally informed and supported—sweeping the scene for threats, checking in with informants on the ground, and reinforcing security on site with additional snipers and plain-clothes personnel.[5]

Interviewees in Laredo, Nuevo Laredo, and Washington, DC, all made it clear that ensuring everyone's safety was the top priority.[6] At the same time, contemplating a change of location, even if the bridge ceremony was not the Zeta's target, would be equivalent to publicly admitting fear of the "what if."[7] And decision makers, particularly actors based in Laredo, were well aware that recent changes to WBC programming, specifically shying away from organizing charreadas and *callejoneadas* (street parties) in Nuevo Laredo, was already communicating fear.[8] Letting the bridge ceremony play out as planned would signal strength.[9] One city official captured that sentiment with a pithy dig: drug cartel activity was not going to "muscle us off of our own bridge."

This glimpse into the decision-making process that evening reveals where the WBC festivities' border scaffolding characteristics meet contemporary border security issues. It shows how managing the International Bridge Ceremony through moments of acute instability can generate opportunities for leadership on both sides of the border to fine-tune partnerships and crisis scenario action plans.

Preventing transnational organized crime activity from changing the way things have always been done cuts across national identity and jurisdiction to the heart of the politics of border festivals. It also invokes age-old anxieties about authority and the power to make decisions on-site (the border) as opposed to far away (Washington, DC, and Mexico City).[10] Would off-site legislators and federal law enforcement officials have proceeded in the same way as their counterparts at the border did? Probably. As Peter Andreas reminds us, legislators in the United States and Mexico "go to great lengths to project an image of collaboration and cooperation in fighting drugs—an image that has been tarnished by many public embarrassments but is nevertheless sustained with great care in order not to jeopardize their mutual interest in a stable and close economic relationship."[11] While I fully agree with Andreas, this instance is different because that image is protected festively, with costumes, flags, anthems, and abrazos.

This chapter delves deeper into that idea of festive security—one of the book's running themes. The first chapter, for example, alludes to the ways in which individual and collective notions of security are tied to national identity in a border environment.[12] Recall that IORM members drew on George Washington's civil religious legacy to secure Laredo, Texas, for America. Chapter two traces shifts in national identity politics at the border, but it also draws our attention to a different idea of security: how planning the WBC International Bridge Ceremony with certain objectives in mind buoyed the Port of Laredo's economic interests at important junctures (e.g., winning the Meridian Highway bid in the 1920s). Chapters three and four detail the International Bridge reconstruction process after

Hurricane Alice and the tradition of paso libre that followed to highlight how the festivities and the "expectation of ritual" not only protected the port's gateway reputation but also bolstered Nuevo Laredo and Laredo's tourism economies.

Drawing on ethnographic research conducted on both sides of the border, this final chapter continues the task of examining the multiple spaces and opportunities for border scaffolding work that arise as part of WBC preparations.[13] The evidence presented in the following pages highlights the resiliency of the International Bridge Ceremony and the power that the expectation of ritual can yield during sustained periods of border insecurity linked to drug cartel activity (2005–2015). Crucially, it will also show how cross-border partnerships as well as intragroup relationships are not immune to antagonism and separation.

Building on US-Mexico borderlands scholarship that examines cross-border negotiation among nonstate actors, this chapter foregrounds the capacity of civil society organizations to persevere under duress.[14] Unlikely protagonists, members of civil society groups like the WBCA, the IGNC-L, and the CIBV-NL are not policymakers or military strategists.[15] They do not necessarily identify as activists and are hardly ever disenfranchised by enhanced immigration measures. They are not tasked with the obligation to combat drug cartel violence. And yet this analysis shows that while not factored into security planning, their projects and goals overlap in significant ways.[16]

To be clear, this analysis does not discount the work of appointed and elected officials or the strategies of US and Mexican federal law enforcement agencies; nor does it deny that "borders are major loci of state bureaucracies" and that state-sanctioned efforts overtly and covertly protect border residents.[17] It argues that the cross-border work behind coordinating the International Bridge Ceremony, a border enactment that relies on the participation of elected and state-appointed actors, law enforcement officials, business elites, members of civil society organizations, and children, gives rise to "spatial alternatives"—site-specific occasions and practices that can refine, not undermine, contemporary approaches to border security.[18]

The Backdrop: Border Security after 9/11

The attacks of September 11, 2001, introduced specific border security changes and challenges at US-Mexico ports of entry.[19] To be sure, the creation of the Department of Homeland Security (DHS) tested interagency working relationships across the nation.[20] But subsequent legislation such as the Secure Fence Act (2006) placed additional pressure on DHS actors working at ports of entry because they were tasked with magnifying the "physical power of the state"—physical barriers, checkpoints, manpower, surveillance apparatus—while continuing to facilitate the steady and efficient movement of cargo.[21]

One Laredo-based US Customs officer, Gerardo Maldonado, generously walked me through the reality of those changes over the course of several interviews. In terms of reformulating binational cooperation strategies, he recalled, "creating cross-border protocol for bomb threats at the bridge was key in the wake of 9/11 and into the first years of heavy cartel violence. A contract was signed on both sides." "May I see the contract?" I asked. He smiled but didn't smile (if that makes sense). "Access to this contract is limited, as it is law-enforcement sensitive," Maldonado explained. He continued, "Cross-border communication was made a priority. Something as simple as adding two-way radios to the mix, instead of dialing a landline that would result in a phone ringing and ringing in an empty office, expedited planning and response times." He also noted that US agencies wanted to get a handle on things, and Mexican agencies cooperated (in other words, accepted the blurring of jurisdictional lines) because they were dealing with a "hot potato."[22] Drug violence had a firm grasp on Nuevo Laredo, and pedestrian/commuter traffic numbers were suffering.

Mexican president Felipe Calderón's declaration of war against drug cartels in his home state of Michoacán days into his administration in 2006 further complicated Laredo and Nuevo Laredo's security and trade goals. Calderón's sweeping declaration is often highlighted as a watershed moment that exacerbated drug-related violence in Mexico.[23] Statistical analyses of Calderón's tenure and that of his successor, Enrique Peña Nieto (2012–2018), show that "disappearances" in Mexico increased over 500 percent in 2007. According to data collected by the Registro Nacional de Datos de Personas Extraviadas o Desaparecidas (RNDPED), between 2007 and 2012, one person disappeared in Mexico every four hours. Between 2013 and 2014, statistics show one person went missing every two hours.[24] Instituto Nacional de Estadística y Geografía (INEGI) data communicates that intentional acts of violence linked to drug trafficking accounted for 31.9 percent of all (known) homicides in 2007, 63.4 percent in 2010, and 53.8 percent in 2011.[25] Those numbers were often higher along Mexico's southern border with Guatemala and its northern boundary with the United States.[26]

In the Port of Laredo's case, drug cartel violence had already escalated before Calderón took his swing at the cartels.[27] As one of the hemisphere's busiest inland ports, Laredo and Nuevo Laredo had long since grown accustomed to hosting an ever-changing roster of actors and business interests. The Sinaloa Cartel's decision to shift its drug trafficking operations to the Texas-Tamaulipas border in 2003, for example, instigated a bloody power grab among competing cartels (e.g., Tijuana, Juárez, Sinaloa-Sonora, and the Gulf Cartels) vying for direct access to key distribution routes: the federal and interstate highways that converge at the Port of Laredo (discussed in chapter 2).[28] Street warfare in Nuevo Laredo between cartel members and Mexican law enforcement officers intensified. Neo-laredenses, as well as refugees and economic migrants making their way from the interior of Mexico and Central America to the United States, confronted violence—beheadings, mass shootings, kidnappings, disappearances, and extortion—with increased frequency.[29]

Alarm bells began to ring in 2004.[30] International and national news coverage often included words like "insanity" and phrases like "war zone" to depict violence on the border at the Port of Laredo.[31] Local newspapers like *El Mañana de Nuevo Laredo* and the *Laredo Times* informed public perception, as much with their periods of silence as with their day-to-day coverage. Similar to other places in the Republic of Mexico, journalists became targets. Marking the onset of Nuevo Laredo's battle with drug cartel violence, *El Mañana* journalist Roberto Javier Mora García was stabbed outside his home in 2004. One of eight (confirmed) journalists to be killed in Mexico in 2011, María Elizabeth Macías Castro, editor of the Nuevo Laredo–based newspaper *Primera Hora* and a blogger who used the code name "La Nena de Nuevo Laredo," was decapitated in September.[32] Drug cartels' use of *narcomantas* (large signs or banners displayed in public) to claim responsibility for violent acts and to threaten competitors or noncompliers, further complicated journalists' work.[33]

Broadcasting on a different frequency, congressional testimony provided a platform for border officials and business elites to educate federal legislators about drug cartel activity and the threat of "spillover" violence.[34] In addition to sharing firsthand details, expert witnesses used the opportunity to angle for more resources or even advocate for scaled-back security strategies. One Laredo-based bank president offered the following testimony before the US Congress in 2006:

> The "build-a-wall and throw-them-out" mentality is in essence a "denial-of-admission agenda" that is anti-immigrant, anti-tourist, and anti-commerce.

> We cannot continue to abuse our neighboring countries through excessive border security sending a "don't come" message when all these visitors want to do is spend money and add value to our economy.[35]

Border business actors were keen on promoting the logic of smart security, but talk of spillover violence—often described as involving aggravated assault, home invasions, auto theft, kidnappings, and extortion—handily upstaged their efforts. Complicating matters further, understandings of what constitutes spillover violence varied according to the speaker's home base. South Texas legislators and law enforcement officials, for example, had a decidedly different take on the gravity of the threat than did their colleagues in Washington, DC.[36]

Drug cartel violence took center stage, but it is important to remember that border populations were still learning how to negotiate post-9/11 security shifts. It is also important to clarify that the border was not the only place where things changed. As geographer Matthew J. Coleman reminds us, the "devolutionary trend in immigration enforcement" after 9/11 led to "the expansion of interior [immigration] enforcement via state and local authorities."[37] Those living adjacent to an international boundary line, however, were subject to increased surveillance and checks—a constant source of anxiety for "mixed-status" families.[38] In some cases, as Jason Ackelson notes, "the biggest change in North American border communities appears to be psychological . . . a general feeling of increased separation and heightened difference."[39] Drug cartel violence, or, more precisely, the fear of spillover violence, certainly incited separation plans, but it did not exempt Port of Laredo officials from their WBC responsibilities, which included embracing in the middle of their International Bridge.[40]

Violence Takes Hold

In 2004 International Bridge Ceremony participants exchanged abrazos surrounded by extra security. As should be anticipated by now, Master of Ceremonies Ignacio Urrabazo Jr.'s statement on the bridge that year followed a standard script: "The significance of this ceremony is that two great countries that fought for their independence and two great cities that have established long relationships and strong values meet again at this bridge ceremony."[41] The photo of the abrazo shared by Miguel Hidalgo (Rogelio Rojas Cordova) and George Washington (WBCA president Robert Summers) that accompanied celebration coverage that year did not look particularly different from photos of years past. Nuevo Laredo newspaper *El Mañana*'s coverage of the event, however, told a different story: "Desorganización casi total y ausencia de reconocidos personajes de Laredo, restaron lucidez a la ceremonia anual del 'Abrazo Internacional de las Fiestas de George Washington,' afectadas además por estrictas medidas de seguridad" (In addition to being affected by stricter security measures, the annual WBC International abrazo ceremony lost its shine this year because it was disorganized and lacked the participation of high-profile individuals).[42]

Enacting the abrazo ritual may have sent mixed messages about the reach and impact of drug cartel activity at the Port of Laredo. After all, if George Washington and Miguel Hidalgo could still share an embrace on a hyper-public international stage, then circumstances may not actually be that bad. But any lingering doubts about the severity of the situation were dispelled by a wave of violence in 2005. During a particularly gruesome six-month period in Nuevo Laredo, seventeen police officers were slain and a well-known radio journalist was murdered.[43]

Mexican president Vicente Fox (2000–2006) launched "Operation Safe Mexico" after Nuevo Laredo's chief of police was gunned down in June of that year. But that initiative did not get very far.[44] Legislators in Tamaulipas took to reinvesting in public investigation resources so that "ciudadanos pueden realizar todo tipo de denuncias, sobre todo delitos del fuero común, como robo a domicilio, asalto y allanamiento de morada" (citizens can [freely] report any type of complaint, especially out of the ordinary crimes such as home robberies, assault, and trespassing).[45] That strategy also proved ineffective.

Between 2008 and 2011, state authorities consistently discussed the need for military equipment and additional resources like *unidades motrices* (motor vehicles), *el suministro e instalación de 26 torretas y 26 sirenas* (the supply and installation of sirens and gun turrets), *radios de comunicación* (radios), *aparatos auditivos* (audio equipment), *equipamiento de uniformes para seguridad ciudadana* (uniforms and accessories), and *chalecos balísticos* (bulletproof vests). In 2011 they moved to make legislative changes to reinforce "*el cumplimiento de mandatos judiciales en material de cateos*" (the legality of home invasions [by federal authorities]) and the regulation of "*servicios privados de seguridad*" (private security services).[46]

Unsuccessful campaigns to increase public trust generated skepticism and disorientation on a wider scale.[47] Neolaredenses with enough resources, for example, moved permanently to the United States with an E1 "trade" visa or an E2 "investor" visa, which are basically platinum-express green cards.[48] E1 and E2 visa holders can live and work in the United States under the condition that they carry on "substantial" trade or make "substantial" investments in the US economy.[49] Some of those "new refugees" relocated their entire business operations to Laredo or further into the interior of the United States.[50]

Manuel Guzmán, a retired civil servant from Nuevo Laredo who had recently relocated to Laredo, explained that the situation produced "*una preocupación excesiva o psicosis*" (excessive concern or psychosis). Many people did everything to move because they were scared for their lives: because "*le pasó algo*" (something happened to them), or "*conoce a alguien*" (they know somebody), or "*que lo oyó cercano*" (found themselves in close proximity to violence). Fear, he emphasized, took on a life and an economy of its own. Having a bodyguard, for example, became "trendy"; it became a marker of status.[51]

Raymundo Ríos Mayo, a historian who maintains houses on both sides of the border, also used the word "psicosis" to explain the situation. But discussing how violence can trouble the idea of patriotism's proper geography, he clarified: "Están equivocados, están equivocados en ese sentido. Los factores primordiales acaules que son los de la inseguridad en México, eh . . . deben de tomarlos en cuenta no es que toda la gente que han venido a radicar aquí quiera venirse para acá" (They are mistaken, they are mistaken in that respect. The key factors driving insecurity in Mexico, well . . . we should remember that the people who have relocated [to Laredo, to the United States] did not necessarily want to make the move).[52] Violence does not make relocation a choice; it makes it imperative.

Driving around Nuevo Laredo in the fall of 2013, I was able to note how insecurity had impacted built environments differently in the two Laredos. A "trail of abandoned houses" in some of Nuevo Laredo's wealthier areas revealed the class dimensions of insecurity.[53] With closed and boarded-up nightclubs, bars, markets, and restaurants sandwiched between unyielding tertiary sector businesses like dentists' offices, pharmacies, and currency exchanges, the streets of Nuevo Laredo's downtown district confirmed commercial ruin. In stark contrast, building permit requests soared and home sales and property values increased in Laredo during the same period.[54] Put bluntly by one of my interlocutors in Nuevo Laredo: "Laredo is growing while Nuevo Laredo is dying."[55]

Los Dos Laredos

Media coverage of border violence in Nuevo Laredo that linked the two Laredos or suggested that they were the same place increasingly frustrated actors in Laredo (particularly because law enforcement statistics did not corroborate that narrative).[56] One city employee recalled staff meetings in which colleagues asked: "How do we get ourselves out of this? . . . We can't take on the national media."[57] Unsure how to respond to mounting negative publicity, city staff continued to circulate statistics and emphasize the strong presence of multiple federal, state, and municipal law enforcement groups (the DEA, the US Marshals, CBP, and the FBI, to name a few). Comparing Laredo crime rates with those of other border towns, as well as cities in the interior of the United States with similar population size, became an all-hands-on-deck project.[58] Several studies of border insecurity have made clear that deploying crime statistics to mold public opinion and to neutralize negative media attention is well-tread territory.[59] That includes disproportionately publicizing successful interdiction efforts to project some semblance of border control.[60]

A sharp decline in pedestrian, vehicle, and bus traffic at the Port of Laredo's two noncommercial bridges—the Gateway to the Americas International Bridge and the Juárez-Lincoln International Bridge—prompted municipal staff in Laredo to begin disentangling promotional campaigns featuring "Los dos Laredos." It is difficult to determine when that byname became codified, but offering a couple of examples from the year 1985 can help us imagine what that sequence of words strived to do.[61] That year, Henry Cisneros, then mayor of San Antonio, received the first "Los Dos Laredos International Award" at a ceremony staged in the middle of the Juárez-Lincoln International Bridge. Arranged by José L. González and Víctor Oliveros (both still employees of the Laredo Health Department) and described as a "contribution of the venerable Washington's Birthday Celebration Association to the Dieciséis de Septiembre Festival," that border enactment not only hit all of the right public relations notes but also followed through on ritual niceties (e.g., inviting Laredo leaders to cross the bridge and to join the festivities in Nuevo Laredo).[62] Earlier that year, Nuevo Laredo's Tecolotes (owls) baseball team became the Tecolotes de los dos Laredos).[63] Given this history, walking back from a "Los dos Laredos" mind-set (on paper) undermined decades of joint publicity work, including lucrative margarita (flashy) and prescription drug (subtle) tourism campaigns.[64]

The decision to let go of "Los dos Laredos" was not ideal, but the reality of rapidly declining figures was panic-inducing.[65] Recall that the municipality of Nuevo Laredo receives a smaller cut of bridge revenue, approximately two hundred thousand pesos a month after monies are funneled through federal channels via the Caminos y Puentes Federales de Ingresos y Servicios Conexos (CAPUFE) and the State of Tamaulipas. As a bridge co-owner, the City of Laredo has more control. Administrators are able to channel 50 percent to the city's general fund thanks to the City of Laredo Resolution #98-R-164 passed in the mid-1990s. That steady income stream helps keep Laredo's tax base low and makes the city attractive to outside investors. When Laredo bridge officials did the math, the numbers confirmed the crisis. Revenue fell from $357,677 in February 2007 to $244,095 in February 2008, confirming a total loss of $133,582—a 34 percent drop—from one year to the next. And half of that amount—$66,691—would not make its way into the city's general fund.[66]

City of Laredo tourism and convention staff members I interviewed recalled struggling to develop promotional strategies that took a step back from advertising Laredo and Nuevo Laredo together as a "Two Nation Destination." One employee noted that publicizing separately, particularly after years of "selling ourselves [Laredo and Nuevo Laredo] dually" through programs like the Western Hemisphere Travel Initiative and with "joint [conference] booths" and "joint [conference] tours" was hard but deemed necessary.[67] Those difficulties were being discussed and managed elsewhere in the city. Council members voted unanimously to change the name of the city's official guide from "Laredo/Nuevo Laredo Official Visitors Guide" to the "2009 *Laredo* Visitors Guide" (emphasis added).[68] The detail of omitting Nuevo Laredo from the cover of a glossy magazine may seem inconsequential, but it paved the way for modifications in more public settings. In 2011, for example, LCC members voted to remove "Nuevo Laredo" from city-limit mile markers. In 2012 a "Laredo Is Safe" campaign led to the placement of billboards throughout Texas along the southbound lanes of I-35.[69]

Several bridge ceremony participants with whom I spoke did not mince words when expressing their disappointment. It was not unusual to hear that it was "*un insulto borrar a Nuevo Laredo de las carreteras texanas*" (removing Nuevo Laredo from highway mile-marker signs was insulting).[70] A former presidente municipal and past bridge ceremony participant was not surprised. He saw the situation as proof that the relationship between the two cities is imbalanced. He acknowledged "*los niños inculcan hermandad*" (the [abrazo] children inculcate brotherhood). But, he qualified, "*la ceremonia es una situación robótica*" (ceremony participants just go through the motions).[71] He went on to explain that it will always be difficult to achieve any sort of equilibrium through the ritual because there are eight city council members from Laredo and twenty-one *regidores* (councilmen) from Nuevo Laredo; not everyone is able to share an embrace.

Recent bridge ceremony volunteers were quick to note glaring as well as less obvious imbalances. The difference in the quality of the flags exchanged in the middle of the bridge was a popular talking point because it could make people chuckle. One IGNC-L representative explained, "It's true." The Mexican flags were "[made of] silk and dignified." The "US flags looked like they were purchased at the Dollar Store. . . . They were made in China."[72] Other disparities are less light-hearted. In 2015, for example, US law enforcement officials formed a human chain on the bridge immediately after the ceremony (see image, next page) to prevent unauthorized entry by Mexican journalists or any other kind of crossing slippages.

Border Festival Hazard: Tunnel Vision

There is no denying border violence affected Port of Laredo residents unevenly. Neolaredenses were not only blamed for the spillover violence, but they were also on the receiving end of *spill-across* violence—daily firefights, strict curfews, and emergency protocol measures that played out across Nuevo Laredo, not just in or around "hot-zone" plazas. Between 2010 and 2013, Presidente Municipal Benjamín Galván Gómez, whose administration faced enormous challenges (for example, receiving heads packed in ice chests, dealing with bodies hanging from bridges, and narcomantas that mentioned him specifically), linked his plans to reclaim Nuevo Laredo's historic city center to the WBC festivities. In 2012 he announced: "Nuevo Laredo no solo participará con representantes en los festejos del natalicio de George Washington, organizados por el gobierno de Laredo, Texas; sino que se sumará a la celebración mediante una tardeada en las calles céntricas de la localidad" (Nuevo Laredo will not only participate in the [Washington's Birthday] festivities, organized by the City of Laredo, by sending representatives but will also add to the celebration by hosting an afternoon party in the central streets of our city).[73]

Consider that the expectation of ritual may have already obligated Galván Gómez to keep an open mind when it came to the WBC. As was custom, he took his place during the International Bridge Ceremony during his tenure as presidente municipal. In addition, LULAC Council No.

Hands-on border security. Law enforcement officers form a barrier immediately after the International Bridge Ceremony to prevent unlawful entry into the United States from Mexico, 2015. Courtesy of Elaine A. Peña.

12 honored him as Señor Internacional from 2013 (along with then–San Antonio mayor Julián Castro, who became secretary of housing and urban development during the Obama administration and later a one-time 2020 presidential hopeful). I was able to speak to Galván Gómez briefly after his presentation to Laredoans about the state of affairs in Nuevo Laredo at TAMIU's Binational Center. He was well protected and in demand, as can be imagined, but he very kindly listened to my WBC/border collaboration project elevator pitch, which actually happened in an elevator. I remember feeling a bit claustrophobic because it was just me, him, and his bodyguard (who was giving me a mixed side-eye—fierce and annoyed). Galván Gómez, on the other hand, remained unfazed. We spoke for a good fifteen minutes after getting off the elevator, a conversation in which he stuck to his talking points. He emphasized that participating in the festivities, in as many capacities as possible, was a pleasure. And he reiterated that it is good for Nuevo Laredo to keep that bond alive.[74]

Shortly after serving his three-year (nonrenewable) term as presidente municipal (2011–2013), Gálvan Gómez was reported missing in February

2014, and his body was found a month later in the trunk of a car near Monterrey, Nuevo León. While his murder was not related to his participation in the festivities, it puzzled me that his death was not acknowledged by WBCA actors or by LULAC Council No. 12 members who had recently honored him during their Noche Mexicana gala in 2013.[75] Galván Gómez had participated; he gave acceptance speeches, toasted, and networked. One longtime WBC associate, who seemed genuinely annoyed by my question, explained: "He served his purpose. The celebration honors a lot of important people every year but then it forgets about them."[76]

Losing track of participants was a reoccurring theme, but the acuteness of disremembering could vary based on the country of residence and access (or lack thereof) to cross-border mobility options such as dual citizenship or visa privileges. Many neolaredenses with whom I worked could share specific details about timelines and the steps that they took to protect themselves and their loved ones. This includes never using the same route twice, traveling in different nondescript cars (but which had good engines), and using trusted drivers on a rotating basis. Along with specifics, elements of critical reminiscing could arise with neolaredenses who continued to call Nuevo Laredo home. Maribel López, a stay-at-home mom, lamented the fact that before the violence took hold, her city regularly hosted a *charreada*, a *callejoneada*, and a *rejoneada* (bullfight on horseback, Portuguese style). As long as she could remember there had been the custom of "fiestas pareja—fiestas del lado mexicano, corrida do toros, convivíamos juntos" (parties on the Mexican side of the border, bullfights, we would do it together). But, she clarified, "*Los Americanos coordinaban todo*" (The Americans would coordinate everything).[77]

In turn, many residents in Laredo could not pinpoint the year they had stopped feeling safe or when they stopped "going across." Several WBC associates I interviewed wondered out loud about crossing the bridge: Six years? Eight? Ten? Having to think about the question brought a real sense of sadness to our conversations. Especially because the norm, as has been established in previous chapters, had been to "go across" at least once a week if not daily to see family, shop, or have fun as they, their parents, and their grandparents had done for decades. It is important to note that asking active WBCA/IGNC-L members about their cross-border work did not differ in significant ways from the interviews I conducted with celebration planners of yesteryear. But older generations' reflections were often sharper; the past was not rendered as idyllically.

Having served the association since the early 1960s and most prominently in the 1970s, one former WBCA executive recalled going to Nuevo

Laredo often, "sometimes two or three times a day." He explained, "There was no traffic, no one bothering me or anything in customs or anything. *Revisaban el carro pero, pásele* (They would check the car, but they would let us pass). There was no violence. . . . [Thoughtful pause.] Yeeahhhh, occasionally there was a bar fight but, *it was a fistfight*, not even knives, much less guns, and *much less AK-47s*" (emphasis original).[78] Nostalgia was pervasive intergenerationally, but the bottom line was always made clear: it was drug cartel violence that changed the two Laredos, not the people themselves. Across conversations I found that reflecting on violence in the present can engender collective ideas of a past that may have never quite existed.[79]

If and when travel to Nuevo Laredo was necessary (for instance, formally inviting an official to participate in the festivities), active WBC associates easily admitted that they were "scared to death."[80] Over the course of dozens of formal interviews and informal conversations, it became increasingly clear that fear of spillover violence—reports of missing children, news of kidnapping and extortion, first- and second-hand accounts of assault, as well as the aural evidence just across the river (gunfire and/or air surveillance)—encouraged self-quarantining measures and generated protest activity that would have been unthinkable only a decade earlier.

Heading Off Protest

An example of spillover violence that many Laredoans could recall, regardless of their relationship to the WBC festivities, is tied to the establishment of a citizen's group called Laredo's Missing. William Sleymaker founded the group soon after his stepdaughter went missing the night of September 17, 2004, after attending a concert in Nuevo Laredo. Sleymaker and other parents with missing children used the organization to challenge what they perceived as local law enforcement's inadequate investigation methods.[81] In addition to drawing media attention to the situation via mainstream media outlets like *People* magazine, the group used the International Bridge Ceremony to publicize their cause.[82] Laredo's Missing staged a silent protest the morning of the 2006 abrazo ceremony at the US entrance of the Juárez-Lincoln International Bridge.[83]

Walking by the protest that morning alongside local and state officials, honored guests, media, and law enforcement officers, I understood why demonstrators did not have to raise their voices. Their choice of loca-

Laredo's missing. A silent protest staged at the foot of the Juárez-Lincoln International Bridge on the US side of the border, 2006. Courtesy of Elaine A. Peña.

tion spoke for them. As the ceremony participants walked along Zaragoza Street toward the bridge, directly in their line of sight and less than ten feet away, it was impossible not to notice large signs embossed with photos of missing children. Their presence made a particularly strong statement because it highlighted the stark and painful irony of featuring abrazo children to reaffirm border friendship. Nevertheless, the ritual did not budge; choreography and protocol shielded the event. Reading from a prepared speech, Laredo mayor Betty Flores did not acknowledge the group or speak of the issue on the bridge.[84]

It is important to note that singling out the International Bridge ceremony as a protest site is fairly uncommon. But the celebration at large, because of its ability to attract high-profile politicians or power players in the making, has inspirited demonstrations and mobilized action among groups who feel disenfranchised by the WBC festivities and/or by state politics for decades. SMW member Sally Brennan recalled, for example, that she saw people holding placards outside of the society's pageant in 1969. The signs read "They dance while the poor starve" and "Let them eat cake." To her knowledge that was the first and only time the event had ever attracted negative attention. She took a long pause and then admitted that she felt uncomfortable discussing it because she did not know if the society had ever talked about it on the record. Pivoting away from the subject gracefully, she concluded, "But we [Laredoans] are not really the protesting type." Shifting into a discussion of why Laredo may be different,

Sally did note that racism does not exist in Laredo like it does in the Valley (for example, in Brownsville, Texas).[85]

Her response, while cautious and somewhat evasive in that she uses racism as a catch-all term for class inequality, still resonated with the responses of other festivity organizers and participants I interviewed from that generation. When I asked Mr. Delgado about the "no discrimination" narrative that is often associated with Laredo, he explained that the first time he encountered prejudice was when he transferred to the University of Texas in Austin as a junior in the early 1960s. Delgado recalled that he was taken aback his very first day on campus when he saw the words "Mexicans eat shit and bark at the moon" scribbled above a urinal. This was shocking for him because in Laredo, he explained, "everybody knew everybody, from the richest to the poorest, from the barrios to the 'Heights' neighborhood. . . . There was no barrier. I [had] never experienced discrimination, I didn't even know what that was. . . . And why wasn't it in Laredo, to answer your question, Laredo, the Jewish community, the Arab community, Lebanese like the Kazans, the Arabs like the Jacamanes, they were all merchants; the Jewish community, the bankers, uh the ranchers, they all mixed. Intermarried; there was no discrimination. The city council always had two Anglos. . . . There was always one patrón. Albert Martin [father of Pepe Martin]."

Rallies staged during WBC celebrations in the 1960s were informed by antidiscrimination politics and mostly oriented toward Texas legislators.[86] The most overt examples of inward, intrastate, or intragroup protest unfolded in support of Chicano (politicized Mexican American) causes. In 1967, for example, Texas governor John Connally's presence at the WBC festivities prompted demonstrations because he had refused to meet with César Chávez and had thwarted farmworker rights activists marching toward Austin in the fall of 1966.[87] It is important to factor in that Connally, a conservative Democrat at the time, was considered a friend of the festivities even before he succeeded Price Daniel as governor of Texas in 1963. One particularly vivid account I heard about his participation involves him stealing the spotlight during the 1964 Noche Mexicana gala. Governor Connally was shot and severely wounded while riding in President John F. Kennedy's motorcade that fateful day in November 1963 in Dallas, Texas. While this is a dark detail, my interlocutor was ready to poke fun at the situation. Barely able to suppress his laughter, he recalled a mariachi group making their grand entrance to start things off, with Governor Connally marching close behind in a charro hat and with his arm in a sling. This is the type of story that attendees "would tell their children and

John Connally (with arm in sling) photographed with George and Martha Washington during the Washington's Birthday Celebration, 1964. Connally served as governor of Texas from 1963 to 1969 and was later US treasury secretary, 1971–1972. He had been wounded in Dallas three months earlier during the assassination of John F. Kennedy, November 22, 1963. Courtesy of the Webb County Heritage Foundation, Laredo.

grandchildren about." "*He milked that sling! People said that he was already healed but he wore it anyway*" (emphasis original).[88]

In the 1980s Texas Governor Mark White's participation in the celebration attracted "nearly 300 unhappy teachers" chanting "We Want White" and "We got you there, we'll get you out." Educators from across the state set up camp across the street from Governor White's hotel to protest the Texas Exam of Current Administrators and Teachers.[89] Around the same period, but informed by different political grievances, the participation of high-ranking Mexican officials generated acts of civil disobedience in Nuevo Laredo. Bridge ceremony coordinator Víctor Oliveros vividly recalled an incident while riding in a bus from the Palacio Municipal—the location of the pre-abrazo ceremony breakfast in Nuevo Laredo—to the Juárez-Lincoln International Bridge in the early 1990s. A group of colonia residents with land requests stopped the bus en route, effectively demanding an audience with then-governor of Tamaulipas Américo Villarreal Guerra (1989–1993). Governor Villarreal got off of the bus and spoke to them for about ten minutes. It is unclear whether that conversation produced results, but it did change how bridge ceremony coordinators transported Mexican guests in the future. From then on, bus drivers were instructed to change up their routes.[90]

More recently, in 2014, prolife groups gathered near the building where Noche Mexicana was taking place to protest the presence of one of that year's Señora Internacional honorees—Texas state senator Wendy Davis. Davis was targeted that year because of her stance on a woman's right to choose, specifically her thirteen-hour filibuster of Texas Senate Bill 5 in June 2013.

It is also important to acknowledge that the WBC International Bridge Ceremony can inspire quiet political action. Across the festivities, there are practices that absolutely need to stay the same (e.g., the *correct* way a debutante should bow during the SMW pageant). But in terms of costume or adornment, there is room for discreet innovation and intervention. The same day that prolife groups protested state senator Davis's presence, one of the abrazo children representing Mexico walked to the center of the bridge wearing a china poblana dress featuring the Virgin of Guadalupe, not an eagle (as is customary).[91]

Doing something different, changing a detail here or there, is an intimate decision taken among family members with the knowledge that dresses and sombreros will travel and be seen even after the children outgrow them. A former abrazo mother explained at a photo session that she and the dressmakers, who have shops on both sides of the border and have helped designed several of the Mexican abrazo children costumes since the mid-1990s, decided to add monarch butterflies to one of the base layers of the china poblana dress her daughter wore. They wanted to show support for the work of immigration reform groups that had adopted the symbol.[92] The idea behind integrating monarch butterflies, which migrate between Mexico (Michoacán) and Canada every year "without papers," into the design was fully realized that morning on the bridge. Moreover, as the costumes tour regionally, nationally, and internationally, that discreet show of support can have an influential afterlife.

Living the Mission

Acts of macabre violence, separation campaigns, self-quarantining, and silent protests challenged the resolve of WBCA actors, particularly when coordinating binational events required travel between the two Laredos.[93] The IGNC-L and CIBV-NL—two groups that pride themselves on continuing the international goodwill work that previous generations had set in place—had to factor in personal security issues when attempting to "live the mission" during this period.[94]

Since the IGNC-L chapter's founding in 1956, Christian-oriented charity work or "living the mission" has involved attending to the needs of children in Nuevo Laredo—a goodwill technique that doubles as a publicity device to encourage greater interest in the organization.[95] Alongside the responsibility to help "needy children" in Mexico, IGNC-L members are also encouraged by leadership within the upper echelons of the organization and at the chapter level to "fight bad press," which often involved refuting perceptions of Mexico that emphasized violence and danger. In 1977, for example, an IGNC *carta noticiosa* (news bulletin) circulated among chapters on both sides of the border. The front page of the bulletin rallied for a collective effort to restore Mexico's image:

> Most of us have been asked many times the question if it is safe to travel in Mexico, what about Mexico? Hasn't the Peso dropped out to the bottom and the farmers are killing anybody who looks like an American? What about the disappearance of the people in Acapulco? The killings in Sinaloa? And so forth. . . . IGNC members should all join in the campaign to try to straighten out this problem and fight the bad press, both in Mexico and the USA. We have to clean the bad image left by the sensational news in the USA about Mexico.[96]

IGNC organizations may have invested in countering those narratives since the 1970s, but post-9/11 border security shifts and drug cartel violence made living that part of the mission more complicated. For example, insurance coverage limitations restricted plans to travel to Mexico and Nuevo Laredo among private-sector executives as well as any city, county, or federal employees.

Despite those constraints and a steady decline in membership, a handful of IGNC-L members still attempted to complete the organization's annual service act of delivering gifts to a hospital and an orphanage in Nuevo Laredo.[97] Unlike previous years, successful expeditions were made with personal guards and sometimes nuns "who used to pray before the trip." Some years Nuevo Laredo's presidente municipal would provide a police escort. When the process of delivering too many gifts at one time in one car became too dangerous (visible packages attracted unwanted attention), mission logistics became more intricate.[98] In consultation with hospital staff, IGNC-L members pursued what anthropologist David Spener would call "*trabajo de hormiga*" (ant labor). That work involved a hospital staff member making several trips to Laredo to pick up gifts "little by little."[99] Prewrapped in Laredo by IGNC members, the hospital employee would cross with the gifts and take them home. When the time came to deliver the gifts, IGNC members would make their way to where the gifts were being stored and then transport them to the hospital in an ambulance. Taking extra steps and extra precautions did not make the trip any less scary, but it got the job done.

The close proximity of violence also impacted relationships and ways of getting things done within those organizations. The selection process to pick the abrazo children, for example, came under intense scrutiny. Often on the minds of IGNC-L and CIBV-NL members years in advance, deciding who gets to choose the abrazo children has always been a contentious affair. The perks of being an abrazo child are many: they may get to meet the president of the United States in the White House (as was the case in March 2008); they perhaps get to follow in their mother's or father's footsteps; they get to represent their country in their best dress (which can include travel to Mexico City and Guadalajara to procure custom-made charro hats and bespoke belt buckles); they receive congratulatory notes on letterhead from respected public officials; and they may even get to see life-size cutouts of themselves in costume.[100] Moreover, they can claim a place in the history of the WBC festivities and a set of social privileges that can be passed on to their own children.

Previously decided by the president of the WBCA, IGNC-L and CIBV-NL members only (re)gained the right to choose their child representatives in 1988. The process became an issue once again in the 2010s with the permanent relocation of neolaredenses on the US side of the border. In the past, abrazo children representing Mexico went to school in Laredo but lived in Nuevo Laredo. But now all of the abrazo children, representing both the United States and Mexico, live in the United States. In practice this means that the Mexican abrazo children have to wake up extra early to travel to Nuevo Laredo to join the rest of the Mexican delegation for breakfast at the Palacio Municipal. Traveling on the bus that leaves from the Palacio Municipal ensures that ceremony participants representing Mexico are standing on the correct side of the bridge.[101]

Dealings with WBCA officers who were keen on renegotiating the terms of the selection process complicated things further. One CIBV-NL associate explained the chapter's general frustration: if the WBCA gets to choose the children who will represent Mexico, "*se va el concepto*" (the ritual loses its point). In other words, if a US-based organization has the power to select who represents both the United States and Mexico, then what is the point of a binational ceremony? "There is no relationship."[102]

Those tensions can put immense pressure on the abrazo children. The rules of participation and representation had to be spelled out more clearly, which often put a damper on rehearsals and meetings. Respecting patriotism's proper geography requires that Mexican abrazo children live in Nuevo Laredo, Tamaulipas, Mexico. Spanish should be their native language. Or, at the very least, the children representing Mexico should be able to speak Spanish to avoid widespread embarrassment at public events where the children were expected to exchange words along with abrazos. American abrazo children should live in Laredo. Their mother tongue should be English. It is nice if they are able to speak Spanish, but it is not necessary.

IGNC-L and CIBV-NL abrazo parents are working through those expectations separately, but they have also set their sights on achieving important public-facing goals together. Making the most of the situation, members have decided to coordinate joint fundraising events. Cohosting a casino night, for example, could bring in tens of thousands of dollars in one night instead of thousands of dollars over a few months.[103] Working together is more efficient and definitely generates more money for each group's preferred charities, but it remains to be seen if those extra-WBC interactions can mitigate the abrazo children selection process.

Border Scaffolding Meets Homeland Security

The planning and execution of the International Bridge Ceremony dovetails with border security realities in other noteworthy ways. WBCA leadership took to inviting important or powerful individuals from Washington, DC, to participate in the abrazo ritual during this volatile period. Several high-ranking DHS officials took part in the bridge ceremony between 2008 and 2016 as honorary bridge ceremony speakers: Commissioner W. Ralph Basham (2008), Commissioner Alan D. Bersin (2010), Commissioner David V. Aguilar (2013), Commissioner R. Gil Kerlikowske (2015), and DHS Secretary Jeh Johnson (2016). In conversation with state-level elected officials, WBCA executive committee members invited those particular actors because of their involvement in favorable border initiatives (e.g., the Southwest Border Strategy and the River Vega Project).[104]

Having Secretary Johnson give remarks on the bridge and then walk among parade-goers without an obvious security detail communicated control and order on the border during a period of heightened instability. Circulating an official press release with an excerpt of his speech reinforced that message far beyond the border:

> There is no amount of overheated rhetoric, hurtful and offensive commentary, or hot air, that can blow this bridge down. . . . A year from now, no matter what happens the rest of this year, this bridge will still be here. No matter what happens over the next year, a year from now two children from the United States and two children from Mexico will meet on this bridge and give each other a hug. The youth of our two countries have been doing this here for over 100 years, and they will do it for 100 more.[105]

The participation of authority figures like Secretary Johnson served federal interests as much as it served port-of-entry interests. Quite different from a president's or a first lady's visit to a border detention center, bringing in DHS leaders so that they can assess the situation for themselves also permits port boosters to showcase meticulously curated examples of border cooperation. Moreover, by agreeing to take part in the bridge ceremony, the border patrol can confirm their investment in community/local affairs and tactfully manage negative press linked to "excessive use of force" reports.

The participation of high-level officials does not deliver border security. That is not the point of the ceremony. But the abrazo ritual compels face-to-face interaction and requires embodied as well as spatial in-

Abrazo children embrace in the middle of the Juárez-Lincoln International Bridge as Border Patrol agents applaud, 2014. Gisella Rose Carranza Gutiérrez and Eduardo Andrés Lerma Bazán represent Mexico. Isabella González and Frank Riley Puig represent the United States. Courtesy of Elaine A. Peña.

vestments. And that combination of place and practice invites profound ways of recognizing and thinking about borders, lines, and boundaries. As one past bridge ceremony speaker put it when describing the value of the abrazo ceremony, "International relations require engagement. . . . We cannot look at the border as a juridical line. This is all part of a maturation process."[106]

Border Enactments, Not Walls

The International Bridge Ceremony cannot safeguard border residents against the material, physical, or emotional realities of drug trade–related violence. But we should not sell the ritual short. In contrast to "security theater," which places the responsibility of maintaining the appearance of a safer environment primarily in the hands of the Transportation Security Administration, or "border theater," which explores how artistic interventions can interupt "technologies of security" at the border proper, the abrazo ritual provides a wide range of border actors with a recurring opportunity to jointly assess insecurity issues.[107] Moreover, the bridge ritual's capacity to distinguish Mexican space and US space nonviolently and to facilitate bilateral coordination during times of crisis makes it a powerful, if underappreciated, example of festive security.

CONCLUSION

Why Study Border Enactments?

You are closer to home when you are further away.
GLORIA ANZALDÚA, "ON THE PROCESS OF WRITING *BORDERLANDS/LA FRONTERA*," 2009

¡Viva George! pivots away from expected tropes and presumptive border policy thinking to enliven key debates and theoretical work in comparative border studies, US-Mexico borderlands history, and the anthropology of infrastructure. From its in-depth analysis of spatially imagined identity claims codified during the celebration's early decades (Laredoans and neolaredenses playing Indian, playing colonial, and playing Mexican) to its explanation of how a stand-alone ritual—the WBC International Bridge Ceremony—doubled as a platform for the legal extension of documentation-free border-crossing privileges for close to two decades (1957–1976), *¡Viva George!* is not a typical US-Mexico borderlands book.

Unlike much of recent scholarship that emphasizes pathos, poverty, illegality, and violence, *¡Viva George!* takes a calculated risk in drawing attention to WBC festivities and to cross-border festival planning processes. Through vivid historical accounts, ethnographic insights, and interdisciplinary analysis, it critically engages (but does not fixate on) all that is politically incorrect about the WBC festivities, past and present.

Admittedly, it has been difficult to sidestep what seems incorrigibly wrong-headed at several points in the research process. But I hope this interdisciplinary analysis of the history of the celebration cuts through my subjectivity. In taking that route, I hope to inspire readers to think with my interlocutors as opposed to dismissing them offhand. My choices of style and tone are not meant to silence or undermine the significance of those challenging border histories; rather, they are intended to open up discussions of what is possible in a border environment.

The goal I had in mind as I drafted each chapter was first to familiarize the reader with the idiosyncratic ways that border actors can relate to each other, and then to explain the underlying political logics and economic interests that have ensured the celebration's longevity. In the process I developed the concept of *border enactments*: face-to-face engagement staged at or across a physical boundary line and choreographed to communicate political desire or dissent to an international audience. In addition, I have explored corollary ideas surrounding what I call the "expectation of ritual" and "border scaffolding" to ground the research across time periods and political and economic shifts.

Accounting for how border actors have made use of all available resources—including festively repurposing border infrastructure during times of crisis (in the aftermath of a natural disaster or in spite of border violence)—is a timely exercise, particularly when arguments for or against border wall construction dominate political debates. This study shows how and why the Port of Laredo has never needed a border wall. The place where the children embrace differentiates American and Mexican populations symbolically but *effectively enough* to avoid having to compromise trade and security relationships that actually produce quantifiable benefits. Smart border security practices should pay attention to those details, to the strengths and limitations of each border place because a one-size-fits-all approach is inadequate. Any crossing point, authorized or unauthorized, will be more secure if lines of communication remain open and operational among the widest variety of border actors.

Paying attention to how borderlanders invent national histories and play at racial/ethnic identities can also help us understand why insisting that immigration is a national security threat is as unfounded as it is dangerous. Neglecting the complex ways race, ethnicity, class, citizenship, and patriotism intersect in a binational environment makes it very easy to assume that border zones are battle areas. And that myopic line of thinking has far-reaching repercussions and mortal consequences. It can tacitly endorse human rights violations (e.g., cage-like detention standards prevail because detainees are not citizens) as well as inspire acts of domestic terrorism that find their stamps of approval in supremacist interpretations of what constitutes "real American" identity. Ordering identifiably white and African American shoppers to get out of harm's way so that he could kill Mexican people exclusively, as a gunman did in El Paso, Texas, on August 3, 2019, for example, reveals how conflating immigration and national security trades in place-specific solutions.[1] Attempting to demarcate and police the racial and ethnic contours of American identity with the logics of early twentieth-century exclusionist policies is a losing battle and will not make anyone safer.

Critically examining multiple facets of border culture—including the whimsical ways that state and nonstate border actors maintain contact and cooperate under duress, however out of touch or out of place their methods may seem—has a place in those conversations. And not only in a North American context but also globally. In light of ever-increasing news coverage of border situations that invoke explicit "othering" strategies (e.g., Hungary's pro-fence political campaigns; the anti-immigration undertones of Great Britain's exit from the European Union; the Rohingya crisis at the Myanmar-Bangladesh border), ethnographic and historical studies of cross-border rituals can help us confront global challenges in more informed ways.

To be clear, I am not suggesting that border enactments guarantee political action or spur social change. Indeed, at first glance (and given the fact that border environments are often characterized with citizenship, class, and linguistic prejudices), a border enactment can easily be perceived as little more than a tone-deaf political charade. While that reading has its own merits, it elides a discussion of the time-consuming, cross-border coordination work that goes into staging a border enactment. Whether periodic (e.g., Wagah ceremony, loudspeaker blasts across the DMZ) or as a one-off occurrence (Speaker of the House Nancy Pelosi exchanging an embrace with Tamaulipas governor Francisco García Cabeza de Vaca during the WBC International Bridge Ceremony in February 2019), state and nonstate border actors take on onerous backstage planning and logistics work, often months in advance or even year-round, to bring border enactments to fruition.

The Washington's Birthday Celebration may be idiosyncratic and highly particular to the two Laredos, but border enactments are not. Applying those ideas to border contexts with very different dynamics can show us how actors on the ground blur lines of authority and defy predictable, top-down crisis-resolution narratives. Encouraging broad-based participation, making full use of cross-border sources of knowledge, and recognizing border festivals as communicative acts are also viable options. And while highly unconventional, recognizing a border enactment's scaffolding potential can innovate how we think about and tackle global challenges linked to border security, immigration, and trade. In light of national and supranational conversations about mass migration and climate change, locating potential cross-border cooperation strategies along a wider spectrum of social actors and spaces, however whimsical, is both relevant and necessary.

Notes

List of Abbreviations

AGN	Archivo General de la Nación, Mexico, DF
BLAC	Benson Latin American Collection, University of Texas at Austin
CAPUFE	Caminos y Puentes Federales de Ingresos y Servicios Conexos
CBP	US Customs and Border Protection
CIBV-NL	Consejo Internacional de Buena Vecindad–Nuevo Laredo
CLSO	City of Laredo Secretary's Office
DHS	Department of Homeland Security
IGNC-L	International Good Neighbor Council–Laredo
INEGI	Instituto Nacional de Estadística y Geografía
INS	Immigration and Naturalization Service
IORM	Improved Order of Red Men
JFMM	Junta Federal de Mejoras Materiales
JPL	John Peace Library, University of Texas at San Antonio
LBS	Laredo Bridge System
LCC	Laredo Chamber of Commerce
LCCP	Laredo Chamber of Commerce Papers
LGHC	Luciano Guajardo Historical Collection, Laredo Public Library
LMT	*Laredo Morning Times*
LPL	Joe A. Guerra Laredo Public Library
LT	*Laredo Times*
LULAC	League of United Latin American Citizens
LWT	*Laredo Weekly Times*
NACP	National Archives, College Park, MD
RMML	Red Men Museum and Library, Waco, Texas
SMW	Society of Martha Washington
SPN	Secretaria del Patrimonio Nacional
TAMIU	Texas A&M International University, Laredo
WBC	Washington's Birthday Celebration
WBCA	Washington's Birthday Celebration Association
WBCAP	Washington's Birthday Celebration Association Papers, Laredo
WCHF	Webb County Heritage Foundation, Laredo

Introduction

1. One of the key takeaways in this work is that it is fairly easy to accept the idea that plurality, at least in theory, is built into a democratic nation's DNA. However, paying attention to the way democracies stage-manage difference at international boundary lines, especially when immigration and citizenship issues are at play, can reveal other national priorities.

2. For recent studies that underline those pressures see, for example, Rosas, *Barrio Libre*; Correa, "After 9/11"; Correa-Cabrera, "Security, Migration"; Holmes, *Fresh Fruit*; Payan, Staudt, and Kruszewski, *War That Can't Be Won*; De León, *Land of Open Graves*; Rael, *Borderwall*; Vélez-Ibáñez and Heyman, *US-Mexico Transborder Region*; and Peña, *Material Religion*.

3. I describe residents of Laredo, Texas, and Nuevo Laredo, Tamaulipas, as Laredoans and neolaredenses respectively. Port of Laredo refers to both the municipality of Nuevo Laredo and the City of Laredo. While not without its limitations, the term "Port of Laredo" avoids reinforcing ideas of natural cross-border kinship, or what Pablo Vila calls "sister city" metaphors and tropes. I use the term to highlight Laredo and Nuevo Laredo's interdependent economic ties and interest in regional infrastructure development. See Vila, *Crossing Borders*, 233.

4. For a journalistic account of SMW debutant participation in the parade, see Swartz, "Once Upon a Time"; see also, *Las Marthas* (2014), directed by Cristina Ibarra.

5. Rosaldo, *Culture and Truth*, 39.

6. See, for example, Green, *Celebration of Heritage*. For a brief but informative discussion of the celebration alongside Laredo history, see Shanks, *Laredo: Reflections*.

7. See "Washingtons' [*sic*] Birth-day 22 of February," 1870, leaflet, Box 203, LGHC.

8. Stoss, "Border Ball."

9. City of Laredo officials used the International Bridge as a place to meet and greet WBC guests. In 1900, for example, Laredo's acting mayor Floyd crossed the Rio Grande in a special car on the electric train, picked up the Nuevo Laredo mayor Juan de la Garza, and drove him to the parade reviewing stand. WBCA, 1898, Vertical File, Drawer 1, Stan Green Papers, WCHF (hereafter cited as Green Papers, WCHF).

10. The ceremony is presently overseen by the WBCA and jointly organized by members of the IGNC-L and the CIBV-NL. Chapters 4 and 5 of this book assess the work of those organizations, particularly how leadership changes and intergroup negotiation dynamics have affected the ritual.

11. Lomnitz et al., *El fondo de la forma*, 1990.

12. Here I borrow Danilyn Rutherford's distinction between a "public" and an "audience." Rutherford does not treat the "feeling of expanded agency that people experience when they sense themselves adopting a widely shared viewpoint" as a foregone product defined by presence or absence but as a process in which varied attention shifts the intensity of communication. She nuances Michael Warner's differentiation between audiences (i.e., embodied and proximate) and publics, which are rarely ever on-site but maintain "a shadowy existence around a published work." Moreover, Rutherford helpfully reminds us, "even when a group of individuals shares a patch of sidewalk, much work must be done to turn them into addresses or overhearers, let alone tellers of a tale. Alongside the materiality of bodies, more or less available to a scene of interaction, one must pay heed to the materiality of signs, be

they etched in newspapers, lit up on computer screens, or pulsed through the air." In other words, any analysis of spectatorship—thinking critically about acts of watching or participating en masse—should factor in knowledge exchange and circulation off-site and en route. Rutherford, *Laughing at Leviathan*, 16–17. For a discussion of Warner's work on publics in relation to Noche Mexicana, see Manuel Cuellar, "La escenificación de lo mexicano," 124.

13. Lefebvre, *Production of Space*, 59.

14. Performance theorist Shannon Jackson's work on art and social change—especially her idea that "art forms that help us to imagine sustainable social institutions"—has helped me develop the concept of border scaffolding. Jackson explains that through "the infrastructural operations of performance, we might find a different way to join aesthetic engagement to the social sphere, mapping a shared interest in the cofounding of insides and outsides, selves and structures. To emphasize *the infrastructural politics of performance*, however, is to join performance's routinized discourse of disruption and de-materialization to one that also *emphasizes sustenance, coordination, and re-materialization*." Jackson, *Lines of Activity*, 29 (emphasis mine). Jackson's work offers a master class in performance historiography and a robust theorization of scaffolding.

15. One of the first descriptions of Laredo as a "gateway" was put forth by Texas legislator Edward Rex Tarver. See Tarver, *Laredo, the Gate Way*.

16. Lomnitz uses Mexican nationalism to recalibrate Benedict Anderson's influential idea of "imagined communities" (see *Imagined Communities*) in truly brilliant ways. Lomnitz, *Deep Mexico*, xiv.

17. Foucault, *Security, Territory, Population*.

18. Rappaport, *Ritual and Religion*, 32. See also Turner, *Dramas, Fields, Metaphors*.

19. Roy Rappaport's tenacious analysis of ritual, particularly the ways in which he links anthropological and performance-oriented approaches in chapters 2 and 4—"ritual form" and "enactments of meaning"—has helped me refine several aspects of this project. See Rappaport, *Ritual and Religion*, especially 23–68 and 107–138. Anthropologist Saba Mahmood's critical examination of spontaneity and ritual inspired me to find my own place in debates about feeling, emotion, and ritual. See Mahmood, "Rehearsed Spontaneity." Richard Schechner's and Victor Turner's individual work, as well as their joint efforts, opened up my thinking about ritual from the earliest days of this project. See, for example, Turner, *Anthropology of Performance*; Schechner, *Between Theater and Anthropology*; Turner, *Dramas, Fields, and Metaphors*; Schechner, *Environmental Theater*; and Turner, *Ritual Process*. For a critical overview of the role of performance theory in the study of ritual see Grimes, "Performance Theory."

20. Anthropologist Stanley Tambiah clarifies, "Ritual [as opposed to play, which produces a winner] usually specifies in advance not only the procedural rules but also the sequence of events, and in this sense stands in stark contrast to the unpredictable and unequal outcome of sports." "Performative Approach to Ritual," 118.

21. Using infrastructure as one of the guideposts for the project has several benefits and just as many challenges. Recent discussions in the anthropology of infrastructure, for example, have grappled with the "humble" French engineering term's overwhelming capaciousness. Academics have consistently widened the scope of their projects in the past decades to analyze not only physical infrastructure such

as dams and roads but also support systems that take the form of fiber-optic information superhighways, television networks, and people. Public works such as dams, roads, and plants may serve as classic examples of infrastructure, but as Laura Bear reminds us, they too can "demand our attention" in unexpected ways (Venkatesan et al., "Attention to Infrastructure," 7). Renewed interest in the subject draws our attention once again to the "enchantment" (Harvey and Knox, "Enchantments of Infrastructure") and "aloofness" of infrastructure (Appel, Anand, and Gupta, *Promise of Infrastructure*, 11) as well as to the ways in which infrastructure can be "spectacular" (Schwenkel, "Spectacular Infrastructure"). Brian Larkin has shown in his study of postcolonial Nigeria, radio stations and television networks can be analyzed as technical infrastructure (*Signal and Noise*). AbdouMaliq Simone proposes a "people as infrastructure" approach in his study of marginalized populations in South Africa ("People as Infrastructure"). In addition to refining the literature, these shifts continue to signal that infrastructure is not always national nor is it necessarily public. Studies of export processing zone infrastructure and "global cities" made that point clear, most notably in the 1990s, and continue to capture the attention of scholars across the social sciences, humanities, schools of architecture, and public planning. See Carse, "Keyword: Infrastructure," for an overview of the history and use of the term; see also Larkin, "Politics and Poetics"; Harvey and Knox, *Roads*; and Appel et al., *Promise of Infrastructure*. See Laura Bear's motion for a materialist analysis of the political in Venkatesan et al., "Attention to Infrastructure," 7. See O'Neill and Rodgers, "Infrastructural Violence," for a closer look at infrastructural violence. For globally focused perspectives, see Herzog, "Cross-National Urban Structure"; Sassen, "Spatialities and Temporalities"; Shapira, "The Border"; and Easterling, *Extrastatecraft*.

22. See, for example, Löfgren, "Concrete Transnationalism"; Yang, "Geopolitics of Cross-Boundary Governance"; Yoder, "La infraestructura del transporte"; Hodges, "Building Across the Borderline"; and Peña, "Paso Libre." For an analysis of the role of virtual walls in border policing, see Heyman, "Constructing a Virtual Wall."

23. See, for example, Berdahl, *Where the World Ended*; and Kim, *DMZ Crossing*.

24. See, for example, Amir, "On the Border"; Kallius et al., "Immobilizing Mobility"; and Dominguez and Metzner, "Special Section on Nativism."

25. Newman, "Lines That Continue."

26. Lawrence A. Herzog's published research, which has applied cross-border attention to architecture and landscape at the Mexico-US border for decades, his dynamic public presentation style, and his eye for the visual have all set the bar very high. I have referred back to his work throughout this process. See, for example, "Cross-National Urban Structure," *From Aztec to High Tech*, and "Political Economy of Tourism."

27. Jusionyte, "Called to 'Ankle Alley,'" 98; Rael, "Boundary Line Infrastructure," 76.

28. As anthropologist Robert Álvarez reminds us, Mexico-US border studies could use a perspective change. "The notion of borders and bridges," he proposes, "provides a specific verticality and a new dimension . . . a different analytic to disrupt (not replace) the entrenched epistemology of the border." "Borders and Bridges," 31. See also, for example, Lugo, "Theorizing Border Inspections"; and Chapin, "Reflections from the Bridge."

29. Diana Taylor's work, particularly *The Archive and the Repertoire*, continues to

influence my thinking about materiality and ephemerality in the study of knowledge production and transmission.

30. For work on "Charro Days," see Wooldridge and Vezzetti, "Founding of Charro Days"; and Knopp et al., *Charro Days in Brownsville*. For an excellent overview and analysis of transborder festivals along the Texas-Tamaulipas border, see Oliveras-González, "Fiestas transfronterizas."

31. Rael, *Borderwall*, 125–129.

32. Ngai, *Impossible Subjects*.

33. For a behind-the-scenes look at Laredo business community member's response to and anxiety about Operation Intercept, see Correspondence, Letter from Vidal M. Cantú to LCC Members, October 2, 1969, Box 255, J. C. "Pepe" Martin Jr. Papers, LGHC (hereafter cited as Martin Papers, LGHC). For a sense of President Nixon's awareness of "border beauty and friendship day[s]" during that period as well as his perspective on festive border enactments in South Texas, which he hails as "a splendid showcase of voluntarism at work" and "a unique and inspiring precedent in international cooperation to solve joint problems that transcend physical boundaries," see Western Union telegram from Richard Nixon to J. C. Martin, April 19, 1969, Box 255, Martin Papers, LGHC. For multidisciplinary and cross-border reflections on the "war on drugs," see Payan et al., *War That Can't Be Won*. For a robust analysis of Operation Intercept, see Kate Doyle, *Operation Intercept: The Perils of Unilateralism*, National Security Archive, https://nsarchive2.gwu.edu/NSAEBB/NSAEBB86/.

34. Martínez explains, "Between 1950 and 1955 the US government successfully pressured millions of Mexicans to leave the United States 'voluntarily' as part of an aggressive, quasi-military campaign known as 'Operation Wetback.' . . . At the conclusion of the campaign, US officials asserted that the 'wetback problem' had been solved once and for all. Contrary to that claim, however, undocumented immigration actually swelled during the late 1950s and throughout the 1960s and 1970s. . . . The perception that a foreign 'invasion' was underway led to an increasingly acrimonious national debate in which Mexican immigrants became the main targets. Thus, the eruption of the Tortilla Curtain incident in 1978–1979 followed years of frustration in the United States over the persistence of the border problem." "Border Conlict," 269. See Andreas, *Border Games*, for an eye-opening analysis of border security funding cycles.

35. Rael, "Boundary Line Infrastructure," 80. For a compelling discussion of how artistic interventions can illuminate and interrupt border security rituals, see Amoore and Hall, "Border Theater."

36. Michele Sleighel, "Braids across Border: How Women in El Paso Are Fighting Back on Inauguration Day," *Ms.blog*, January 18, 2017, http://msmagazine.com/blog/2017/01/18/el-paso-women-using-braids-send-message-washington/.

37. Khushbu Shah, "There Was a 'Giant Picnic' at the US-Mexico Border," CNN, October 11, 2017, https://www.cnn.com/2017/10/10/us/border-wall-picnic-trnd/index.html. See also Jones, *Open Borders*, which features that border enactment on its cover.

38. The following chapters nod to examples of border enactments produced outside of North America. The Wagah ceremony staged at the Indian-Pakistan border, for example, shares several qualities with the WBC abrazo ceremony. It features mili-

tary personnel from both countries using synchronized choreography to close a border gate, but on a daily basis. For a close analysis of the Wagah ceremony, see Menon, *Performance of Nationalism*, 22–54. For other examples of border enactments, see Gómez-Peña, "Cruci-Fiction Project"; Berdahl, *Where the World Ended*; Darian-Smith, *Bridging Divides*; Eagles, "Organizing Across"; Dornbach, "Remains of a Picnic"; and Simpson, *Mohawk Interruptus*.

39. Cited in Harms, "Tale of Two Revolutions," 481. Harms specifies that the border picnic is part of western European narrations of Hungary's move away from communism. For a discussion of the picnic's ties to nostalgic views of the Danubian confederation of nations, see Dornbach, "Remains of a Picnic," 258.

40. See Pratt, *Imperial Eyes*; and Roseberry, "Social Fields."

41. For studies that speak to the Port of Laredo's uneven landscape, see, for example, Ward, *Colonias and Public Policy*; Medina, "Cardboard Collectors"; and Richardson and Pisani, *Informal and Underground Economy*.

42. For analyses of the WBC, see Klein, *Baseball on the Border*; Dennis, "Washington's Birthday"; Young, "Red Men"; Ceballos Ramírez, "Los dos Laredos"; Momen, "Remembering Laredo"; Cantú, "Dos Mundos"; Oliveras-González, "Fiestas transfronterizas"; and Peña, "De-Politicizing Border Space," "More Than a Dead American," "Paso Libre," and "Reveling in Patriotism."

43. Peña, "De-Politicizing Border Space."

44. Hobsbawm, "Introduction," 12. Hobsbawm, for example, nods to the colors worn by athletes of the German gymnastic movement in the 1890s to pinpoint an instance in which the transformation of German nationalism could be identified but which had largely gone unnoticed.

45. Burke, "Performing History," 41–42; see also Turner, *Ritual Process*; Geertz, *Negara*; Cannadine, "Context, Performance"; Anzaldúa, *Borderlands*; Bonfil Batalla, *México profundo*; Anderson, *Imagined Communities*; Guss, *Festive State*; Lomnitz, *Deep Mexico*; de la Peña, "Anthropological Debates"; Taylor, *Archive and Repertoire*; Wimmer and Glick Schiller, "Methodological Nationalism"; García Canclini, *Culturas híbridas*; and Shannon O'Neil, *Two Nations Indivisible*. I also found it helpful to read personal essays, short stories, and poetry about nation and patriotism based on Nuevo Laredo. See, for example, Federico Schaffler, *Escencia de patriotismo* (paperback); Gregorio Z. Cabeza, *Breves notas de un confín de la patria* (pamphlet); and *Places, Events, Beliefs, People and Poetry of Northern Mexico and the Border (1920–1986)* (pamphlet), all in Box 18–Nuevo Laredo, LGHC.

46. Interview, August 20, 2013.

47. Peña, "More Than a Dead American."

48. Newman and Paasi, "Fences and Neighbours," 198.

49. See Vélez-Ibáñez, *Hegemonies of Language*, for reasons to think regionally about borders.

50. See Conquergood, "Performing as a Moral Act" and "Rethinking Ethnography."

51. I have sought inspiration and guidance from studies of expressive cultures set at the US-Mexico border. See, for example, Anzaldúa, *Borderlands*; Paredes, *"With His Pistol in His Hand," George Washington Gómez*, and *Folklore and Culture*; Limón, *Dancing with the Devil*; Gómez-Peña, "Cruci-Fiction Project" and *Dangerous Border Crossers*; Madrid, *Transnational Encounters*; and Rivera-Servera and Young, *Performance in the Borderlands*.

Chapter 1. Playing Indian, Playing Colonial

1. My account draws from the Souvenir Program and the following descriptions of the 1898 celebration: Joseph Netzer, Letter, n.d., Box 203, WBCA, LGHC; Netzer, "Origin"; Seb S. Wilcox, "Official Program of the Washington's Birthday Celebration," 1947, Wilcox Papers, John Peace Library, UTSA (hereafter cited as Wilcox Papers, JPL); Stephen Gould, Records of the Fourth Council of the Great Council of Texas, July 1898, 204, Red Men Museum and Library, Waco (hereafter RMML); S. D. Moore, Records of the Fourth Council of the Great Council of Texas, Aug. 1898, pp. 192–193, RMML; WBCA, 1898, Vertical File, Green Papers, WCHF; and WBC-Histories, WCHF.

2. In 1906 Sánchez not only played himself as mayor but also helped plan the Indian attack on city hall. Highlighting the violent nature of the spectacle, newspaper coverage specifies that while over three hundred soldiers stationed at Fort McIntosh fought bravely alongside local law enforcement officers and ranchers, an avalanche of Indians "*perpetraron una carnicería atróz*" (instigated a brutal massacre). The Indians (Yaqui Tribe No. 59 members in costume) eventually "killed" all of the troops and ranchers, saved the captives, and captured the city. "Las Fiestas del 22 de Febrero," *El Demócrata Fronterizo*, January 20, 1906.

3. Building on David Montejano's work, historian Elliot Young identified Sánchez as a member of Laredo's "gente decente" class in his analysis of the WBC, race, and power in the early twentieth century. Montejano explains that "in Laredo there are many influential Mexican citizens and they can't be treated like a *pelado*. The treatment given to Mexicans depends partly on the individual Mexican, who may be of high class, and partly on numbers; in Laredo there are so many you have to give them social recognition." Young, "Red Men, Princess Pocahontas," 248. See also Foley, *From Peones to Politicos*, for a robust analysis of citizenship and class in South Texas. For a parallel conversation about the connections between "whiteness" and property ownership in Texas, see Gross, "Texas Mexicans." For a classic analysis of overlap across property, race, and power, see Harris, "Witness as Property."

4. Deloria, *Playing Indian*, 34.

5. There is a rich body of scholarship that examines how "playing Indian" need not necessarily rely on America's colonial relationship with Great Britain. Josefina María Saldaña-Portillo's book *Indian Given* (2016), for example, shows how imagining Native American identity via cinematic representation, land surveys, and legal or institutional decisions about racial categories and human value have not only confined and inflicted violence upon the figure of the Native American but also determined indigenous peoples' dispensability.

6. Juan Mora-Torres provides a rich overview of that transition period. He explains, "Mexicans who did not want to live under the US flag, including a good portion of Laredo's residents, crossed the Río Bravo and founded a new settlement, Laredo-Monterrey, which later became Nuevo Laredo. At the same time, many residents of Matamoros crossed the river and founded Brownsville. . . . For those on the US side of the boundary, the 'other side' represented an abundance of commercial opportunities. For most Mexicans on the southern side of the Bravo, the 'other side' was the source of violent groups who threatened the existence of their *patria chica*." *Making of the US-Mexico Border*, 22–23.

7. For additional insight, see, for example, Richer, *Reseña histórica*; Salinas Domín-

guez, *Orígenes de Nuevo Laredo*; Hinojosa, *Borderlands Town*; Ceballos Ramírez, *La fundación de Nueva Laredo*; Green, *Laredo: 1755–1920*; Adams, *Conflict and Commerce*; Valerio Jímenez, *River of Hope*; and Díaz, *Border Contraband*.

8. Baumgartner, "Line of Positive Safety," 1110; Paredes, *Folklore and Culture*, 26.

9. Violence between "las Botas" (the boots) and "los Guaraches" (the sandals) after the 1886 spring elections has been well documented. Scholars agree that political alliances shifted with the arrival of the railroads. Troubling clear-cut logics of border class, ethnicity, and kinship, established Mexican elites and Anglo-American newcomers could find themselves vying for power as a Bota (boot) or as a Guarache (sandal). Underlying tension around ethnicity and class lines surfaced when the Botas celebrated their victory over the Guarraches by staging a mock funeral for the latter party. That victory lap through the streets of Laredo left twenty-five dead and forty wounded. Arguably, elite Mexicans played second fiddle to Anglo-Americans in a "bipartisan coalition called the Independent Club" that held its ground in Laredo through the 1970s. See Hinojosa, *Borderlands Town*, 118–120; for a detailed analysis of the election, see Thompson, *Warm Weather*.

10. Schechner explains: "In environmental theater there is a shift in that the spectator and performer often share the same space, sometimes they exchange spaces, and sometimes the domain of the performer is larger than that of the spectator, enclosing the spectator within the performance. . . . *This tendency is taken even further in restored villages and theme parks where the visitor enters an environment that swallows him*." *Between Theater and Anthropology*, 96 (emphasis mine).

11. Nugent, "Cyclical History," 223–224.

12. Frederick Jackson Turner's analysis of 1890 US Census data and his public remarks on the subject in 1893 set off alarm bells across the United States. He declared that the United States "can no longer be said to be a frontier line," and "the frontier line, which its maps had depicted for decade after decade of the westward march of the nation, could no longer be described." The rub here is that without land to settle or colonize, how would the United States be able to continue developing its unique American qualities? In this case study, IORM members were deciding how to proceed in real time. F. J. Turner, "Frontier and Section," 42, 154. For insightful explorations of "American" subject formation in a "frontier" environment, see Weber, "Conflicts and Accommodations"; Slotkin, *Regeneration through Violence*; Reséndez, *Changing National Identities*; Yokota, *Unbecoming British*; and Grandin, *End of the Myth*. For transnational and hemispheric-focused analyses, see Adelman and Aron, "Borderlands to Borders"; Truett et al., *Continental Crossroads*; Gutiérrez and Young, "Transnationalizing Border Studies"; Johnson and Graybill, *Bridging National Borders*; Hämäläinen and Truett, "On Borderlands"; Kramer, "Power and Connection"; and Chang, *Pacific Connections*.

13. Deloria, *Playing Indian*, 8.

14. Here I am following the lead of historian David Cannadine in his analysis of the British monarchy and the meaning of ritual in the modern period (1820–1977). He notes, "In order to rediscover the 'meaning' of royal ritual during the modern period, it is necessary to relate it to the specific social, political, economic, and cultural milieu within which it was actually performed. With ceremonial, as with political theory, the very act of locating the occasion or the text in its appropriate context

is not merely to provide the historical background, but actually to begin the process of interpretation." See "Context, Performance," 105.

15. The publication of Lindsay's *Official History* greatly expanded on M. H. Gorham's *The History of the Improved Order of Red Men* (1884). Both were sold by subscription. The key difference between the two is that Gorham's text describes Washington's importance to the Society of Red Men, not the Improved Order of Red Men. See also Davis, *History of the Improved Order of Red Men.*

16. IORM membership reached 133,485 in 1895 and 194,785 in 1900. The number of state tribes in 1895 and 1900 also offers a sense of potential distribution numbers and locations. Every state but Vermont, Oklahoma, Mississippi, the Canal Zone, and the Hawaiian Islands had at least one tribe by 1900. California, for example, had thirty-nine registered tribes in 1895 and fifty-four in 1900; Colorado had twenty-two and then sixty-five; Missouri had ten and then twenty; Georgia had thirty-three and then twenty-one; the District of Columbia had four and then eight; Massachusetts had one hundred and four and then one hundred. The Philippines had one tribe in 1900. See Record of the Great Council of the United States IORM 9.4 (1895), and Record of the Great Council of the United States IORM 9.2 (1900), RMML.

17. See Lindsay, *Official History*, especially chapter 2, "Primitive Red Men."

18. Ibid., 49.

19. Ibid.

20. Morgan, *League of the Iroquois*, 178–179.

21. Ibid., ix.

22. Deloria, *Playing Indian*, 76. See also Modern, *Secularism in Modern America*, especially 183–238; and Bieder, "Grand Order of the Iroquois."

23. Deloria, *Playing Indian*, 90.

24. Paton, *Ceremonies for Celebration*, 744.

25. See R. S. Gregory, D. M. Stevens, and J. W. Bissikummer, *Record of the Great Council of the United States* 10, no. 1 (1896): 163, RMML.

26. Deloria, *Playing Indian*, 68.

27. Ibid., 144.

28. "Ceremonies of the Great Council of the US of the Improved Order of Red Men" (1918), 13, RMML. See also Paton, *Ceremonies for Celebration*, 6.

29. Lindsay, *Official History*, 200.

30. See "Celebrating the 22nd of Snow Moon," Council Brand 22.29 (1896), p. 1, RMML.

31. Previously under Louisiana's jurisdiction because of flailing membership numbers, Texas became autonomous in 1896. Records of the First Council of Texas, IORM, March 1896, p. 7, RMML.

32. Stephen Gould, Records of the Third Council of the Great Council of Texas, IORM, August 1897, p. 106, Special Collections and Archives, TAMIU (hereafter cited as SCA, TAMIU).

33. Between August 1896 and August 1897, Barnes and fellow recruiters established forty-five tribes in Texas. Some had a short life span (sometimes a couple of months). Others, like Yaqui Tribe No. 59, enjoyed visibility for a longer period. See "List of Tribes Organized in Texas," Records of the Fourteenth Council of the Great Council of Texas, IORM, August 1909, p. 168, RMML.

34. The ideal start-up kit included over twenty items such as "roll books" and "application blanks." The most expensive item on the list was the "question book for tribes," which cost $3.15. "Printed constitutions" and "Copies of Proceedings G.C. of Texas" were the most affordable purchases at 5 and 10 cents, respectively. See "Supplies to be Furnished at the Organization of a Tribe or Council," Records of the Sixth Great Council of Texas, May 1900–1901, p. 210, RMML. See also Records of the Second Council of the Great Council of Texas, August 1896, pp. 36–37, RMML.

35. On May 26, 1897, for example, the Laredo Yaqui Tribe No. 59 paid $25 in charter fees and, on July 8, 1897, $38 in per capita tax and adoption fees. For evidence of additional expenses, including "supplies and rituals, etc." fees, see "Table: Statement of Receipts," Records of the Fourth Council of the Great Council of Texas, August 1898, RMML.

36. Those tableaux also reflect the Red Men organization's particular vision of time based on Christopher Columbus's presence in the New World, instead relying on the specified number of years after Christ's birth (AD). To calculate and/or understand time as understood by members of the IORM, one must subtract 1491 from the current year. For example, AD 2010 - 1491 = GSD 519. I would like to thank David Lintz, director of RMML, for explaining the significance of the "Great Sun of Discovery" (GSD).

37. For a discussion of the Port of Laredo's economic profile during that period, see Carlos Cuellar, "House of Armengol," 78; and Adams, *Conflict and Commerce*, 147–149. See also Dewey, *Pesos and Dollars*; and Díaz, *Border Contraband*.

38. See *Dallas Morning News*, June 26, 1896, "Red Men Lodge," Vertical File, ITC.

39. For a discussion of naming practices, see Barnes, Records of the Second Council of the Great Council of Texas, August 1896, pp. 43–45, RMML. For an insightful account of Lipan history, see Nancy McGown Minor, *Turning Adversity to Advantage: A History of the Lipan Apaches of Texas and Northern Mexico, 1700–1900* (Lanham, MD: University Press of America, 2009).

40. See "Yaqui Tribe #59, from the papers of the late Joseph Netzer," 1897, Box 7, File 2, Wilcox Papers, JPL. See also Records of the Great Council of Texas, June 1902 [Hot Moon 410], pp. 14–19, RMML.

41. Green, *Border Biographies*, 133. For more biographical information, see Special Souvenir Edition, *Laredo Daily Times*, July 15, 1895, Box 200.8, LGHC; and "Washington's Birthday Celebration Histories," Vertical File, WCHF.

42. Future Red Men, and border residents generally, had several options after 1880: Creath Memorial Baptist Church (est. 1881), the Christ Episcopal Church (est. 1883), the Primera Iglesia Bautista Mexicana (est. 1883), the Laredo Seminary–Methodist Episcopal (est. 1883), and St. Peter's Church (established in 1897 for English-speaking Catholics) joined San Agustín Catholic Church (est. 1762) and the First United Methodist Church (est. 1871). Jewish Red Men brothers Ike Alexander, J. Alexander, Leon Daiches, Charles Moser, Elias Ross, J. Wormser, and Adolf Saft would celebrate on the second floor of the Western Union Building on Flores Street, which was located across the street from city hall. For more information see *Laredo Methodist Centennial*, 1871–1971 (1971); Betty Causey, *One Hundred Years of Ministry of the First Baptist Church of Laredo, Texas, 1881–1981: A Century of History* (1981); L. R. Elliott and Harlan Julius Matthews, *Centennial Story of Texas Baptists* (1936); Esterina Samudio Pulido, *100 Years History of the Primera Iglesia Bautista Mexicana of Laredo,*

Texas, 1883–1983: A Centennial of History (1983); Alfredo Náñez, *Historia de la Conferencia Río Grande de la Iglesia Metodista Unida* (1981); and Stanley C. Green, *A History of Laredo's Jewish Community* (1992). These texts may be found at WCHF and LGHC.

43. Born in Frankfurt-am-Main, Germany, on May 1, 1863, Netzer acquired his expertise as a plumber traveling throughout Germany, Austria, Serbia, and Russia before migrating to the United States in 1879. He joined the US Army at Baltimore, Maryland, traveled west as a ranking officer, and eventually settled in Laredo in 1889. He joined the IORM in 1897 and quickly moved up the ranks, serving as Great Sachem of Texas in 1909. He died in Laredo in 1937. Using the in-state and cross-border networks he developed as the de facto director of the WBC, Netzer was able to earn a handsome profit as the owner of Laredo's biggest hardware store. His fortune and reputation, however, eventually took a turn for the worse. The FBI scrutinized Netzer's business practices, particularly the revenue that agents suspected he had generated from selling munitions during the Mexican Revolution. For more on Netzer's biography, see Frank Johnson, *History of Texas*, 1633; and Green, *Border Biographies*, 100–102. For a discussion of Netzer's legal and bankruptcy woes, see Garza, "On the Edge of a Storm," 49–50; Peña, "Reveling in Patriotism," 199–202; Díaz, *Border Contraband*, especially 65–88; and Dewey, *Pesos and Dollars*.

44. Mary Genevieve Wilcox, "Some Social, Political and Economic Problems of a Border Town," master's thesis, University of Texas, 1934, p. 4, Box 1, Folder 8, Wilcox Papers, JPL.

45. "Año de 1869 Sesión Especial de la Corporación," City of Laredo Minute Book A, May 15, 1867–October 13, 1877, Box 4.5.1, LGHC.

46. Jo Anne Balzar and Jerry Thompson, "City Hall and Market House," Mercado Building—City Hall, 1982, Vertical File, Cabinet 6, WCHF. See also Leyendecker & Cavazos Architects and Carol Gunter, "Design Standards and Inventory of Significant Buildings—Old Mercado District, Laredo, Texas," in ibid.

47. The fraternity paid $18 per month to Thomas Farrell. The lease stipulates that "said premises is to be used by the lease as a council chamber for the lodge for purposes and that the lessee may sublet the same or the use thereof to other fraternal organizations or lodger in its discretion for similar use by them." Lease, M. G. Benavides, Deputy, Webb County, Texas, 1900, Farrell Building Vertical File, Cabinet 2, WCHF. It is also worth mentioning that local Red Men members and esteemed guests used that space to contemplate adding the "Republic of Mexico" to the "Reservation of Texas." Indeed, state-level Red Men often used special rail rates offered by the Texas-Mexican railroad during the WBC to travel on to Monterrey, Nuevo León. See Record of the Great Council of the United States 10.2, September 1897 [Corn Moon GSD 406], p. 451, RMML.

48. The *Laredo Times* published several IORM-related announcements between the founding of Yaqui Tribe No. 59 and the first celebration. See, for example, "The Improved Order of Red Men recently organized in this city held another meeting last night," June 2, 1897; "Attention!! Red Men! Work in Chief's Degree tonight at 8 o'clock sharp. Reception of Great Sachem S. D. Moore, who visits our tribe tonight. A full attendance desired," November 12, 1897; "The Red Men began last night to rehearse at Market hall for the play they propose to put on the night of the 21st," February 10, 1898; "Red Men Attention! Council Fire of Yaqui Tribe No. 59, IORM will be kindled at the 8th run of the 11th Sun, Snow Moon. Work in Adoption De-

gree. Visiting Chiefs fraternally invited," February 11, 1898; and "The Red Men are rehearsing in Market Hall every night for the play they will put on next Monday night," February 15, 1898. I have offered headlines to give more of a detailed sense of their backstage planning.

49. "Washington's Birthday Celebration," 1898, Souvenir Program, Box 7, File 1, Wilcox Papers, JPL.

50. City Council Minutes, February 14, 1898, Book 3 (January 4, 1894–November 11, 1918), CLSO.

51. "Washington's Birthday Celebration," 1898, Souvenir Program, Box 7, File 1, Wilcox Papers, JPL.

52. "Long Talk of Great Sachem S. T. Howard," Records of the Great Council of Texas, Spec. session of IORM, May 1901, pp. 34–35, RMML.

53. Herberg, "America's Civil Religion," 78.

54. Similar to the protagonists of Catherine Albanese's *Sons of the Fathers*, they understood the power of "high theater": how "orations and processions, liberty songs and 'new' ballads, tolling bells and mock funerals, standardized toasts, huzzas and feu de joie, [can] provide a taste of the heady wine of living myth which mere words can no longer supply." Albanese, "Sons of the Fathers," 12. For a detailed explanation of the IORM's relationship to George Washington and an analysis of the WBC as a form of civil religion, see Peña, "More Than a Dead American," especially 64–67. For foundational articulations of the concept, see Bellah, "Civil Religion in America" and *Broken Covenant*. Particularly interesting in light of this book's binational focus is Bellah and Hammond, *Varieties of Civil Religion*, 40–85. For critical studies of the term see, for example, Albanese, *Sons of the Fathers*; Demerath and Williams, "Civil Religion"; and Gorski, *American Covenant*.

55. Peña, "More Than a Dead American," 62–63.

56. See discussion of "environmental theater" above (Schechner, *Between Theater and Anthropology*).

Chapter 2. Playing Mexican

1. "Celebration Began Today with Favorable Weather; Concerts on Plazas, Movies and Carnival Attractions; Tomorrow will be Prize Fights, Bullfights, Noche Mexicana on Program; Banner Day in on Monday," *LT*, February 21, 1925.

2. "Laredo Washington Celebration, Its Origin and Development after 25 Years," *Houston Post*, February 17, 1924.

3. "Las Fiestas del 22," *El Demócrata Fronterizo*, February 25, 1905.

4. "Coolidge, Obregon Invited to Laredo for Feb. 22 Fete," *Houston Post*, February 3, 1924.

5. For a detailed history of Laredo's built environment, see *City of Laredo Historic Preservation Plan*, Resolution No. 96-R-031 (passed by the city council and approved by the mayor on March 25, 1996).

6. This description is based on accounts of the preparation leading up to Noche Mexicana and coverage of the event; see "Everything in Readiness for Celebration Shortly," *LT*, February 14, 1925; "Celebration Began Today with Favorable Weather; Concerts on Plazas, Movies and Carnival Attractions; Tomorrow will be Prize Fights,

Bullfights, Noche Mexicana on Program; Banner Day in on Monday," *LT*, February 21, 1925; and "Celebration Most Colorful and Best with Thousands of Visitors on Hand," *LT*, February 24, 1925.

7. "Being Neighborly," *LT*, February 24, 1925.

8. "Matias de Llano, President of Ass'n," *LT*, February 24, 1925.

9. For biographical information about M. de Llano, see Barrera, "Matias de Llano." I would also like to thank the Jackson family for taking the time to speak with me about de Llano's life. For a promotional overview of Laredo's resources, including a profile on de Llano, see *Laredo: The Gateway City*, published by the *Laredo Times* in 1925, which can be found in the Texas Collection, Baylor University, accessed April 4, 2014. For details about inducements for businessmen from Mexico, see "Plans for the Celebration Now Being Fast Arranged," *LT*, February 5, 1925.

10. "Veni, Vidi, Yaqui," *Laredo Daily Times*, February 22, 1898.

11. Slated to host hundreds of their associates in May, the Laredo branch of the advertising club requested that Noche Mexicana scenery be left up permanently. See "A Humble Suggestion," *LT*, February 24, 1925, and "Noche Mexicana Festival Adds Number New Features," *LT*, May 13, 1925.

12. "Our Celebration," *LWT*, February 28, 1926.

13. "Las Fiestas del 22," *El Democrata Fronterizo*, February 25, 1905; see also Box 203, File 1: WBCA Notes, LGHC.

14. "Official Programme," *LWT*, February 13, 1910.

15. "Laredo Pays Tribute to Father of Country for Fourteenth Time," *LWT*, February 26, 1911.

16. Fraternal groups living and recruiting in Laredo at the turn of the twentieth century like the Masons also influenced political networking, the port's economic security, and identity formation on the border. Religious diversity in Laredo, as evidenced by brick-and-mortar places of worship, which at that time included Christ Church Episcopal, Presbyterian Church, Baptist, San Agustín Catholic Church, Methodist, Christian, and St. Peter's Catholic Church, also informed those identification processes. As well, the multiracial military presence at Fort McIntosh after Reconstruction may have affected the way residents identified and categorized themselves and others based on phenotypic and linguistic characteristics (e.g., Anglo Blacks or Hispanic Blacks). For an in-depth look at the presence of black squadrons in Laredo (particularly during 1870–1900), see Jorge O. González, "The Black Experience in Laredo: 1755–1919," master's thesis, Laredo State University, 1986.

17. Geertz, *Negara*, 13.

18. For more information about those activities, see *El Demócrata Fronterizo*, March 18, 1905; "El Parque Juárez: LLAMAMIENTO AL PATRIOTISMO (una mejora importante)," *El Demócrata Fronterizo*, February 3, 1906; and "Circular. El Parque Juárez," *El Demócrata Fronterizo*, February 3, 1906.

19. For planning details and coverage of the landmark event, see "Celebramos el Centenario," *La Crónica*, March 5, 1910; "La Celebración del Centenario," *La Crónica*, March 12, 1910; "Ligera reseña de la expléndida celebración del Primer Centernario de la Independencia Mexicana en Laredo, Texas," *La Crónica*, September 24, 1910; and "To Establish Insurance Branches," *LWT*, October 1, 1911. See also Perales, *En defense de mi raza*, for the remarks offered by N. Idar at the Primer Congreso Mexicanista hosted in Laredo. For scholarly analyses of the event, see Limón, "El primer

congreso mexicanista"; Foley, *Peones to Politicos*, 68; Hinojosa, *Borderlands Town*, 120; and Orozco, "Origins of LULAC."

20. The motion reads: "The Application of Melaquiades Garcia, Secretary Centennial Celebration Committee for permission to erect in the center of Independence Plaza a monument to the Memory of Miguel Hidalgo y Costilla Mexico's liberator as a testimonial of profound respect and grateful veneration for his achievements in [sic] behalf of the sacred cause of human liberty was read and on motion granted provided that they submit the plans and specifications to the Council for Approval before erecting." Other issues on the agenda include excess property valuation, the placement of lights on Lexington Street, and a verbal petition by members of the Elk Club requesting "relief from the payment of taxes erroneously assessed against them," which was subsequently granted. Minutes, City Council Meeting, January 8, 1914, Book 3 (January 4, 1894–November 11, 1918), p. 577, CLSO. For a list of Yaqui Tribe No. 59 members, see "Yaqui Tribe #59, from the papers of the late Joseph Netzer," 1897, Box 7, File 2, Wilcox Papers, JPL; and Records of the Great Council of Texas, June 1902 [Hot Moon 410], pp. 14–19, RMML.

21. For a contemporary example, see, for example, Kaiser and Nikiforova, "Borderland Spaces."

22. Guss, *Festive State*, 12. Performance theorists Angela Marino and Manuel Cuellar critically engage Bakhtin's notion of carnival while working through their idea of fiesta epistemologies. They argue that Bakhtin's carnival is "disruptive and chaotic. . . . It ignores the constitutive acts of the fiestas themselves, the structures that sustain them—cultural, social or economic—and the transmission and transformation of epistemologies." "Fiesta Performance," 131. See also Roper, "Blackface at the Andean Fiesta," 387.

23. "Official Program," *LWT*, February 4, 1912.

24. This account is based on newspaper coverage of the WBC festivities. See "Committees Are Busy," *LWT*, February 18, 1912; and "Father of His Country Is Honored," *LWT*, February 25, 1912.

25. Mrs. J. A. Applewhite was also the chairman of the float committee when she portrayed Pocahontas. Her husband, Mr. John A. Applewhite, had recently made the news in Laredo after debuting a five-passenger 1912 Buick "with all the latest improvements and attachments." See "Little Locals," *LWT*, January 28, 1912.

26. Geertz explains: "The crucial task of legitimation—the reconciliation of this political metaphysic with the existing distribution of power in nineteenth-century Bali—was effected by means of myth; characteristically enough, a colonizing myth. . . . Like the myth of the Founding Fathers in the United States, or of The Revolution in Russia, *the myth* of the Majapahit Conquest *became the origin tale by means of which actual relations of command and obedience were explained and justified.*" *Negara*, 14 (emphasis mine).

27. This point will take center stage in chapter 5.

28. Roach, *Cities of the Dead*, 27–28.

29. Newspaper coverage of the event affirmed that idea with positive feedback. "One of the most noticeable features of the celebration today," one report read, "is the fact that both Laredos—Mexicans as well as Americans—are celebrating for 'our sister city' across the river in honoring the natal day of Washington with a joint celebration." "Father of His Country Is Honored," *LWT*, February 25, 1912.

30. Incidentally, having the attack unfold in such a way that US military stood ready under their side of the bridge but did not (or were unable to) intervene helpfully countered news reports of US military intervention at other ports of entry such as El Paso and Ciudad Juárez. "Troops to Cross Border if Needed," *LWT*, February 25, 1912.

31. "El 22 de Febrero," *La Crónica*, January 29, 1910.

32. In addition to profiting from the celebration, we should also consider that the promise of spectacle could potentially undermine monotony of conflict. "En vano buscamos el los periódicos de México algunas noticias de interés; no traen sino inverosímiles noticias de revolucion, los que puedan darlas, y asuntos artísticos o literarios los demás. TODO LO ABSORVE LA REVOLUCION, Y TODO OCULTA EL MIEDO." (We seek in vain to find newsworthy items in the Mexican dallies; all they report are implausible chronicles of the revolution, those who are in a position to provide them, and the rest only offer artistic or literary notices. THE REVOLUTION ABSORBS EVERYTHING, AND EVERYTHING IS HIDDEN BY FEAR.) While hardly a substitute for peace, or border parity for that matter, the occasion, for better or for worse, offered spectators a different experience. *El Demócrata Fronterizo*, February 25, 1911 (emphasis in original).

33. In his analysis of festive forms and the theatre of the state in Bali, Geertz proposes: "Political power inhered less in property than in people; was a matter of the accumulation of prestige, not of territory. The disagreements between the various princedoms, as recorded in edicts, treaties, and legends, or as remembered by informants, were virtually never concerned with border problems, but with delicate questions of mutual status, of appropriate politesse (the instant cause of one important war was an impolitely addressed letter about an insignificant matter) and of rights to mobilize particular bodies of men, even particular men, for state ritual and, what was really the same thing, for warfare." *Negara*, 24.

34. Dated February 18, 1913, the letter reads: "The City Council of Nuevo Laredo supported by the revolutionary commission and the military forces will co-operate in carrying forward the previously arranged program for the 22nd of February in this city and will assist in every way possible in making the celebration a grand success as far as it pertains to Nuevo Laredo carrying out her part of the program." For more details, see "Madero Agrees to the Naming of a Provisional President," "Geo. Washington's Birthday Fittingly Commemorated," and "The Day We Celebrate," all in *LWT*, February 23, 1913.

35. Celebration boosters continued to request that "representative citizens" in Nuevo Laredo work on subcommittees, but English- and Spanish-language newspaper coverage and WBC archives show that the international bridge ceremony was not staged between 1913–1919. See "Announcement of Proposition to Stage Big Celebration in February Is Looked upon with Favor," *LWT*, January 2, 1916. US authorities acknowledged that neolaredenses "live in a constant state of dread and fear of uprising," but they would close the bridge to prevent a mass exodus of people from seeking shelter in Laredo. But WBC programming still included events and travel to Nuevo Laredo. In 1916, and even amid reports of American and British citizen deaths in Chihuahua, for example, organizers not only arranged boxing matches and bullfights but also fielded written requests from tour groups interested in catching "a glimpse of the ruins [property damage resulting from revolution violence] left by

the evacuating federals in Nuevo Laredo." See "Misleading the People" and "Interest in Celebration Is Shown by Many Letters," *LWT*, February 13, 1916; and "Roosevelt Will Be Asked to Use His Influence to Change Mexican Policy," *LWT*, January 16, 1916. The only times WBC planners scaled back the festivities on the US side of the border were in 1915, in light of the Plan of San Diego, and during World War I, out of respect for their brothers fighting in Europe. See "Persistent Inquiries Are Being Received Here," *LWT*, January 13, 1918. For an extended analysis of the WBC and cross-border negotiation during the Mexican Revolution, see Peña, "Reveling in Patriatism." For an overview of the festivities in 1921, see "Nuevo Laredo Is Arranging Program for Celebration," *LWT*, February 13, 1921.

36. Red Men member and WBC chairman Joseph Netzer sent out invitations on official letterhead stating: "The parade and all other features will be on a more elaborate scale than ever before. You may rest assured that your presence and co-operation will be highly appreciated." See "Sixteenth Annual Celebration of Washington Birthday a Success," *LWT*, March 1, 1914. See also, Letter, Joseph Netzer, February 1914, John Keck, personal collection (reviewed July 10, 2014).

37. "Laredo Pays Tribute to Father of Country for Fourteenth Time," *LWT*, February 26, 1911. For a terrific history of border baseball as well as an excellent analyis of nationalism and identity in the two Laredos, see Klein, *Baseball on the Border*.

38. The *Laredo Weekly Times* reported, "The picture was a fine one and one could readily recognize Laredo people lined on the banks of the river or assembled about the international bridge on the American side." During the actual attack on Nuevo Laredo on January 1, 1914, day tourists from San Antonio, Corpus Christi, and other parts of Texas assembled in Laredo along the river to witness the violence in Nuevo Laredo from a safe distance. The public screening offered residents and visitors the opportunity to experience the revolution (perhaps again) through a different medium. See "Immense Crowds Were Out," *LWT*, March 1, 1914; and "Many Came to See Battle," *LWT*, January 11, 1914.

39. The newspaper article noted that while the Kickapoo had traveled from their "reservation" in Coahuila, Mexico, originally, tribe members made their home in the former Indian Territory (now Oklahoma). "Kickapoo Indians in Laredo," *LWT*, February 14, 1915.

40. Peña, "Reveling in Patriotism," 199. See also "Beginning of Celebration," *LWT*, February 23, 1913.

41. See "1914 WBC notes," Drawer 1, Stan Green/WBCA Vertical File, Washington Birthday Celebration Historical Collection, WCHF. See also "Official Program: Washington Birthday Celebration, February 20 to 25, Inclusive," *LWT*, February 8, 1914.

42. Gender expectations made themselves known in different contexts. In addition to taking on Pocahontas selection committee work, they headed parade float committees. A decade later a "women's executive committee" was organized once the WBCA received its state charter. The women were active at the Port of Laredo and facilitated regional communication with chambers of commerce in Cotulla, Pearsall, San Antonio, Austin, Waco, Dallas, Fort Worth, Beeville, Corpus Christi, Brownsville, Alice, Hebbronville, and Eagle Pass. See "Are Relying on the Women to Assist the Committee," *LWT*, February 6, 1916. See also Ledger, January 24, 1924, Minutes of Meeting, Board of Directors, LCC Minute Book 2, p. 194, Box 142A (hereafter LCC MB2), LGHC.

43. Ledger, November 27, 1918, Minutes of Meeting, Board of Directors, LCC Minute Book 1, p. 4, Box 142A (hereafter LCC MB1), LGHC.

44. "Laredo Preparedness," *LWT*, February 27, 1916.

45. "For Annual Celebration Washington's Birthday," *LWT*, December 28, 1918.

46. Ledger, January 19, 1919, Minutes of Meeting, Board of Directors, LCC MB1, p. 11, LGHC.

47. The LCC sought the counsel of festival organizers operating in other parts of the state, such as the Cotton Palace Exposition team in Waco, to learn about organization and finances. In the meantime they streamlined their involvement; fussing over a decision to pay $7.50 to have the front of their office decorated during the festivities. See Ledger, February 3, 1921, Minutes of Meeting, Board of Directors, LCC MB1, p. 152, LGHC; Ledger, February 17, 1921, ibid., 159; and Ledger, March 3, 1921, ibid., 162.

48. Ledger, December 22, 1921, Minutes of Meeting, Board of Directors, LCC MB1, p. 225, LGHC; Ledger, January 19, 1922, ibid., 233; Ledger, February 23, 1922, ibid., 246.

49. Soon after the LCC's constitution and bylaws were adopted on November 27, 1918, neolaredense business elite were invited to join. Ledger, November 27, 1918, Minutes of Meeting, Board of Directors, LCC MB1, p. 4, LGHC. For discussions of the creation of a "Mexican-American Branch," see Ledger, October 28, 1918, ibid., 7–10.

50. Led by M. S. Saldaña and M. C. Cadena, members of Nuevo Laredo's business elite created an independent Cámara de Comercio (chamber of commerce) in 1921. There was little resistance to the idea in Laredo, particularly after chamber secretary Fred W. Mally returned from the Confederation of the Chambers of Commerce of Mexico at Juárez in February 1921 and reported that most border cities had two chambers. Ledger, April 21, 1921, Minutes of Meeting, Board of Directors, LCC MB1, p. 172, LGHC. See also, Ledger, February 11, 1921, ibid., 157; and Ledger, September 24, 1920, Minutes of Adjourned Weekly of Board of Directors, ibid., 123.

51. Ledger, January 19, 1919, Minutes of Meeting, Board of Directors, LCC MB1, p. 12, LGHC; Ledger, February 19, 1920, ibid., 92; Ledger, April 18, 1920, ibid., 97.

52. "Celebration Aftermath," *LWT*, February 28, 1926.

53. A fire thought to be "incendiary" destroyed the international footbridge on April 25, 1920. *LWT*, May 2, 1920. Rebuilding the bridge was not an LCC project or a City of Laredo project because the Laredo Bridge Company owned the US side of the structure. Curiously enough, chamber members agreed to the disposal of the "minutes of the special meetings, concerning the burning of the International Foot Bridge. . . . All that was necessary to read, and record, of these special meetings, was the resolution adopted by the meeting." See Ledger, May 6, 1920, Minutes of Meeting, Board of Directors, LCC MB1, p. 101, LGHC; and Ledger, May 20, 1920, ibid., 187.

54. While the route itself is centuries old, the rise of automobile culture and the creation of the International Meridian Highway Association in 1911 generated newfound interest in the road's business potential. It even acquired the moniker "North America's Main Street" when design plans, which cut a vertical line from the US-Mexico border at Laredo up toward the US-Canada border at Winnipeg, were made public. Promotional materials such as pamphlets and letterhead signaled the Meridian Highway's hemispheric aspirations. Stationary printed in 1928, for example, reads "The Pan-American Highway—The Main Street of North and South

America. Under Construction in Ten Nations, International Meridian Highway—US 81, Canada 14, Mexico 1, Main Street of North America." Moore, Freeman, and Dudley, *Meridian Highway in Texas*, 59. For more information about the construction of the Meridian Highway and the Pan-American Highway at Laredo see, for example, Desay, "Landscape Types"; Amanda Johnson, "Feeling the Drive"; and Gruel Sández, "La inauguración de la Carretera Panamericana."

55. Ledger, February 2, 1922, Minutes of Meeting, Board of Directors, LCC MB1, pp. 238–239, LGHC. For regional coverage of the bridge ceremony, see *Houston Post*, February 18, 1922; and *Liberty Vindicator*, March 3, 1922.

56. Ledger, February 9, 1922, Minutes of Meeting, Board of Directors, LCC MB1, p. 243, LGHC.

57. Ledger, February 2, 1922, Minutes of Meeting, Board of Directors, LCC MB1, pp. 238–239, LGHC.

58. As historian Mae Ngai reminds us, "The Immigration Act of 1917 doubled the head tax and imposed a literacy test, erecting the first barriers to entry, but unlawful entry was limited, as the Labor Department exempted Mexico from the requirements during the war. It was not until 1919 that Mexicans entering the United States were required to apply for admission at lawfully designated ports of entry." *Impossible Subjects*, 64.

59. With that said, it is important to note that chamber members' international thinking did not support racial diversity. They denied the presiding elder of the African M.E. Church's request asking for the "endorsement and encouragement of immigration of negroes into the southwestern portion of Texas." Siding with the Pastors' Association of Laredo, they agreed that "it would be an inopportune time for a colonization scheme in Laredo on account of the negro not being able to compete with the Mexican labor successfully, where the latter is at home, and also on account of other conditions prevailing in this community at this time." Board members accentuated that point the next year when discussing real estate issues: "The average laboring man, or the negro and Mexican do not add much to the real estate values of property within the city. It is the men with money, who operates [sic] with it, and invests [sic] that money, that will mean something to Laredo from a business standpoint, as well as real estate." See Ledger, February 9, 1922, Minutes of Meeting, Board of Directors, LCC MB1, p. 244, LGHC; and Ledger, February 1, 1923, ibid., 60.

60. Ledger, March 2, 1922, Minutes of Meeting, Board of Directors, LCC MB1, p. 249, LGHC. The chamber also had to worry about discussions of routes by way of Saltillo to Zacatecas to Aguascalientes to Mexico City as well as trade gains made by Eagle Pass, who had taken to offering lower tariffs on wheat and grain. See, for example, ibid., entries for February 23, 1922, p. 246; March 9, 1922, p. 251; April 13, 1922, p. 261; and August 24, 1922, p. 2.

61. The LCC agreed unanimously to pay a $30 membership/annual dues fee to join the Confederation of Chambers of Commerce in Mexico, which had amended their constitution to permit American chambers to become members. See Ledger, February 15, 1923, Minutes of Meeting, Board of Directors, LCC MB2, p. 70, LGHC; and Ledger, March 8, 1923, ibid., 80.

62. The WBCA officially received its state charter on February 2, 1923, with no capital stock. L. Villegas, Sam Mackin, and W. J. Sames were named as the incorporators. See "Charters," *Austin American*, February 3, 1923. The WBCA's first meeting

was scheduled on April 23, 1923, at the Hamilton Café. Ledger, April 19, 1923, Minutes of Meeting, Board of Directors, LCC MB2, p. 95, LGHC. For a discussion of the charter at the municipal level, see Ledger, December 28, 1922, ibid., 37; and Ledger, February 8, 1923, ibid., 66.

63. Seb S. Wilcox, historian and court reporter for the Texas District 49 in Laredo, authored the stenographic report. Ledger, March 8, 1923, Minutes of Meeting, Board of Directors, LCC MB2, p. 82, LGHC. For additional details, see "Dedication of the International Bridge, Laredo, Texas, and Nuevo Laredo, Tamaulipas, Mexico, Washington's Birthday, February 22, 1922," Wilcox Papers, Box 5, File 14, JPL; and Minutes, November 17, 1958, Regular Meeting of the Board of Trustees of the Laredo Bridge System (1946–1959), p. 393, Box 144, LGHC. See also Shanks, *Laredo: Reflections*, 39.

64. See "An Open Letter," *LWT*, February 7, 1926.

65. "Highway Convention," *Bellville Telescope*, February 7, 1926.

66. "An Open Letter," *LWT*, February 7, 1926; "Huge Celebration Planned at Laredo Beginning Feb., Anniversary of American Independence to Be Observed with Parades," *Austin American*, February 14, 1926.

67. "Being Neighborly," *LT*, February 24, 1925.

68. See Tenorio-Trillo, *Mexico at the World's Fairs*, especially 48–63.

69. For insightful discussions of "playing" and "acting" in other contexts, particularly in film and on television, see, for example, Herrera, *Latin Numbers*; and Bial, *Acting Jewish*.

70. Deloria, *Playing Indian*, 36.

71. Ibid., 34.

72. Michel de Certeau uses the act of reading to explain the concept of poaching. He explains that the reader "insinuates into another person's text the ruses of pleasure and appropriation: he poaches on it, is transported into it, pluralizes himself in it like the internal rumblings of one's body. Ruse, metaphor, arrangement, this production is also an 'invention' of the memory. Words become the outlet or product of silent histories. The readable transforms itself into the memorable." Playing Indian or Mexican in this context does not rely on the act of reading, but the underlying sentiment of de Certeau's idea remains intact. Identity can be absorbed in a moment, with attention and action. And that moment enables "the reader" to invent his/her/their past. *Practice of Everyday Life*, xxi.

73. Vila, *Crossing Borders*. For a discussion of the analytic value of twin towns, see Nugent, "Border Towns," 557–558.

74. Manuel Cuellar, "La escenificación de lo mexicano," 123.

75. Ibid., 125; see also 135–136.

76. Marino and Cuellar, "Fiesta Performance," 124.

77. Manuel Cuellar notes that when presented together, Noche Mexicana newspaper coverage, both articles and images, "incorpora discursivamente a una estética nacional o que de lo contrario serían simples diseños y decoraciones populares." "La escenificación de lo mexicano," 127.

78. Tenorio-Trillo, *Mexico at the World's Fairs*, 202. See also Brading, *Prophecy and Myth*, 71–80. For a study that sheds important light on the limitations of Díaz's approach to modernization and Mexico's built environment/construction projects, see Connolly, *El contratista de Don Porfirio*.

79. Piñon, *Searching for America*, 150–151. For a discussion of the importance of the "charro" figure in a transnational context, see Cohen, *Braceros*, 75.

80. "Two-and-one-half hours of orchestra and band concerts and speeches honoring the two Laredos" were broadcast that year. See *Washington's Birthday Celebration Official Program 1935*, p. 11, WBCAP. For additional information, see Raymundo Rios Mayo Papers on Nuevo Laredo, Box 10.5, File: Nuevo Laredo, LGHC; Documents on the origin of Life Downs, Box 213, File: Life Downs, LGHC; Border Olympics (minutes, schedules, correspondence, finances), Box 258, File: Border Olympics, 1932–2013, LGHC; and Promotional Brochure re: Sixth Annual Fair and Exposition in Nuevo Laredo, August 1963, Highlights on Tourism, International Travel Guide, Box 187b, LCC, 1963, Martin Papers, LGHC.

Chapter 3. Hurricane Alice and the International Bridge Closure Crisis

1. For examples of bridge ceremonies at the US-Mexico border, see Cadava, *Standing on Common Ground*, 37; Miller, *On the Border*, xi; and Stamp, *Bridging the Border*, 126. For examples beyond North America, see Gluckman, "Analysis of a Social Situation," 5; Darian-Smith, *Bridging Divides*, 101; and Löfgren, "Concrete Transnationalism?," 67.

2. Kang, "Crossing the Line," 168.

3. Mize et al., "Consuming Mexican Labor," 33–34; see also Ngai, *Impossible Subjects*, 153.

4. Jackson, *Lines of Activity*, 26.

5. Letter, September 11, 1957, LCC president Chester C. Wine to L. H. Hewitt, Commissioner, US Section, International Boundary and Water Commission, LCCP.

6. "Laredo-Nuevo Laredo braced today for the worst flood on record," *LT*, June 29, 1954.

7. Report, Telefonea del C. Ing. Eduardo Chávez, Secretario de Recursos Hidraulicos, desde Nuevo Laredo, Tamaulipas, July 1, 1954, AGN, FO0396 SPN, SC222 JFMM, 1923–1980, 561.3/39. See also Koebel and Sonesson, 1, found in misc. papers, LCC offices.

8. Arreola, *Tejano South Texas*, 153; and Adams, *Conflict and Commerce*, 168.

9. Minutes, February 18, 1956, Regular Monthly Meeting of the Board of Trustees of the Laredo Bridge System (1946–1959), pp. 1–2, Box 144, LGHC; Correpondence, Dr. Jesús López Lira, Administrador de la Aduana Fronteriza Nuevo Laredo, Tamaulipas, to Enrique Rodríguez Cano, Secretario de la Presidencia de la Republica, Asunto: Construción del Puente de Pontones, July 27, 1954, AGN, FO0396 SPN, SC222 JFMM, 561.3/39; "Unificará los Esfuerzos para Reconstruir las Ciudades Afectadas," *La Prensa*, July 9, 1956.

10. Correpondence, Rafael Garza González, Vice-Presidente Cámara Nacional de Comercio, to Presidente, Secretario Particular, Asunto: Construcción del Vado en Nuevo Laredo, December 29, 1954, AGN, FO0396 SPN, SC222 JFMM, 561.3/39; Correspondence, Antonio Ramiro, Jr., Secretario Particular, to Director General de Caminos, Asunto: Construcción del Vado en Nuevo Laredo, January 12, 1955, ibid. See also "Low-Level Bridge to Be Officially Opened Tuesday," *South Texas Citizen*, February 11, 1955.

11. Several of my interlocuters described J. C. Martin Jr. as a "patrón" who maintained close ties with national and state power brokers in Washington, DC, and Austin. One university professor recalled, "Everyone bowed down to him, which isn't really related to the WBC, but it is a bit." Things are different now, he added. "It [the celebration] is 'purely local,' which is not a bad thing, but it is different." Another interviewee clarified Martin's power on the ground: "You couldn't get a job if you were opposed [to the municipal status quo]. You couldn't work at a bank or at a utility company, you could not get a job as a school teacher, helloooo." For more on patron democracy see Piñon, *Patron Democracy*, 101–102; and Miller, *On the Border*, 61–62.

12. Telegram, July 1, 1954, Lyndon B. Johnson to Hugh S. Cluck, LCCP.

13. Telegram, June 29, 1954, Joe M. Kilgore to J. C. Martin Jr., LCCP; Telegram, June 29, 1954, Lloyd M. Bentsen to J. C. Martin Jr., LCCP. For subsequent discussions, see US Congress, Senate, Committee on Appropriations, *Rio Grande International Dams Program: Hearings before the Committee on Appropriations, Vol. 2*, 84th Cong., 1st sess., 1955, p. 552.

14. Report, Dirección General de Información, Asunto: Flood Response Efforts, July 8, 1954, AGN, FO0396 SPN, SC222 JFMM, 561.3/39.

15. "Local residents recall 1954 flooding," *LMT*, July 4, 2004.

16. Correspondence, Antonio Ramiro, Jr., Secretario Particular to Director General de Caminos, Asunto: Iniciar los trabajos de construción, November 24, 1954, AGN, FO0396 SPN, SC222 JFMM, 561.3/39; Correspondence, Antonio Ramiro, Jr., Asunto: Acelerar los trabajos de la reconstrución, December 1, 1954, ibid.

17. Texas Highway Department, *Laredo Urban Transportation Study*, 17.

18. Promotional Report, 1956, *Laredo, TX*, 3, LCCP. For corresponding statistics in Nuevo Laredo, see JFMM 1958, p. 39.

19. Between November 1955 and November 1956, Brownsville/Matamoros almost doubled their collections revenue. The *Laredo Times* reported, "Laredo continued far in the lead, with $237,279.27 last month, compared with $114,431.51 for November 1955. Brownsville, with $160,847.91 last month, showed a heavier percentage gain over only $76,768.37 collected for the same month of last year." See "Port Leads in Customs Collections," *LT*, December 11, 1956.

20. When Foreign Relations Committee members asked Texas senator Ralph W. Yarborough why Texas-Tamaulipas border cities wanted authority to construct an international bridge without congressional approval, he explained in plain terms: "Increased production of cotton in Mexico is hurting the Texas cotton farmers, the growers of that cotton in Mexico, for as far as two or three hundred miles down into the interior, come up and cross the bridges and buy a tremendous amount of personal goods, maybe as many as 10 to 12 suits of clothes per person at a time, to last for 2 or 3 years, from the merchants on the American side. That has led to a demand for more of these bridges." See International Bridges, Hearings before the Committee on Foreign Relations, Senate, 86th Cong., 9–10 (1959). For a history of cotton production in South Texas, see Walsh, *Building the Borderlands*.

21. Border residents and legislators alike recognized the value of steady pedestrian traffic. In the summer of 2014, I had the pleasure of interviewing a businessman who in 1948 had opened a retail and general merchandise store at the foot of the US side of the bridge. He recalled that register tape during that period would often show upwards of two thousand customers a day. Bestselling items included

Butter Krust bread and Palmolive soap. He emphasized that maintaining "high volume of sales per square foot" depended on product availability, the actual layout of the store (i.e., use of vertical space to simultaneously store and display goods), and efficient border-crossing facilities. He also added that more people meant more arrests. He recalled that "eight to twelve people would go to jail for petty theft" each day of the celebration. Interview, July 11, 2014.

22. Correspondence, Arq. Carlos Lazo, Secretario de Comuncaciones y Obras Públicas de México, to Secretario Privado de la Presidencia de la República, Bridge Reconstruction Request Letter, June 14, 1955, AGN, FO0396 SPN, SC222 JFMM, 561.3/39; Correspondence, Carlos Lezama Guttiérrez, Director General de Camino, to Lic. Horacio Teran, Gobernador Constitucional del estado de Tamaulipas, Asunto: Relativo al Puente Internacional de Laredo, June 9, 1955, ibid.

23. Significantly underbidding their American competitors, Concretos S.A. of Monterrey, Mexico, offered \$335,000 USD to construct the 48,200 square-foot structure (approximately \$7/sq. ft. compared to \$12.50/sq. ft.). Koebel and Sonesson (1956), 3, misc. papers, LCC.

24. Ibid., 4.

25. "Donación del Laredo Bridge System para el Puente Bajo Internacional," *La Prensa*, January 26, 1956.

26. Letter, December 21, 1955, J. C. Martin Jr. to Manuel de Anda Carranza, Oficina de Transito Federal (Nuevo Laredo), Re: Mexican noncommercial vehicles exemption from Texas license provisions, Box 256, Martin Papers, LGHC.

27. "Ha Quedado Terminada la Mitad del Puente Internacional Urbano," *La Prensa*, April 5, 1956.

28. Minutes, June 11, 1956, Regular Monthly Meeting of the Board of Trustees, LBS (1946–1959), p. 327, Box 144, LGHC. See also Tom Green, "City Files for Urban Renewal Funding," *LT*, February 21, 1957; and "Urban Renewal Parley Is Set This Afternoon," *LT*, January 21, 1958.

29. Minutes, August 13, 1956, Regular Monthly Meeting of the Board of Trustees, LBS, p. 333, Box 144, LGHC.

30. Parties from both sides including Mexican engineers Jesús Fernández Guerra and Juvencio Guttiérrez, the directors of Concretos, S.A., and International Bridge Reconstruction Committee members from Nuevo Laredo: engineer Luis Guzmán Garduño, president of the Mexican delegation; engineer J. de Jesús González Aparicio; and engineer Guillermo Verduzco attended the ceremony. Engineers Andrew M. Gault, Louis Kowalski, and Leopoldo P. Botello—LBS trustees and "International Bridge Committee" members—were also present. See "Las Fiestas en Nuevo Laredo," *La Prensa*, September 19, 1956.

31. Mayor Martin sent invitation letters to key officials like governor of Texas Allan Shivers to secure his attendance and to governor of Tamaulipas Horacio Terán Zozaya. Announcements of the potential participation of US president Eisenhower and Mexican president Ruiz Cortínes in the bridge inauguration ceremony also made the rounds. Correspondence, November 28, 1956, Bridge Inauguration Invitation Letter from J. C. Martin Jr. to Allan Shivers, Martin Papers, LGHC; and Correspondence, October 16, 1956, Ezequiel D. Salinas, 111th District Court of Texas, to J. C. Martin Jr., Martin Papers, LGHC. See also "Una Entrevista de Eisenhower y Ruiz

Cortínes en Laredo, al Inaugurarse el Nuevo Puente Internacional," *La Prensa*, October 14, 1956.

32. "Mexico Refuses to Accept Span until Completed," *LT*, December 9, 1956; "Se Efectuó la Entrega de la Mitad del Puente Urbano Local," *La Prensa*, December 14, 1956.

33. *Revista Mensual* (1948), 1.

34. Ibid., 1, 4.

35. See Minutes, August 28, 1947, Special Meeting of the Board of Trustees, LBS, p. 56, Box 144, LGHC; Minutes, January 16, 1950, Regular Monthly Meeting and Annual Meeting of the Board of Trustees and Minutes of the Annual Meeting for 1949 of the LBS, p. 112, ibid.; Minutes, May 19, 1947, Eighteenth Meeting of the Board of Trustees, LBS, p. 48, ibid.; and Minutes, March 17, 1947, Sixteenth Meeting of the Board of Trustees, LBS, pp. 38–39, ibid.

36. Memo, November 12, 1956, J. C. Martin appointed head of bridge committee, Martin Papers, LGHC; Memo, December 1, 1956, New International Bridge Inauguration Plan, Martin Papers, LGHC.

37. Piñon, *Patron Democracy*, 108–112.

38. Ibid., 130.

39. It was often easier for border residents to use expanded local authority than to rely on faraway federal regulations and governing customs. Such was the case with regional initiatives like Zona Libre (1858–1905), which took effect in the wake of Mexican president Comonfort's dissolution of the constitution and congress (1855–1858). Devised in 1858 by Tamaulipan governor Ramón Guerra to take control of cross-border trade and scale back migration out of Mexico, Zona Libre exempted payment of import duties for cargo while it remained "in the fiscal or private warehouses" and for goods sold for consumption "as far as the limit of the respective municipal jurisdictions." Driven by improvised cross-border creation, the policy fostered "mutually dependent" economic opportunities that cut across the international boundary line. It also attracted political backlash. Zona Libre's unilateral qualities were particularly unsettling for DC-based legislators, diplomats, and military officials, who were not accustomed to being passive targets of their neighbor's policy initiatives. See Margolies, *Spaces of Law*, 58–59, 74; see also Bell and Smallwood, *Zona Libre*; and Mora-Torres, *Making of the US-Mexico Border*.

40. "El Puente entre los dos Laredo," *La Prensa*, February 19, 1957.

41. "Ha Quedado Terminada la Mitad del Puente Internacional Urbano," *La Prensa*, April 5, 1956. See also, City of Laredo, *General Fund* (1955), 1.

42. In early February 1957, for example, Mayor Martin traveled to Washington, DC, to negotiate Urban Renewal Act funds. While not explicitly linked to bridge construction efforts, guaranteeing access to federal dollars lessened the sting of chamber members' earlier proposal to raise toll fare to "match Federal funds" and to help subsidize "Urban Renewal work." See "City Files for Urban Renewal Funding," *LT*, February 21, 1957; Report, July 30, 1956, "A Workable Program for Urban Renewal," Martin Papers, LGHC.

43. Arreola, *Tejano South Texas*, 152; and Adams, *Conflict and Commerce*, 167. See also Wine (1969), misc. papers, LCC.

44. Annual Report, LCC 1950–1951, p. 4, LCCP; "Laredo Fete Draws 4 Mexican

Governors," *El Paso Herald-Post*, February 21, 1957; "Laredo y Muevo [sic] Laredo Exención de Pasaportes Para Los Ciudadanos Mexicanos Que Vengan a Esta Ciudad Durante las Fiestas de Washington," *La Prensa*, February 23, 1957.

45. "Van a Cambiar todas las tarjetas para cruzar la frontera por permisos de un carácter permanente," *La Prensa*, October 5, 1956. See also "12,000 Passports Issued by Mexico," *Waco Herald-Tribune*, November 25, 1956; and "Mas de 40,000 Personas han Solicitado las Nuevas Tarjetas para el Cruce de la Frontera," *La Prensa*, March 30, 1957.

46. NL 1960a, American Consul Ben Zweig to Foreign Service Inspector Lee E. Metcalf, File: Nuevo Laredo (1960–1960), Statements to Facilitate Inspection: Section 4, Consular Affairs, Sub-Section C: VISAS, March 25, 1960, p. 1, Record Group 59 (hereafter RG 59), General Records of the Department of State, 1763–2002, Box 84, File: Nuevo Laredo (1960), NACP.

47. NL 1955a, American Consul Walter W. Orebuagh to Foreign Service Inspector Herbert S. Bursley, Statements to Facilitate Inspection: Section 4, Consular Program (Continued), October 28, 1955, p. 1, RG 59, General Records of the Department of State, 1763–2002, Box 84, File: Nuevo Laredo (1955), NACP.

48. Goffman, *Strategic Interaction*, 18–19.

49. Minutes, Special Meeting of Laredo City Council, February 18, 1957, Minute Book 10 (September 6, 1955–August 25, 1960), City Manager's Office, Laredo; Minutes, February 18, 1957, Regular Monthly Meeting of the Board of Trustees, LBS, pp. 348–349, Box 144, LGHC. For public announcements, see *LT*, February 21, 1957; and *La Prensa*, February 22, 1957.

50. Ordinance, February 18, 1957, Record of City Ordinances (October 20, 1953–June 7, 1960), Book 9, pp. 195–196, City Manager's Office, Laredo. For media coverage of a free-bridge option, see M. Durán, "El Puente entre los dos Laredos," *La Prensa*, February 19, 1957.

51. "Issuance of Celebration Passes for Three Days," *LWT*, February 6, 1921.

52. Goffman *Strategic Interaction*, 24.

53. Ibid., 95.

54. Ibid., 96.

55. Washington's Birthday 1928, 6, LGHC.

56. *Revista Mensual* (1952), 6–7. See also, Report, Bessie F. Lindheim presented to the Table, Collected History, Pan-American Roundtable of San Antonio Records, undated, MS 3 Box 26, JPL.

57. Washington's Birthday 1953, p. 13, LGHC.

58. See, for example, Cadava, *Standing on Common Ground*, 23.

59. Guss, *Festive State*, 12.

60. Appel et al., *Promise of Infrastructure*, 11.

61. Paso libre may have resulted in a loss of revenue that year, but LBS trustees were well aware that opening the bridge increased pedestrian traffic. Continuing to offer paso libre in the future would have a positive economic impact. Here is a snippet of their conversations: "The Manager then reported on the dates of February 21 and 22 when no toll charges were made for passengers crossing the bridge. He reported that a careful traffic count had been made just as if tolls were being charged with the result that Foot Passenger traffic would have amounted to $1,774.20 while other traffic, with the exception of Freight, would have paid $3,276.75; a total of

$5,050.95 worth of traffic which passed Free. The Manager pointed out that some of this traffic would probably not have passed at all if the bridge had not been free; another part of this traffic would have passed with the use of tickets which would have brought revenue in the amount of approximately 4 cents apiece; and still other parts of the traffic would have passed on Free Passes and therefore could not be counted as a loss of cash. The Manager reported that there was practically no comment on the part of the Public as they passed the toll booth, either on the two days with Free Tolls or the succeeding days when toll charges were again put into effect." Minutes, March 18, 1957, Regular Meeting of the Board of Trustees, LBS, p. 350, Box 144, LGHC.

62. American Consul Ben Zweig to Foreign Service Inspector Lee E. Metcalf, Statements to Facilitate Inspection, Subject: Part 2, Information and Educational Exchange Program, March 25, 1960, p. 1, General Records of the Department of State, 1763–2002, Box 84, File: Nuevo Laredo (1960), NACP.

63. American Consul James C. Powell Jr. to Foreign Service Inspector Herbert S. Bursley, Statements to Facilitate Inspection, Subject: Part 2, Information and Educational Exchange Program, February 3, 1953, pp. 1–2, General Records of the Department of State, 1763–2002, Box 84, File: Nuevo Laredo (1953), NACP; American Consul Walter W. Orebuagh to Foreign Service Inspector Herbert S. Bursley, Statements to Facilitate Inspection, Subject: Part 2, Information and Educational Exchange Program, October 28, 1955, File: Nuevo Laredo (1955), ibid.; American Consul Ben Zweig to Foreign Service Inspector Fulton Freeman, Statements to Facilitate Inspection, Subject: Part 2, Information and Educational Exchange Program, March 26, 1958, p. 1, File: Nuevo Laredo (1958), ibid.

Chapter 4. Paso Libre

1. The Mexican federal agency Secretaria de Comunicaciones y Transportes and the City of Laredo International Bridge department have managed their respective ends of the bridge since the privately owned Laredo Bridge Company was dissolved in 1946. For information about ownership shifts in Laredo, see Minutes, February 18, 1946, First Meeting of the Board of Trustees, LBS, pp. 1–4, Box 144, LGHC.

2. Letter, Robert M. Bayre, State Department, Office of Caribbean and Mexican Affairs, to Mr. Cantu, May 13, 1963, Re: Labor and "commuter" situation, Box 187, File: Kilgore, Joe M., Martin Papers, LGHC; and Letter, Joe M. Kilgore to J. C. Martin Jr., May 15, 1963, Re: Commuters situation, Box 187, File: Kilgore, Joe M., 1963, Martin Papers, LGHC. For Bracero Program crossing figures at the Port of Laredo, particularly in the aftermath of Operation Wetback, see Spener, *Clandestine Crossings*, 42.

3. "Tremendous Crowds Here," *LT*, February 23, 1962.

4. For an overview of Port of Laredo population statistics between 1850 and 1990, see Lorey, *US-Mexico Border Statistics*, 36–38, 46–49.

5. In their study of border elites and community integration, Jonathon W. Sloan and Jonathon P. West calculated that Nuevo Laredo's annual growth rate since the mid-1950s averaged about 4.5 percent. They also found that "over 33 percent of Nuevo Laredo's population are migrants who have been attracted to the border city because of the comparatively better jobs and living conditions available there and

the opportunities to attain legal or illegal jobs in the United States." "Community Integration," 454.

6. Arreola discusses the regenerative impact of a "staging area" in his analysis of Mexico-US borderlands history. He explains: "The flood of potential crossers in towns creates business opportunities that spawn a new kind of commercial landscape replete with lodgings, food stalls and the all-important public telephone so *pollos* can contact and communicate with *polleros*." Arreola, *Mexico-US Borderlands*, 343.

7. "Bridge Revenue Highest in History: Annual Net Take Totals $282,382," *LT*, January 22, 1958.

8. After retiring from the INS, Skinner made his mark on Laredo politics as an alderman. "Allen Skinner Aids Visitors During Fiesta," *LT*, February 18, 1970.

9. Interview, July 5, 2014. The "Council of the Five States"—Tamaulipas, Nuevo Leon, Coahuila, Chihuahua, and Texas—was incorporated in 1956 as a nonprofit and nonpolitical organization under the legal name the International Good Neighbor Council (referred to in Spanish as el Consejo Internacional de Buena Vecindad). That cooperative body followed in the footsteps but internationalized the Texas Good Neighbor Commission (TGNC), which was established by Texas governor Coke R. Stevenson in 1943 to advance the equal treatment of Latin Americans (especially Mexicans) in Texas. The TGNC was allowed to expire in 1991, but the IGNC and CIBV organizations remain active and have expanded their reach to additional states in the United States and Mexico.

10. Chalfin's fieldwork with employees across different border/entry sites (e.g., wet port, airport) in Ghana resonates with here. She argues, "The border is not a reflection of territorial sovereignty but a space to reflect on the project of territorial sovereignty." Customs officers' daily tasks (such as stamping passports and inspecting cargo shipments) materialize territorial sovereignty in important ways. Chalfin, Neoliberal Frontiers, 58–59.

11. See, for example, *Laredo Times*: "Visa Waiver Set Feb. 23–26," February 21, 1961; "Joint Waiver Scheduled for Cinco de Mayo," April 19, 1961; and "Bridge Waiver for Three Days," September 14, 1961.

12. For more on being, doing, showing, and studying showing, see Schechner, *Performance Studies*.

13. Report, May 20, 1963, Minutes of a Regular Meeting of the Board of Trustees, LBS, Box 187, File: Laredo Bridge System–Minutes 1963, Martin Papers, LGHC. See also, Report, September 16, 1963, in ibid.

14. Manning the bridge with extra warm bodies in uniform, either to project border control or to create a welcoming environment after a spell of bad press, was a tried and true image-management strategy. In an attempt to repair Laredo's reputation in 1929, for example, chamber members discussed hiring and stationing bilingual bridge "handshakers" on the US side of the bridge. This fix was dreamt up after Inaugural Yaqui Tribe No. 59 member and district attorney John Valls nearly caused an international fiasco: he threatened to arrest former Mexican president Plutarco Elias Calles, who at that time held diplomatic immunity in the United States, for the death of two Mexican military officers whose bodies were found near Laredo in 1922. See Ledger, August 1, 1929, Minutes of Meeting, Board of Directors, LCC MB3, pp. 37–38, Box 142B, LGHC; and Ledger, September 5, 1929, ibid., p. 42, LGHC. See also, "Stimson to Prevent Arrest of Calles," *New York Times*, December 14, 1929.

15. Crossing the bridge at Laredo regularly during research, Spener, a "light-skinned, blue-eyed middle-class Anglo," remembers thinking, "So, this is what apartheid looks like." *Clandestine Crossings*, 11.

16. Ginsberg, *Howl*.

17. Taylor, "Performance and/as History," 71; see also Marino and Cuellar, "Fiesta Performance," 127–128.

18. In 1942 the WBCA dedicated the festivities to the theme of Pan-Americansim. US and Mexican troops marched together on American soil. One hundred and fifty troops from Nuevo Laredo marched "with full equipment in the parade." WBCA president Kyle N. Ervin secured permission from the US War Department and the State Department as well as from Texas governor Coke Stevenson. He secured the troops' participation with permission from several Mexican generals, including Pablo Macías, then secretary of defense. "Mexican Troops to be in Parade," *LT*, February 19, 1942. For lively descriptions of Mexican military participation in the WBC festivities, see "Laredo Welcomes Visitors to Fiesta," *LT*, February 22, 1961; "Mexican Troops Invade Texas by Invitation," *Corsicana Daily Sun*, February 23, 1963; and "Diez Mil Personas en el Desfile de Washington," *El Ciudadano*, February 14, 1978.

19. Interview, August 27, 2013. For backstage details of the shooting of *Viva Max!* in Laredo, see Correspondence, March 3, 1969, and June 2, 1969, Letters from Jim Carter, Manager, Convention and Visitors Bureau, to J. C. Martin, Box 255, Martin Papers, LGHC.

20. Interview, February 22, 2015.

21. Interview, July 5, 2014.

22. A news account from 1970 gives us a glimpse of the diversity of Mexican participation: "Colorfully costumed units from Mexico will include: Leopoldo Naranjo School Band of *Monterrey*, Ignacio Zaragoza College Drum and Bugle Corps, *Saltillo*; *Coahuila* State Normal School Marching units, *Saltillo*; Margil College Drum and Bugle Corps units, *Zacatecas*; *Nuevo Laredo*; Instituto Regiomontano Military Band, *Monterrey*; Febres Cordero College Drum and Bugle Corps, *Guadalajara*; and the University of Nuevo Leon Precision Drill Team, *Monterrey*," *LT*, February 20, 1970 (emphasis mine).

23. Interviews: August 5, 2013; August 16, 2013; August 17, 2013; August 20, 2013; August 28, 2013; September 12, 2013; October 2, 2013; January 14, 2014.

24. Vásquez Guerra's family worked out their visa situation in the 1960s; indeed, she went to high school and both her parents worked in Laredo.

25. Interview, February 2, 2014.

26. Interview, September 26, 2013.

27. For regional news about Bracero Program shifts, see, for example, "Contratación de Braceros Mex.: Presupuesto por 450 Mil Trabajadores," *Tiempo de Laredo*, January 18, 1958.

28. Bridge paid toll figures did not increase in 1969 as in previous years because "Operation Intercept caused a drastic drop in bridge traffic during September, October, and November." For more on the militarization of the US-Mexico border, see, for example, Martínez, "Border Conflict," 269–270; and Andreas, *Border Games*, 35. For a detailed analysis of "low-intensity conflict doctrine," see Dunn, *Militarization*. For an excellent study of the widespread economic impact of border policies such as "prevention through deterrence," see Durand and Massey, "Costs of Contradictions," 239.

29. As should be expected, Nuevo Laredo and Laredo have very different demographic profiles and thus invest their resources differently. For snapshots of Nuevo Laredo's public service and urban planning goals during paso libre, see Dirección General de JFMM, *N. Laredo, Cd. Aleman, Reynosa, Matamoros, Tampico*, Mexico, 1960, BLAC; *Norma Acción y Proyeccion de Adolfo López Mateos en la Frontera, Dinámica de Una Ciudad: 1958–1964*, Tamaulipas: JFMM, 1964, BLAC; and García Cortés, *Nuevo Laredo*. For a glimpse of cross-border planning after the termination of paso libre, see Report, January 21, 1982, Comité de Planeación de los dos Laredos/Joint Planning Committee of Both Laredos, Box 171, File 11, LGHC.

30. Both Laredos benefited, but Laredo, Texas, had more control over its share. So the possibility that "bridge traffic may surpass 10 million in 1970" must have felt like an incredible payoff for city administrators. Indeed, the number of persons paying to cross into the United States increased from 10,324,864 in 1973 to 10,971,220 in 1974. The LBS added $843,892 to the city treasury in 1973 and $962,048 in 1974. See "Record Number Crosses Bridge," *LT*, January 4, 1970; and "Bridge Tolls Record Broken," *LT*, February 6, 1975.

31. Car travel into Mexico became more lucrative during paso libre, particularly because Antonio I. Mortera, then manager of Pemex Travel Club and federal tourist chief in Nuevo Laredo, announced that PP Petroleros Mexicanos had stacked major tourist travel routes in Mexico with Gasolmex (90 octane gasoline). This included Nuevo Laredo's main highway: Mexican Federal Highway 85, which connects to US I-35 at Laredo. For more details about tourism promotion planning in Nuevo Laredo during paso libre, see, for example, "Recepcion del Nvo. Comité Local de Turismo: De Nvo. Laredo lo preside Don Pedro Molano," *Tiempo de Laredo*, January 30, 1958; and "Good Year for Border Economy Seen," *LT*, February 12, 1970.

32. In 1967, for example, 7,703 laborers were admitted into the United States, but 107,695 unauthorized Mexican migrants were expelled. Between 1968 and 1973, 1,985,695 undocumented Mexican immigrants were "returned to Mexico." Lorey, *US-Mexico Border Statistics*, 105.

33. "Officials of Fiesta go to Mexico," *LT*, January 20, 1971, WBCA Scrapbook No. 1, WBCAP; Jim Parish, "Hemisphere's 'Most Impressive Ceremony': Dr. Cigarroa to Emcee at Bridge," 1971, WBCA Scrapbook No. 1, WBCAP; and "Periscope," *LT*, February 22, 1961. It is also important to mention that the festivities were broadcast internationally as early as 1935. That year the celebration program announced that the bridge ceremony would be broadcast "over 27 Mexican Stations and NBC system in the United States. Two and a half hours of orchestra and band concerts and speeches honoring the two Laredos," *Washington's Birthday Celebration Official Program 1935*, p. 11, WBCAP.

34. "Paso libre a Laredo, Tex," *El Continental*, February 17, 1960; "Mexican Troops Invade Texas by Invitation," *Corsicana Daily Sun*, February 23, 1963; and "Friendship at Border Celebrated," *Austin American*, February 21, 1965.

35. See, for example, "US to Waive Visa, Passport Rule for Fete," *LT*, February 16, 1958; "Visa Waiver Set Feb. 23–26 for Washington Celebration," *LT*, February 1, 1961; "Tremendous Crowds Here," *LT*, February 23, 1962; "Paso libre Anuncia el Cónsul Cash," *El Ciudadano*, February 1, 1968; "Visas Waivered for Celebration," *LT*, February 18, 1970; "Crossing Rumors Said False," *LT*, February 16, 1972; "Open Bridge Set for WBCA Fiesta," *LT*, January 25, 1973; Gilberto Zardeneta, "Desde Hoy se Concede

el Paso libre," *El Tiempo de Laredo*, February 15, 1973; and "Bridge to Be 'Open' for Fiesta," *LT*, January 28, 1975.

36. "Paso libre' Anuncia el Cónsul Cash," *El Ciudadano*, February 1, 1968.

37. In the early days of paso libre, for around two months after the ceremony, the BP would reinforce checkpoints with additional personnel. One agent I spoke with explained that the checkpoint north of Laredo existed in the 1970s, but it was not always in full operative mode. "Border Patrol Sets Roadblocks," *LT*, February 16, 1975; and "Visas Waivered for Celebration," *LT*, February 18, 1970.

38. "Crossing Rumors Said False," *LT*, February 16, 1972.

39. "El Turismo Continúa Aumentado," *Tiempo de Laredo*, January 19, 1973.

40. Squint, *Border Patrol Diary*, 20.

41. Interviews: August 13, 2013; February 25, 2014; July 14, 2014; phone interview, September 22, 2014.

42. Operating with Cold War sensibilities in 1963, Chester Wine (WBCA) and José F. Muguerza (IGNC/CIBV Monterrey) handled the recruitment of star students from Monterrey, Ciudad Victoria, Saltillo, Torreon, and San Luis Potosí to attend science classes in Laredo and participate in the WBC festivities. The theme of that year's celebration was "Scientific and Industrial Development through International Cooperative Education." For details see "Neighbor Council Asked to Join in Fete Project," *LT*, February 3, 1958; "Invitación a Estudiantes de México: Auspiciara el Consejo de Buen Vecino," *Tiempo de Laredo*, February 4, 1958; and "Good Neighbor Gesture: Mexican Students Will Attend Science Classes," *LT*, February 16, 1958.

43. IGNC-L members may not have overseen the bridge ceremony's choreography or participated in every cross-border coordination meeting, but they were able to use that event as well as other highlights of the festivities to champion their organization's mission. In 1958, for example, Muguerza arranged for Texas governor Price Daniels and colleagues like Deryood Manford, Presidente del Consejo Estatal de Ingenieros Hidráulicos, and William Allcorn, Comisionado de Bienes Raíces del Estado, to travel by private plane to Monterrey after the WBC festivities. Wives were also invited to travel. See "El Gob. de Texas, visitará Monterrey, el 23," *Tiempo de Laredo*, February 13, 1958. The IGNC was also highly invested in Texas governor Connally's participation in the festivities. See, for example, CIBV/IGNC, *Boletin Mensual*, year 12, no. 6, Monterrey (July 1966): 6; and CIBV/IGNC, *Carta Noticiosa*, no. 90, Monterrey (March/April 1976): 2, both at BLAC.

44. González, who passed away in 2006, oversaw the bridge ceremony for over three decades. For an elegant reflection of his work and his enthusiasm for cross-border coordination, see, for example, Correspondence, February 27, 1975, and March 26, 1976, Letters from José L. González, Organizador de la Ceremonia del Puente Internacional, to Presidente Municipal de Nuevo Laredo Lic. Carlos Enrique Cantú Rosas, Víctor M Oliveros Collection, File: Bridge Ceremony, Box 239, LGHC (hereafter cited as Oliveros Collection, LGHG).

45. Diagram, Oliveros Collection, LGHC. A few words about Mr. Oliveros: *He is wonderful*. I would not have been able to put this puzzle together without his help.

46. Interview, September 26, 2013.

47. I learned about the importance of protocol firsthand when I attended a workshop led by Texas state senator Judith Zaffirini (D-Laredo) in September 2013. And although it was published after the end of paso libre, protocol followed during the

era of paso libre matches up fairly well with the rules outlined in Zaffirini's handbook. Judith Zaffirini, *Protocol Handbook*, 2nd ed. Laredo: Zaffirini Communications, 2001–2002. See also Judith Zaffirini, *English-Spanish Vocabulary for the Laredo National Bank*, 2nd ed., 2002. A copy of this publication may be found at the Harold R. Yeary Library Special Collection Room, Laredo Community College.

48. De Certeau, *Practice of Everyday Life*, 97–98.

49. Having children participate in, and many times lead, border enactments, is a strategy used at border-crossing points around the world. See, for example, Darian-Smith, *Bridging Divides*, 102–103; Aggarwal, *Beyond Lines of Control*, 26; and Venken, *Borderlands Studies*.

50. The bridge ceremony experienced an upgrade with the inclusion of the abrazo children in 1969. The performances on the bridge also got stronger during that period. One bridge ceremony that made its way into most of my conversations with elders was the 1975 ritual in which the Norad Band (based in Colorado Springs) interpreted Mexico's national anthem and la Banda de la Marina de la Ciudad de México interpreted the US national anthem. Laredoans and neolaredenses alike agreed that the Mexican band was superior that day. Several people emphasized that they were extraordinary. Also, Queen Elizabeth II had invited them to play for her. See Correspondence, March 7, 1975, Letter from Presidente Municipal de Nuevo Laredo Lic. Carlos Enrique Cantú Rosas to José L. González, Organizador de la Ceremonia del Puente Internacional, Oliveros Collection, LGHC.

51. For more about border-crossing spectacles and media coverage, see Andreas, *Border Games*. He argues that press coverage of Banzai runs at San Ysidro, California, in 1994—"the dramatic footage of men, women, and children dashing across the border and weaving through busy traffic"—were exploited for political gain and cited to secure additional border enforcement monies. *Border Games*, 88.

52. Lomnitz, "Chronotopes," 209.

53. Conversation, February 21, 2015.

54. Stanley Tambiah explains: "Those of us who have done detailed studies of complex rites and ritual cycles are keenly aware of various kinds and patterns of repetition that occur, sometimes boring us with their seemingly insistently unvarying recurrence, and sometimes subtlety stimulating in us a sense of creative variation and attentive expectation . . . but [that redundancy] can be demonstrated to be interesting and complex in the work that it does." "Performative Approach," 134.

55. Minutes, International Bridge Ceremony Committee Meeting, April 3, 1975, Oliveros Collection, LGHC.

56. In 1971, for example, José L. González, administrator of the Laredo–Webb County Health Department, attended the meeting as a special guest representative of the "Health Committee." See CIBV/IGNC, *Carta Noticiosa No. 35*, Monterrey (May 1971), p. 2, BLAC.

57. See Correspondence, n.d., Handwritten note from José L. González to J. C. Martin Jr., and a copy of "The Left Arm of Public Health," speech delivered at the US-Mexico Border Public Health Convention, Santa Fe, NM, June 5, 1969, Box 255, Martin Papers, LGHC.

58. Speech, June 5, 1969, "The Left Arm of Public Health," Box 255, pp. 6–7, Martin Papers, LGHC.

59. For an overview of public health projects in Laredo, see Box 19, File: Health, Víctor Oliveros Border Health Papers, LGHC.

60. Unlike many of his predecessors, Texas governor Rick Perry was never a sure bet. This meant that the bridge ceremony could not count on the participation of state governors between 2002 and 2015. Incidentally, Perry won his first bid for governor against Tony Sánchez (a Democrat), who was one of Laredo's most prominent international bankers. Interview, September 12, 2013.

61. The tradition of inviting the heads of state of each country can be traced back to 1905. IORM member John Valls invited his good friend President Porfirio Díaz (who politely declined). "Las Fiestas del 22," *El Democrata Fronterizo*, February 25, 1905. See also Box 203, File 1: WBCA Notes, LGHC. In 1966 Lic. Ignacio D. Silva represented Mexican president Gustavo Díaz Ordaz. Newspaper clipping, "Nuevo Laredo y Tamaulipas Representan a México en las Fiestas de Washington," *La Verdad* (Nuevo Laredo), 1966, Box 210, File 6, LGHC. I would like to extend a special thank you to past WBCA president John Keck for sharing his personal WBCA correspondence collection with me.

62. Interviews: August 20, 2013; August 21, 2013; September 20, 2014. For newspaper coverage of some of these trips, see, for example, "Officials of Fiesta go to Mexico," *LT*, January 20, 1971, WBCA Scrapbook No. 1, WBCAP; "Magnon Optimist about 1974 Washington's Fiesta," *LT*, November 20, 1973, WBCA Scrapbook No. 2, WBCAP; "Invitan a Fiestas de Laredo," *El Porvenir*, January 23, 1974, ibid.; "Celebration Group Plans Mexico Trip," *LT*, December 13, 1980, IGNC scrapbook, personal collection; and *Laredo Morning Times*, January 30, 1985, IGNC scrapbook, personal collection.

63. Interview, July 10, 2014.

64. Interview, August 20, 2013.

65. See *LT*, February 18, 1970. For additional publicity/coverage of events in Nuevo Laredo during the early 1970s, see, for example, "Charreada Is Always Popular Event," *LT*, February 15, 1973; and "Traditional Bullfights Feature of Celebration," *LT*, February 15, 1973.

66. LULAC Archives, Part 2: General Collection, Sally Martinez Collection, 1986–1989, Box 3 LULAC Administration-States, Folder 29, Laredo Council, 3, BLAC.

67. Interviews: August 20, 2013; February 4, 2014.

68. Interview, August 20, 2013.

69. Phone interview, September 4, 2013; interviews, September 27, 2013, and August 20, 2014.

70. Interview, August 14, 2013.

71. Interview, February 19, 2014.

72. Interview, September 10, 2013.

73. Interview, February 13, 2014.

74. Mrs. Gutiérrez did insist, and rightly so, that I not use her actual phone number in this book. Just in case.

75. For ads asking for a maid to stay in Laredo, see, for example, *Tiempo de Laredo*: "Avisos de Ocasión," February 16, 1962; "Avisos Clasificados," February 18, 1972, and February 20, 1972. For ads that signal relocation to places like Houston, see, for example, "Avisos de Ocasión: Sirvientas," *El Diario*, January 26, 1967; "Avisos Clasifica-

dos," *Tiempo de Laredo*, January 25, 1971; "Avisos de Ocasión," *LT*, January 1, 1975; and "Avisos de Ocasión," *LT*, January 28, 1975.

76. Discussing border security concerns before and after NAFTA, a former CBP agent explained that there is a general assumption about border cities like Laredo and Nuevo Laredo: "They know how to handle the border." With that said, the oldest problem pre-NAFTA was apprehending "illegal aliens working on farms near the border." He called this a "border-centric problem." Trade and smuggling became major talking points in the 1970s. It was only with the growth of the market economy, he specified, that 'illegal immigration' and what came to be known as 'the Browning of America' became a 'national problem.' . . . We [Americans] needed to feed the hunger of our market economy with service jobs, landscaping." Interview, May 27, 2015.

77. Pisani and Yoskowitz, "Maid Trade." For research on domestic work patterns and conditions in South Texas and at other US-Mexico ports of entry, see, for example, Ruiz, "By the Day"; Mattingly, "Job Search"; Hondagneu-Sotelo, *Doméstica*; and Richardson and Pisani, *Informal and Underground*.

78. It is interesting to note that Michael J. Pisani and David W. Yoskowitz found that day maids "possess more documents (74.5%) than their live-in maid counterparts (51.7%)" when they conducted their research in Laredo in the late 1990s. "Maid Trade," 573–574. Conducting ethnographic research in Matamoros and Brownsville, David Spener found that "many middle- and upper-class Brownsville women used the *migrapateros* [the term coined by the press in Matamoros to refer to the INS inspectors who would wave cars along] to bring Mexican women across the border to work in their households as domestic servants." *Clandestine Crossings*, 130–131.

79. Interview, December 30, 2015.

80. Phone interview, September 20, 2014.

81. Charles Hillinger, "Border Open for Three Days: Legal or Not, Everyone Is Welcome in Laredo," *Los Angeles Times*, February 22, 1976.

82. Interview, February 13, 2014.

83. Pepe Martin publicized the city's intention to construct a second international bridge as early as 1963. He explained: "*Approximately 80% of all rights-of-way have been secured for the construction of IH-35, an expressway-type facility which is being financed with 90% federal funds and 10% state funds*. Laredo is the terminal point of IH 35 (runs from Canada border to the Mexican border) and the construction of this facility through Laredo will undoubtedly help tremendously to improve Laredo's position as the Gateway to Mexico. *It is expected that the Expressway will be started sometime in late 1963 with a possible completion date as early as 1965*. The program calls for the development of a limited access expressway leading in from the north between Sta. Ursula and San Dario Avenues and provides for several overpasses over important city thoroughfares and railroad crossings. The expressway is to terminate at Victoria St. and will provide frontage roads both on Sta. Ursula and San Dario for one-way travel. Plans for the final design and relocation of utilities [are] presently underway at the Highway Department Engineering office in North Laredo." See News Release, March 26, 1963, p. 4, City Planning Commission Office, City of Laredo, Paul Garza Jr., Director of City Planning, Box 187, File: Press Releases, Martin Papers, LGHC. For details about planning challenges, see, for example, newspaper clipping, "El Ing. Paul Garza y Ross S. Watkins en la Capital," *El Diario*, June 12, 1975, LBS Files, Scrapbook No. 2, Box 5.3.1, LGHC; Jim Parish, "Bridge II Complex Expected to Cost

More than $30 million," *LT*, October 24, 1976, ibid.; and "President Nixon in STDC Region," *Action on the Border*, vol. 2, no. 5, Laredo: South Texas Development Council, November 1972, p. 1, Box 172, File 11, LGHC.

84. Construction began on June 15, 1975. The engineering phase was completed on May 14, 1976, but the bridge was not inaugurated until November 26, 1976. The inauguration ceremony was held up by the absence of *garitas* (sentry posts), pending construction costs/payments, lack of manpower, and a lack of formality (*decreto*). For details about those phases of the project, see newspaper clipping, "En Franca Armonía Harán el Puente," *El Diario*, April 30, 1975, Scrapbook No. 2, LBS Files, Box 5.3.1, LGHC; Newspaper clipping, "New Laredo Bridge Points to Crisis," *San Antonio Express News*, March 30, 1976, Scrapbook No. 1, ibid.; Newspaper clipping, "Humildes Casuchas, al Pie del 2do Puente, Ofrecerán un Mal Aspecto a los Visitantes," *El Diario*, July 23, 1976 (dated by hand), ibid.; Newspaper clipping, "Un Decreto Debe Poner en Servicio el Puente," November 10, 1976 (dated by hand), ibid.; and "Bridge Named after Juarez and Lincoln," *LT*, November 23, 1976, ibid.

85. Paul Garza along with George Rangel led efforts on behalf of the Watkins Bridge Co., the contractor for the American half of the bridge. Cumbres S.A. of Mexico City was the Mexican contractor. See "Bridge II Complex Expected to Cost More Than $30 Million," *LT*, October 24, 1976.

86. Measuring 1,007 feet long and 96 feet wide, International Bridge II was almost twice as wide as International Bridge I. "Bridge II Complex Expected to Cost," *LT*, October 24, 1976.

87. Newspaper clipping, "Por Falta de Garitas aún no Abren Tránsito a Peatones en Puente II," November 30, 1976 (dated by hand), Scrapbook No. 1, LBS Files, Box 5.3.1, LGHC.

88. Newspaper clipping, Odie Arambula, "Judge Garza Gets Fiesta Honor," *LT*, 1976, Scrapbook No. 1, LBS Files, Box 5.3.1, LGHC; see also Guillermo García, "Decision on IH 35 Irks Some," *LT*, November 8, 1974. It is also important to mention that the bridge was not physically linked to I-35, as that part of the construction process had not yet been completed at the time of the bridge inauguration or the WBC festivities in 1977. Newspaper clipping, "Aceleran Derrumbes en Laredo: Unirán el Expressway con el Nuevo Puente," *El Diario*, August 29, 1977, Scrapbook No. 1, LBS Files, Box 5.3.1, LGHC.

89. For media coverage of paso libre's cancellation, see "Aunque sea Por Cortesía, Deben Pedir Permiso, No Han Pedido el Cierre del Puente Nuevo," *El Ciudadano*, February 11, 1977; Newspaper clipping, "Sólo Funcionarios en el Abrazo," *LT*, February 23, 1977, Scrapbook No. 1, LBS Files, Box 5.3.1, LGHC; "Al No Permitir la Presencia del Público, Demostraron Que el Natalicio de Washington en Laredo, es una Fiesta Fenicia," *El Ciudadano*, February 26, 1977; and "Brillante el Desfile, Pero no Hubo Multitudes para Verlo," *El Ciudadano*, February 26, 1977.

90. Program Book, "LULAC Council No. 12 Presents Noche Mexicana (In Memoriam Señor Internacional 1980, Don Pepe Guizar)," 7, LULAC Archives Part 2: General Collection, Box 1, Laredo Council 12, Sponsored Activities, Folder 1: Noche Mexicana (1981), BLAC.

91. LULAC Council No. 12 members contacted the producers of one of Televisa's most popular programs—*Siempre en Domingo*. They arranged for film crews to "record life in Laredo" and to produce a two-hour documentary that was later

shown throughout Mexico, the United States, and Latin America in February 1978. The documentary included a segment about LULAC's Señor Internacional award and highlighted the selection of Mexican luminaries: don Francisco Javier Sauza in 1977 and Raúl Velasco (the host of *Siempre en Domingo*) in 1978. See LULAC Archives Part 2: General Collection, Sally Martinez Collection, 1986–1989, Box 3, LULAC Administration-States, Folder 29: Laredo Council, 3, BLAC. For more information about LULAC Council No. 12's cross-border work, see ibid., Pitín Guajardo Collection, Box 1: Laredo Council 12 Sponsored Activities, Folder 4, News clippings, BLAC.

92. Appointed by President Kennedy in 1961, Judge Garza was the first federally appointed Hispanic judge in the United States. He served as judge of the US District Court for the Southern District of Texas from 1961 to 1974 and chief judge from 1974–1979. In 1979 President Carter appointed him to the US Court of Appeals for the Fifth Circuit. He served there from 1979 to 1982 and as senior judge of that court from 1982 to 2004.

93. Senate Committee on Foreign Relations, "International Bridges" (September 1–4, 1959), Bill Number: 86 S. 2531; 86 S. 2590; 86 H.R. 3180, 68 pp. Summary: Considers H.R. 3180, S. 2531, and S. 2590, to authorize construction of certain international bridges between United States and Canada and between United States and Mexico, subject to approval of other nations involved, p. 64.

94. Interview, May 3, 2016.

Chapter 5. Us, Them, and Festive Security

1. US embassy cable, 10NUEVOLAREDO44, Gun Battle between Mexican Army and Zetas at International Bridge, Feb. 22, 2010. This account is also based on interviews I conducted at the Port of Laredo as well as in Washington, DC, between 2013 and 2017.

2. Interviews: September 26, 2013; May 27, 2015; March 16, 2016.

3. Interview, September 26, 2013.

4. Interviews: September 26, 2013; February 12, 2014; May 27, 2015; August 5, 2015; March 16, 2016.

5. One US State Department official involved in negotiations that evening insisted that the firefight was an isolated event; it was not a targeted attack on the WBC or the International Bridge Ceremony. Echoing the sentiments of many US and Mexican federal-level officials that work on border security issues, he explained that the drug cartels have no interest in engaging the United States. He did not, however, discount the theory that Zeta associates, many of whom had grown up in Nuevo Laredo, were well aware of the WBC festivities. Knowing that additional security would be redirected to the Juárez-Lincoln Bridge the morning of the abrazo ceremony, cartel members may have purposefully initiated a firefight underneath the bridge to direct attention away from activity at an off-site plaza that was up for grabs. Interview, August 21, 2014.

6. This was not the first time the threat of violence had affected the WBC. After 9/11, recurrent bomb threats in 2001 and 2003 closed noncommercial bridges, sometimes up to fifteen times a month. In the event that bridge ceremony organizers could not secure the structure before the WBC, they would have to warn participants

beforehand that the ritual might have to take place in Laredo, Texas. One abrazo parent I interviewed said that she did not mind that modification: "Security comes first." Staging the ceremony on an overpass on the far north side of Laredo (about five miles from the border) would be better than staging it in front of the parade review stand. With the right camera angles, you would not be able to tell that the children were not embracing on the actual international bridge. Interview, August 5, 2015.

7. Interview, February 12, 2014.

8. Interview, May 27, 2015.

9. As demonstrated in previous chapters, those decisions not only protect the integrity of the ceremony that particular year but also reflect the "narrow interests" of market-based actors and law enforcement communities. Payan, "Crossborder Governance," 227.

10. For an example of Laredo making its case for authority, see David Maraniss, "Laredo to Washington: Back Off," *Washington Post National Weekly Edition*, August 4, 1986.

11. Andreas, *Border Games*, 10.

12. For ethnographic studies that explore "American" notions of security and insecurity, see, for example, Lutz, *Homefront*; Low, *Behind the Gates*; Gusterson and Besteman, *Insecure American*; and K. O'Neill, "Left Behind." Studies that highlight the links among insecurity, class, and the built environment were also very helpful. See, for example, Caldeira, *City of Walls*.

13. Ethnographic research for this book primarily took place during the years 2013 and 2014, but I returned to the Port of Laredo multiple times to conduct follow-up interviews and to attend the International Bridge Ceremony. Based in Washington, DC, I was also able to meet with federal-level actors who had participated in the bridge ceremony. I am particularly grateful to former CBP Commissioner Gil Kerlikowske for taking my research seriously.

14. This book joins a handful of cross-border research studies focused on civil society organizations at the Port of Laredo. In contrast, activity at the port of entry at Ciudad Juárez, Chihuahua, and El Paso, Texas, has received rigorous scholarly attention in that respect. For studies that trace cross-border negotiation among nonstate actors at the Port of Laredo, see D'Antonio and Form, *Influentials*; Sloan and West, "Community Integration"; García Ortega and Trujeque Díaz, *El noreste de México*. For research that draws our attention to education, governance, and activism conducted across the border at Ciudad Juárez and El Paso, see, for example, Rippberger and Staudt, *Pledging Allegiance*; Payan, "Crossborder Governance"; and Heyman, "Border Network." For a rich analysis of cross-border business dynamics that crisscross the Tohono O'odham Indian Reservation, Sonora, and Arizona, see Cadava, *Standing on Common Ground*. See Martínez, *Trans-frontier Interaction*; Valenzuela, *Por las fronteras del norte*; and Vélez-Ibáñez and Heyman, *US-Mexico Transborder Region*, all edited volumes, to get a sense of how conversations have developed.

15. Nils Bubandt's idea of "vernacular security," which he defines as "a convenient term for the analysis of different scales of creating imagined communities through a comparison of different but constantly interpenetrating political forms of management of threat and (un)certainty," pushed me to think more broadly about who contributes to border security. "Vernacular Security," 277.

16. Anthropologist Daniel Goldstein argues for the use of research methods that

"explore the multiple ways in which security is configured and deployed—not only by states and authorized speakers but by communities, groups, and individuals—in their engagements with other local actors and with arms of the state itself." "Toward a Critical Anthropology," 492.

17. Heyman, "Culture Theory," 55.

18. Drawing on Joanna Long's work on the concept of "spatial alternatives" to advance their work in Israel and Palestine, Gazit and Latham explain that "foregrounding 'spatial alternatives' is intended to signal a fundamental commitment not only to the study of how spaces in Israel-Palestine are (re)produced according to a range of contested ontologies but also of the ways and dynamics that overlap ontologies might generate spatial co-existence and practical co-operation between the communities. *These spaces—of nonviolent overlapment—can be understood to be where two or more groups are able to: organize their lives on their own terms through their own communal and institutional uses of the same or abutting spaces; and interact in a less securitized and violent manner with one another.* We are keenly aware that the spatialities of interest here are also involved in the production and maintenance of power relations." "Spatial Alternatives," 64–65 (emphasis mine). See also Goldstein, "Toward a Critical Anthropology," 489.

19. Immediately following 9/11, the US border cities like Laredo set enhanced border security measures into motion. Soon after, Nuevo Laredo officials were tasked with making good on Mexico's support plan for the United States. PUNTO DE ACUERDO, Periódico Oficial Número 118, October 2, 2001 (Ciudad Victoria, Tamaulipas), 5.

20. Harris, "From Rhetoric to Reality." I am particularly grateful to Robert Harris for sharing his unpublished thesis with me.

21. Donnan and Wilson, *Borders*, 1. For an updated version of this argument, see Donnan and Wilson, "Borders and Border Studies."

22. Interview, May 27, 2015.

23. International responses to Mexico's drug violence included the Mérida Initiative. Described as a "new paradigm" for bilateral security cooperation between the United States and Mexico that emphasized "shared responsibility," the Mérida Initiative outlined four pillars of action: "disrupting the operational capacity of organized criminal groups, institutionalizing reforms to sustain the rule of law and respect for human rights, creating a 21st century border, and building strong and resilient communities." For some analysts, however, the geography and culture of drug production and distribution had already contoured and escalated Mexico's drug trafficking problem past the point of intervention. See Ribando Seelke and Finklea, *US-Mexican Security*, 6. See also Hernández y Hernández, "Análisis de la política de seguridad." For a critical reading of the Mérida Initiative and US security interests in Latin America, see Delgado Ramos and Romano, "Plan Colombia."

24. For an analysis of violence patterns during Enrique Peña Nieto's presidency, see Campa, "En este Sexenio 13," 9.

25. Molzahn et al., *Drug Violence*, 13.

26. See, for example, Fábregas Puig and González Ponciano, "Mexico-Guatemala"; and Isaacson, Meyer, and Morales, *Mexico's Other Border*.

27. The Port of Laredo moves close to $500 billion dollars in import/export trade annually. See "2012 International Trade Corridor Plan," Texas Department of Trans-

portation (December 1, 2012), http://ftp.dot.state.tx.us/pub/txdot-info/tpp/misc/itcp.pdf; and "Laredo Monthly Economic Indicators 2002–2013," Laredo Development Foundation (September 11, 2013), http://www.ldfonline.org/Economic_Indicators_091113.pdf.

28. For discussions of that shift, see, for example, Payan, *Three Border Wars*, 867–868; Mariñez Navarro and Vivas, "Violence, Governance"; and Correa-Cabrera, "Security, Migration."

29. See, for example, Brophy, "Mexico: Cartels," 255; and Isaacson and Meyer, *Mexico's Other Border*, 37.

30. New terminology accompanied the panic. The term "narcoterrorism," for example, made its way into academic talks, policy debates, and military thinking. See Campbell and Hansen, "Is Narco-Violence Terrorism?," for an explanation of the term; and Kan, "What We're Getting Wrong," for a robust critique.

31. Ballí, "Borderline Insanity." See also Francesc Relea, "El Crimen Organizado Campa en Nuevo Laredo," *El País*, July 25, 2005; Juan Balboa, "Argumenta EU *narcoviolencia* para Cerrar Consulado en Nuevo Laredo," *La Jornada*, July 30, 2005; Jo Tuckman, "In Mexican City It's Free Buses v Bullets," *Guardian*, August 11, 2005; and Ginger Thompson, "Rival Drug Gangs Turn the Streets of Nuevo Laredo into a War Zone," *New York Times*, December 4, 2005.

32. Molzahn et al., *Drug Violence*, 3; for an example of media coverage, see Molly Hennessey Fisk, "Laredo, Texas, Battles an Image Problem," *Los Angeles Times*, April 28, 2013.

33. Campbell and Hansen, "Is Narco-Violence Terrorism?," 161. It is also important to note that even as journalists struggled to tell their stories, they harbored their power to create, corroborate, or challenge common knowledge. Speaking to a very different set of political factors, Ieva Justionyte's study of the media's relationship to violence in the border zone that connects Argentina, Brazil, and Uruguay is relevant here because it shows the site-specific rationale behind periods of silence. She considers how narratives produced by off-site journalists are more likely to highlight fear and anxiety, while local newsmakers, who understand and respect the logic of "*convivencia* (cohabitation and negotiation) and complicity," are often more selective about what they choose to showcase. Reporters based at the site of violence are often well aware that the subjects of their stories are their neighbors and that the truths they uncover produce consequences that reach far beyond the personal and professional lives of those implicated. See Jusionyte, *Savage Frontier*, 172.

34. Cook, "Mexico's Drug Cartels." See also, Testimony, Webb County Sheriff Rick Flores, "Criminal Activity and Violence along the Southern Border," Hearing before the Subcommittee on Investigation of the Committee on Homeland Security, House of Representatives, 109th Cong., 2nd sess., Serial No. 109-96, August 16, 2006, pp. 28–29; Testimony, Mayor Raul Salinas, "Keeping the Border Secure: Examining Potential Threats Posed by Cross-Border Trucking," Hearing before the Subcommittee on Transportation Security and Infrastructure of the Committee on Homeland Security, House of Representatives, 110th Cong., 1st sess., Serial No. 110-50, June 19, 2007, pp. 25–30; and Testimony, Hon. Henry Cuellar, "Border Violence: An Examination of DHS Resources and Strategies," Hearing before the Subcommittee on Border Maritime, and Global Counterterrorism of the Committee on Homeland Security, 111th Cong., 1st sess., Serial No. 111-7, March 12, 2009, pp. 43–45.

35. Testimony, Dennis Nixon, "Criminal Activity and Violence along the Southern Border," Hearing before the Subcommittee on Investigation of the Committee on Homeland Security, House of Representatives, 109th Cong., 2nd sess., Serial No. 109-96, August 16, 2006, pp. 128–131.

36. See, for example, "On the Border and In the Line of Fire: US Law Enforcement, Homeland Security, and Drug Cartel Violence," Hearing before Subcommittee for Oversight, Investigations, and Management and Committee on Homeland Security, House of Representatives, 111th Congress, 1st sess., Serial No. 112-24, March 12, 2011, pp. 21–31, 60–65.

37. Coleman, "What Counts," 907. See also Pallitto and Heyman, "Theorizing Cross-Border Mobility."

38. Correa, "After 9/11." For an illuminating discussion of mixed-status families, see Gomberg-Muñoz, *Becoming Legal.*

39. Ackelson, "Border Security Technologies," 141–142.

40. We should also consider that neolaredenses were experiencing a supercharged version of spill-across violence. Subject to curfews, the closing of businesses, sustained periods of daily firefights, copycat threats, and emergency protocol measures, violence centered around the control of plazas overtook spaces and restricted interaction across the city.

41. "Abrazo ceremony marks 35th," *Laredo Morning Times*, February 22, 2006.

42. "Falta 'feeling' al abrazo," *El Mañana*, February 22, 2004.

43. The situation became so unpredictable that the US State Department closed its consulate office in Nuevo Laredo for one week in August 2005. Sánchez Munguía, "La actual lucha," 99. For an example of media coverage, see Jerry Brewer, "Out-and-out Terrorism on the Border near Laredo," *Houston Chronicle*, August 16, 2005.

44. Confirming suspicions about the depth of Mexico's corruption problem, municipal police officers attacked Fox's soldiers en route from the Nuevo Laredo airport to the city. Marc Lacey, "In Mexican City, Drug War Ills Slip into Shadows," *New York Times*, June 12, 2019.

45. Mexican federal and state-level legislators (re)pledged to increase joint coordination efforts and to channel additional federal monies toward public security in June of that year. See CONVOCATORIA Pública DSP-0002/2004, Periódico Oficial Número 56, May 11, 2004 (Ciudad Victoria, Tamaulipas); ACUERDO 04/05, P.O. Número 66, June 2, 2005 (Ciudad Victoria, Tamaulipas); CONVENIO que modifica al Convenio de Coordinación en Materia de Seguridad Pública, P.O. Número 108, September 8, 2005 (Ciudad Victoria, Tamaulipas). State officials later created the Unidad de Control de Confianza, an evaluation agency designed to confirm the trustworthiness of public and private security personnel. See DECRETO que crea el Centro Estatal de Evaluación y Control de Confianza de Tamaulipas, P.O. Número 17, February 10, 2009 (Ciudad Victoria, Tamaulipas); and ACUERDO 001/2011, P.O. Número 76, June 28, 2011 (Ciudad Victoria, Tamaulipas).

46. Circular Número 001/2011, P.O. Número 76, June 28, 2011 (Ciudad Victoria, Tamaulipas), 10; Decreto No. LX-1496, P.O. Número 150, December 16, 2010 (Ciudad Victoria, Tamaulipas), 17.

47. See, for example, CONVOCATORIA Pública MNLCL-0001/2008, P.O. Número 28, March 4, 2008 (Ciudad Victoria, Tamaulipas), 6; CONVOCATORIA Pública

MNLCL-0002/2008, P.O. Número 42, April 3, 2008 (Ciudad Victoria, Tamaulipas), 10; CONVOCATORIAS Públicas MNLCL-0008/2008, P.O. Número 136, November 11, 2008 (Ciudad Victoria, Tamaulipas), 6–7; CONVOCATORIA Pública MNLCL-0010/2008, P.O. Número 150, December 11, 2008 (Ciudad Victoria, Tamaulipas), 24; CONVOCATORIA Pública MNLCL-003/2009, P.O. Número 51, April 29, 2009 (Ciudad Victoria, Tamaulipas), 14; CONVOCATORIA Pública MNLCL-001/2011, P.O. Número 82, July 12, 2011 (Ciudad Victoria, Tamaulipas), 8; and CONVOCATORIA Pública MNLCL-006/2011, P.O. Número 127, October 25, 2011 (Ciudad Victoria, Tamaulipas), 4–5, 8.

48. Mexican citizens who hold a B1 or a B2 visa are authorized to cross the border for seventy-two hours at a time and travel up to twenty-five miles without having to fill out an I-94 arrival/departure form. I would like to thank José S. Tellez for allowing me to sit in on an immigration tutorial to learn about the cross-border movement of domestic and service-sector laborers with INS-issued Border Crossing Cards (BCC) and DHS-issued (at the time) laser visas: B1 (business) or B2 (tourist) Nonimmigrant Visas (March 2014). Speaking with Mr. Tellez helped me understand the significance of news items printed in the 1970s: "Tourist Permit Extensions to Be Discontinued," *LT*, February 16, 1975. See also "Illegal Aliens Great Burden on the Southwest," *LT*, February 5, 1975; and "Strong Illegal Alien Law Urged," *LT*, February 5, 1975. For big-picture information about NIVs by nationality, issuing office, and classification between 2001 and 2015, see US Department of State, Bureau of Consular Affairs, "Table XVIII: Nonimmigrant Visas Issued by Nationality (Including Border Crossing Cards), Fiscal Year 2001–2010," p. 135; and "Table XIX: Nonimmigrant Visas Issued by Issuing Office (Including Border Crossing Cards), Fiscal Year 2001–2010"; and "Table XVI (B): Nonimmigrant Visas Issued by Classification (Including Border Crossing Cards), Fiscal Year 2011–2015," all at https://travel.state.gov/content/travel/en/, accessed April 21, 2016.

49. It is important to note that they were not the only ones. Violence at other ports of entry on the US-Mexico border during the same period (e.g., El Paso/Ciudad Juárez) prompted an exodus of Mexican business elites out of Mexico. In 2012 the "US government had issued 4,000 investor visas to Mexican citizens . . . the third most in the world, behind only Japan and Germany." See Estevez, "Wealthy Mexicans' Investment"; Morales et al., "Mexican Drug War," 87; and Ríos, "Role of Drug-Related Violence," 202. For media analysis, see Mary Beth Sheridan, "Drug War Sparks Exodus of Affluent Mexicans," *Washington Post*, August 26, 2011.

50. See Cecilia Garza, "The New Refugees: Businesses Moving to Laredo," *Border Research Reports* 9 (2009): 1–19. For insight into the impact of that violence on the built environment and religious practice, see Peña, "Time to Pray." For a take on relocation to a Mexican border city and the idea of "identity escapees," see Campbell, "Escaping Identity," 300.

51. Interview, September 26, 2013.

52. Interview, February 24, 2014.

53. Mariñez Navarro and Vivas, "Violence, Governance," 397.

54. See *Vision 2012: Economic Outlook Report* 14.1 (Laredo, TX: Laredo Chamber of Commerce), 8. See also City of Laredo Building Development Services Department Annual Reports, https://www.cityoflaredo.com/Building/.

55. Interview, February 27, 2014.

56. Hartley and Goonatilake, "Overview of Crime Statistics," 7; see also Kilburn et al., "Is Fear of Crime Splitting?," 32.

57. Interview, March 16, 2016.

58. Graphs prepared by the office of US Congressman Henry Cuellar (D-Dist. 28) communicate safety on the border. Reflecting FBI Uniform Crime Reports statistics, reports show that the total number of murders in Texas border cities like Laredo, McAllen, and Brownsville were lower than in Houston and Dallas, which reported 214 and 143. Further, "Murder Rates in Border Cities compared to select US cities per 100,000 population" (with the national rate holding at 4.5 murders per 100,000 population) shows that it is more dangerous to live in Detroit (45.2) than Laredo (1.2) or Brownsville (0.6). Critiques of this model state that unlike a "National Incident-Based Reporting System," which the FBI implemented after 2013, Uniform Crime Reports do not provide a comprehensive view of crime occurring in a law enforcement agency's jurisdiction. See "2013 FBI Uniform Crime Reports: Texas Cities—Total Number of Murders in 2013," Prepared by Congressman Cuellar's Office (Washington, DC, November 10, 2014).

59. Jusionyte, *Savage Frontier*, 142; see also Andreas, *Border Games*, 36–37.

60. Protecting the "gateway" city's reputation also required the personal investment of customs officers and brokers, international bankers, and transport logistic experts. The action plans they put in place pursued similar goals but used different metrics. Mexican business elites, for example, were much more concerned with resuscitating foreign direct investment in Tamaulipas, which had dropped close to 80 percent between 2006 and 2010. US-based customs and border protection officials focused their efforts on analyzing the ebbs and flows of drug shipments. One US customs agent confirmed that narcotics shipments via commercial transport slowed down tremendously in 2005 (that is, the drugs that were intercepted by CBP agents), while the cartels were figuring out who could do what. The one constant during the period is that commercial trade traffic numbers held steady. See Mariñez Navarro and Vivas, "Violence, Governance," 379; and Correa-Cabrera, "Security, Migration," 75.

61. It is also worth mentioning that monikers such as "Land de Amigos" do similar work. See, for example, the 1960s promotional video "Vacation-Land de Amigos," John A. Paris Collection, Texas Archive of the Moving Image, https://www.texasarchive.org.

62. Newspaper clipping, personal collection; interview, October 1, 2013.

63. Anthropologist Alan Klein notes that the name change was "the first time on record a sports franchise had become binational." *Baseball on the Border*, 111.

64. Winter tours organized by the LCC in the 1940s targeted car owners from San Antonio. As late as 1985, WBCA organizers were facilitating travel from San Antonio with a "Los Dos Laredos" excursion train. During this period of heightened danger, however, neolaredenses would no longer be able to anticipate revenue generated by "prescription medicine tourism"—busloads of older visitors traveling from New Orleans and Houston after Hurricane Katrina to purchase medication at affordable prices and to spend a day in Mexico. For a discussion of border tourism economies, see Arreola and Curtis, "Tourist Landscapes," 241; see also Kearney and Knopp, *Border Cuates*; and Herzog, "Political Economy."

65. I am extremely grateful to City of Laredo Bridge System staff for sharing their statistics with me. For a broader perspective, see US Department of Transportation, Bureau of Transportation Statistics, Border Crossings/Entry Data: Detailed Statistics, PEDESTRIAN, February 2003–2015.

66. The toll fare paid by pedestrians at that time was 75 cents. It is also important to add that those figures do not factor in revenue loss linked to noncommercial single-axle and double-axle traffic.

67. Interview, March 18, 2016.

68. The motion states: "The guide will be produced under the direction of the Laredo Convention & Visitors Bureau in conjunction with PM Design Group relative to style, design, and editorial content for consistency with the *new marketing theme*" (emphasis mine). Motion No. 24 approved (7 in favor, 0 against, 0 abstentions), City Council Meeting M2008-R-019, October 6, 2008.

69. Designing billboards and placing them along highways in Texas is a well-rehearsed strategy. In the late 1960s, for example, Jim Carter, director of the Convention and Visitors Bureau, reported: "We will be working next week to come up with a new ad for our advertising sign boards South of Austin and East of Victoria. Our panel which changes every several months will feature: 'the international flair in shopping in Laredo.'" The panel is also changed periodically for WBC. The billboards' "10-month cost—$2,500. Seen by over 15 million persons." Convention and Visitors Bureau, Box 255, Martin Papers, LGHC.

70. Interview, August 15, 2013.

71. Interview, October 8, 2013.

72. Interview, August 7, 2013.

73. "Celebrará Nuevo Laredo el Natalicio de George Washington," *RN Noticias*, February 13, 2012. See also, "Abrirán Cadillac Bar Y Victoria," *El Mañana*, November 10, 2013.

74. Conversation, September 10, 2013.

75. The only time I heard Gálvan Gómez's assassination acknowledged in public and in an official capacity was not at a WBCA function but at a Fourth of July celebration hosted by the US consul general in Nuevo Laredo.

76. Interview, August 10, 2015.

77. Ibid.

78. Interview, July 5, 2014.

79. See, for example, Taylor, *Disappearing Acts*.

80. Interviews: September 25, 2013; January 14, 2014; August 10, 2015.

81. See Alfredo Corchado Jiménez, "Laredo Man Believes Arrested Zetas Leader Knows Missing Stepdaughter's Fate," *Dallas Morning News*, August 18, 2013. See also Claire Marshall, "Website Seeks US Border Disappeared," *BBC News*, August 9, 2005.

82. Fields-Meyer, "Who Is Stealing Laredo's Young?"

83. Peña, "De-Politicizing Border Space."

84. Previously, however, Mayor Flores had appeared on the *Lou Dobbs Tonight* program, where she insinuated that the missing could be personally connected to the drug cartels. In that case, she said, Laredo could not be held responsible for the disappearances. *Lou Dobbs Tonight*, *CNN*, June 21, 2005 (video). For media analysis of the situation, see Ralph Blumenthal, "Texas Town Is Unnerved by Violence in Mexico," *New York Times*, August 11, 2005.

85. Interview, September 4, 2013.

86. These are just some examples of demonstrations that made the news or continue to circulate in an oral history context. For information about protests in the 1960s and 1970s, see Green, *Celebration of Heritage*, 251–252.

87. "Connally Thwarts Marchers," *El Paso Times*, September 1, 1966. Rumors of a "demonstration by striking farm workers seeking a $1.25 an hour minimum wage" proved unfounded in 1967. "Connally Heads State Group at Festivities," *Corpus Christi Caller-Times*, February 18, 1967. For another take on Gov. John Connally's engagement (or lack thereof) with Chávez protesters, see Piñon, *Searching for America*, 211–213.

88. Phone conversation, June 30, 2014.

89. Tony Vindell, "TECAT Sparks Plaza Rally," *LT*, February 22, 1986. See also Max Albright, "Party on the Inside; Protest on the Outside," *LT*, February 22, 1986.

90. Interview, December 29, 2015.

91. Anthropologist Victor Turner's explanation of social drama in relation to "multivocal symbols of popular powers" in Mexico (such as Miguel Hidalgo or the Virgin of Guadalupe) has always fascinated me. His thinking about the roles of heroes and heroines during times of social crisis informs my analysis here. Turner, *Dramas, Fields, Metaphors*, 153–154.

92. Interview, January 6, 2014.

93. I learned while interviewing past abrazo parents in Nuevo Laredo that the tradition of honoring the abrazo children with separate receptions in Laredo and Nuevo Laredo was not practiced between 2006 and 2013. The last reception in Nuevo Laredo was held on November 20, 2004. Sponsored by the CIBV-NL and the WBCA, that event also commemorated the fiftieth anniversary of the founding of the IGNC. The program featured staple abrazo children events such as the "honores a la bandera" and "himnos nacionales de México y Estados Unidos" and the "presentación de los niños." Highlights included: "Actuación Charra con exhibición de floreo," "Tauromaquia Cómica EL RUEDO," "'Cantinflas II' y la 'Güera Mitotes' bailando y lidiando ganado bravo de Don Refugio Peña," a "Gran Toro Gol, Con la Participación de Alumnos de la Universidad Valle del Bravo," and "Música de Mariachi en Vivo."

94. It is important to clarify that carrying out the organization's mission during this period was not only a problem for members based at the border. Several IGNC chapters based in the interior of the country (for example, in New Mexico and Oklahoma) declined invitations to attend the annual meeting hosted in Laredo. For a brief but insightful explanation of the development of IGNC/CIBV mission goals, see newspaper clipping, "Texas-Mexico Panel on the Border Needs Formed," *Houston Post*, October 10, 1954, Manuel B. Bravo Personal Papers. Mr. Bravo was so kind and helpful. He shared several documents with me relating to the IGNC's history prior to 1954, including a copy of a memorandum titled "Notes on History of International Good Neighbor Council." I was particularly struck by the author's discussion of LULAC and that organization's close ties to the IGNC. He notes, "The LULACs worked with and supported the Good Neighbor Commission. Together they created an entirely new racial atmosphere in Texas—and to some extent in two nations—the fruits of which are only now being harvested" (5). For additional insight, see, for example, Good Neighbor Commission Records, 1949–1950, Dolph Briscoe Center for American History, University of Texas at Austin.

95. CIBV-IGNC, *Boletin Mensual*, year 1, no. 4, Monterrey (December 1956): 7, 12, BLAC. For a glimpse of how the Good Neighbor Commission articulated its Christian mission, which was "put into effect through the initiative of local churches working in cooperation with the civic and cultural clubs, educational institutions and other local organizations," see Pauline R. Kibbe, *Community Organization for Inter-American Understanding* (Austin: Good Neighbor Commission of Texas, 1949), BLAC. The CIBV-NL was not formed until 1979. CIBV-IGNC, *Carta Noticiosa*, no. 106, Monterrey (January–February 1979): 2, BLAC.

96. CIBV-INGC, *Carta Noticiosa*, no. 95, Monterrey (January–February 1977): 1, BLAC.

97. One longtime IGNC member explained that there used to be more incentives to join the organization. Local banks used to offer "service" promotions to employees who volunteered their time working with nonprofit organizations like the WBCA or the IGNC. Eventually, it became necessary to volunteer to get promoted. Today, most committee members are women, and most of them are not familiar with IGNC history. Her take on the situation, which resonates with the opinion offered by other members, is that they want to participate not because they believe in the mission, necessarily, but because they want their kids to be presented as abrazo children. Interview, September 5, 2013. Attending the IGNC-CIBV's biannual meetings in San Antonio (October 2013) gave me additional perspective. There I learned that membership has been on the decline across border chapters (e.g., Reynosa, Piedras Negras, Del Rio) since 2008.

98. That part of the process was always tricky because it is ill-advised not to declare gifts, new goods, or merchandise over $50 USD. For a parallel example, see Rippberger and Staudt, *Pledging Allegiance*, 119.

99. See Spener, *Clandestine Crossings*, 23.

100. The abrazo parents I interviewed agreed that having their children participate involves a lot of work, a lot of traveling, and a lot of money. But at the end of the day, the experience generates immeasurable amounts of joy and pride.

101. There have been times when Mexican participants have missed the breakfast. In 2015, for example, LULAC Señor Internacional honoree representing Latin America, Enrique Martínez y Martínez, then Mexican secretary of agriculture, did not make it to the breakfast at the Palacio Municipal that morning. He had to cross the length of the bridge to join the Mexican delegation, a walk that was made all the more awkward because everyone had already taken their places. Not to worry—the ritual did not notice. LULAC members confirmed that Martínez y Martínez "did not feel comfortable on the bridge." Not necessarily because of security concerns but because of party differences between himself as a member of the PRI and the current administration in Nuevo Laredo, which was in the hands of the PAN. Interview, February 22, 2015.

102. IGNC members controlled the selection process until Velia Uribe became WBCA president in 1981. WBCA president Manuel M. Bravo modified the process during his tenure, which gave IGNC-L and CIBV-NL members the power to choose their own representatives. The CIBV-NL and the WBCA eventually drafted and signed a contract authorizing CIBV-NL members to choose their own representatives. I was privileged enough to be able to attend those meetings with CIBV-NL president Triana Bazán Lerma in the winter of 2014. The paperwork was filed, but intraorgani-

zational disagreements about prerequisite language skills continued to surface. Even then, additional gains were being made, at least institutionally, in terms of recognizing the work (and status) of both IGNC-L and CIBV-NL members. It was clarified at a CIBV/WBCA coordination meeting, for example, that Bazán Lerma's photo would be added to the affiliate organization president's section of the official WBC program book that year. This detail is incredibly important because it signals that a Nuevo Laredo–centric civil society organization—a group that helped staff and coordinate the bridge ceremony for two decades—would be recognized for the first time (on glossy paper) alongside IGNC-L members. Meeting, September 5, 2013.

103. For an interesting parallel, see Vila, *Crossing Borders*, 4–5.

104. Minutes, Board Meeting, September 12, 2007, President's Report, WBCAP. See also Testimony, Chief David V. Aguilar, US Customs and Border Protection, before the House Subcommittee on Homeland Security, on CBP Goals and Objectives, Rayburn House Office Building, April 15, 2010.

105. Press Release, February 20, 2016, "Keynote Remarks by Secretary Johnson at the International Bridge Ceremony (excerpt)," DHS Press Office, Washington, DC.

106. Interview, May 3, 2016.

107. Amoore and Hall, "Border Theater."

Conclusion. Why Study Border Enactments?

1. "'It Feels Like Being Hunted': Latinos across US in Fear after El Paso Massacre," *New York Times*, August 6, 2019.

Bibliography

Archives Consulted

Archivo General de la Nación, Mexico, DF
Archivo Municipal, Nuevo Laredo, Tamaulipas, Mexico
Institute of Texan Cultures, San Antonio
John Peace Library, Special Collections, University of Texas at San Antonio
Laredo Chamber of Commerce
Laredo City Manager's Office
Laredo City Secretary's Office
Luciano Guajardo Historical Collection, Joe A. Guerra Laredo Public Library
National Archives at College Park, MD
National Security Archive, Washington, DC
Nettie Lee Benson Latin American Collection, University of Texas at Austin
Red Men Museum and Library, Waco, Texas
Russell Lee Collection, Dolph Briscoe Center for American History, University of Texas at Austin
Special Collections and Archives, Texas A&M International University, Laredo
Special Collection Room, Harold R. Yeary Library, Laredo Community College
Washington's Birthday Celebration Association Headquarters, Laredo
Webb County Heritage Foundation, Laredo

Sources

Ackelson, Jason. "Border Security Technologies: Local and Regional Implications." *Review of Policy Research* 22, no. 2 (2005): 137–155.

Adams, John A. *Conflict and Commerce on the Rio Grande: Laredo, 1775–1955.* College Station: Texas A&M University Press, 2008.

Adelman, Jeremy, and Stephen Aron. "From Borderlands to Borders: Empires, Nation-States, and the Peoples in Between in North American History." *American Historical Review* 104, no. 3 (1999): 814–841.

Aggarwal, Ravina. *Beyond Lines of Control: Performance and Politics on the Disputed Borders of Ladakh, India*. Durham, NC: Duke University Press, 2004.

Albanese, Catherine L. "Dominant and Public Center: Reflections on the 'One' Religion of the United States." *American Journal of Theology and Philosophy* 4, no. 3 (1983): 83–96.

———. *Sons of the Fathers: The Civil Religion of the American Revolution*. Philadelphia: Temple University Press, 1976.

Álvarez, Robert. "Borders and Bridges: Exploring a New Conceptual Architecture for (US-Mexico) Border Studies." *Journal of Latin American and Caribbean Anthropology* 17, no. 1 (2012): 24–40.

———. "Reconceptualizing the Space of the Mexico-US Borderline." In *A Companion to Border Studies*, edited by Thomas M. Wilson and Hasting Doonan, 538–556. London: Blackwell, 2012.

Amir, Merav. "On the Border of Indeterminacy: The Separation Wall in East Jerusalem." *Geopolitics* 16 (2011): 768–792.

Amoore, Louise, and Alexandra Hall. "Border Theater: On the Arts of Security and Resistance." *Cultural Geographies* 17, no. 3 (2010): 299–319.

Anderson, Benedict. *Imagined Communities: Reflections on the Origin and Spread of Nationalism*. London: Verso, 1983.

Andersson, Ruben. "Time and the Migrant Other: European Border Controls and the Temporal Economics of Illegality." *American Anthropologist* 116, no. 4 (2014): 795–809.

Andreas, Peter. *Border Games: Policing the US-Mexico Divide*. Ithaca, NY: Cornell University Press, 2009.

Anuario de Legislación y Jurisprudencia. Year 2. Mexico: Francisco Díaz de León, 1887.

Anzaldúa, Gloria. *Borderlands/La Frontera: The New Mestiza*. San Francisco: Aunt Lute, 1987.

———. "On the Process of Writing *Borderlands/La Frontera*." In *The Gloria Anzaldúa Reader*, edited by AnaLouise Keating, 187–197. Durham, NC: Duke University Press, 2009.

Appel, Hannah, Nikhil Anand, and Akhil Gupta, eds. *The Promise of Infrastructure*. Durham, NC: Duke University Press, 2018.

Arreola, Daniel D. "The Mexico-US Borderlands through Two Decades." *Journal of Cultural Geography* 27, no. 3 (2010): 331–351.

———. *Tejano South Texas: A Mexican American Cultural Province*. Austin: University of Texas Press, 2002.

Arreola Daniel D., and James R. Curtis. "Tourist Landscapes." In *US-Mexico Borderlands: Historical and Contemporary Perspectives*, edited by Oscar J. Martínez, 236–243. New York: Rowman and Littlefield, 1996.

Austin, John L. *How to Do Things with Words*. 2nd ed. Cambridge, MA: Harvard University Press, 1975.

Ballí, Cecilia. "Borderline Insanity." *Texas Monthly* 33, no. 8, 2005.

Barrera, Sylvia. "Matias de Llano." In *Su vida y su espíritu: Webb County Family Histories*, 114–119. San Antonio: Borderlands Press, 2002.

Bauder, Harald. "Toward a Critical Geography of the Border: Engaging the Dialectic of Practice and Meaning." *Annals of the Association of American Geographers* 101, no. 5 (2011): 1126–1139.

Baumgartner, Alice L. "The Line of Positive Safety: Borders and Boundaries in the Rio Grande Valley, 1848–1880." *Journal of American History* 101, no. 4 (2015): 1106–1122.

Bell, Samuel E., and James Smallwood. *Zona Libre, 1858–1905: A Problem in American Diplomacy*. El Paso: Texas Western Press, 1982.

Bellah, Robert N. *The Broken Covenant: American Civil Religion in Time of Trial*. 2nd ed. Chicago: University of Chicago Press, 1975.

———. "Civil Religion in America." *Daedalus* 96 (1967): 1–21.

Bellah, Robert N., and Phillip E. Hammond. *Varieties of Civil Religion*. San Francisco: Harper & Row, 1980.

Berdahl, Daphne. *Where the World Ended: Re-Unification and Identity in the German Borderland*. Berkeley: University of California Press, 1999.

Bial, Henry. *Acting Jewish: Negotiating Ethnicity on the American Stage and Screen*. Ann Arbor: University of Michigan Press, 2005.

Bieder, Robert E. "The Grand Order of the Iroquois: Influences on Lewis Henry Morgan's Ethnology." *Ethnohistory* 27, no. 4 (1980): 349–361.

Bonfil Batalla, Guillermo. *México profundo: Una civilización negada*. Mexico DF: Grijalbo, 1987.

Brading, David A. *Prophecy and Myth in Mexican History*. Cambridge, UK: Centre of Latin American Studies, Cambridge University, 1980.

Brophy, Stephanie. "Mexico: Cartels, Corruption, and Cocaine: A Profile of the Gulf Cartel." *Global Crime* 9, no. 3 (2008): 248–261.

Bubandt, Nils. "Vernacular Security: The Politics of Feeling Safe in Global, National, and Local Worlds." *Security Research* 36, no. 3 (2005): 275–296.

Burke, Peter. "Performing History: The Importance of Occasions." *Rethinking History* 9, no. 1 (2005): 35–52.

Cadava, Geraldo. *Standing on Common Ground: The Making of a Sunbelt Borderland*. Cambridge, MA: Harvard University Press, 2013.

Caldeira, Teresa P. R. *City of Walls: Crime, Segregation, and Citizenship in São Paulo*. Berkeley: University of California Press, 2001.

Campa, Homero. "En este Sexenio 13 Desaparecidos al Día." *Proceso*, February 7, 2015, 8–19.

Campbell, Howard. "Escaping Identity: Border Zones as Place of Evasion and Cultural Reinvention." *Journal of the Royal Anthropological Institute* 21 (2015): 296–312.

Campbell, Howard, and Tobin Hansen. "Is Narco-Violence Terrorism?" *Bulletin of Latin American Research* 33, no. 2 (2014): 158–173.

Cannadine, David. "The Context, Performance, and Meaning of Ritual: The British Monarchy and the 'Invention of Tradition'." In *The Invention of Tradition*, edited by Eric Hobsbawm and Terence Ranger, 101–164. Cambridge, UK: Cambridge University Press, 1983.

Cantú, Norma. "Dos Mundos: Two Celebrations in Laredo, Texas—Los Matachines de la Santa Cruz and the Washington's Birthday." In *Global Mexican Cultural Productions*, edited by Rosana Blanco-Cano and Rita Urquijo-Ruiz, 61–74. New York: Palgrave Macmillan, 2011.

Carse, Ashley. "Keyword: Infrastructure: How a Humble French Engineering Term Shaped the Modern World." In *Infrastructures and Social Complexity: A Compan-*

ion, edited by Penny Harvey, Casper Bruun Jensen, and Atsuro Morita, 27–39. London: Routledge, 2017.

Ceballos Ramírez, Manuel. "Los dos Laredos: Historia compartida y experiencia de la frontera." In *Encuentro en la frontera: Mexicanos y norteamericanos en un espacio común*, edited by Manuel Ceballos Ramírez, 233–257. Mexico, DF: El Colegio de México, 2001.

———. *La fundación de Nuevo Laredo*. Mexico, DF: Miguel Angel Porrúa, 1989.

Chalfin, Brenda. *Neoliberal Frontiers: An Ethnography of Sovereignty in West Africa*. Chicago: University of Chicago Press, 2010.

Chang, Kornel. *Pacific Connections: The Making of the US-Canadian Borderlands*. Berkeley: University of California Press, 2012.

Chapin, Jessica. "Reflections from the Bridge." In *Ethnography at the Border*, edited by Pablo Villa, 1–22. Minneapolis: University of Minnesota Press, 2003.

Chen, Xiangming. *As Borders Bend: Transnational Spaces on the Pacific Rim*. New York: Rowman and Littlefield, 2005.

City of Laredo. *General Fund, for Year Ending June 30, 1955*. Laredo: Office of the City Secretary, 1955.

Cohen, Deborah. *Braceros: Migrant Citizens and Transnational Subjects in the Postwar United States and Mexico*. Raleigh: University of North Carolina Press, 2011.

Coleman, Matthew. "What Counts as the Politics and Practice of Security, and Where? Devolution and Immigrant Insecurity after 9/11." *Annals of the Association of American Geographers* 99, no. 5 (2009): 904–913.

Comaroff, John, and Jean Comaroff. *Ethnography and the Historical Imagination*. Boulder, CO: Westview Press, 1992.

Connolly, Priscilla. *El contratista de Don Porfirio: Obras públicas, deuda y desarrollo desigual*. Mexico, DF: Fondo de Cultura Económica, 1997.

Conquergood, Dwight. "Performing as a Moral Act: Ethical Dimensions of the Ethnography of Performance." *Literature in Performance* 5, no. 2 (1985): 1–13.

———. "Rethinking Ethnography: Towards a Critical Cultural Politics." *Communication Monographs* 58 (1991): 179–194.

Cook, Colleen W. "Mexico's Drug Cartels." Washington, DC: Congressional Reports Services, October 2007, 1–17.

Correa, Jennifer. "'After 9/11 Everything Changed': Re-formations of State Violence in Everyday Life on the US-Mexico Border." *Cultural Dynamics* 25, no. 1 (2013): 99–119.

Correa-Cabrera, Guadalupe. "Security, Migration, and the Economy in the Texas–Tamaulipas Border Region: The 'Real' Effects of Mexico's Drug War." *Politics and Policy* 41, no. 1 (2013): 65–82.

Cuellar, Carlos. "The House of Armengol: Doing Business on the Rio Grande Border, 1881–1939." MA thesis, Laredo State University, 1990.

Cuellar, Manuel. "La escenificación de lo mexicano y la interpelación de un público nacional: La Noche Mexicana de 1921." In *Mexican Transnational Cinema and Literature*, edited by Maricruz Castro Ricalde, Mauricio Díaz Calderón, and James Ramey, 123–140. Oxford, UK: Peter Lang, 2017.

D'Antonio, William V., and William H. Form. *Influentials in Two Border Cities: A Study in Community Decision-Making*. Milwaukee, WI: University of Notre Dame Press, 1965.

Darian-Smith, Eve. *Bridging Divides: The Channel Tunnel and English Legal Identity in the New Europe*. Berkeley: University of California Press, 1999.

Davis, Robert E. *History of the Improved Order of Red Men and Degree of Pocahontas (1765–1988)*. Waco, TX: Davis Brothers, 1990.

De Certeau, Michel. *The Practice of Everyday Life*. Berkeley: University of California Press, 1984.

De la Peña, Guillermo. "Anthropological Debates and the Crisis of Mexican Nationalism." In *Culture, Economy, Power: Anthropology as Critique, Anthropology as Praxis*, edited by Winnie Lem and Belinda Leach, 47–58. Albany: State University of New York, 2002.

De León, Jason. *The Land of Open Graves: Living and Dying on the Migrant Trail*. Berkeley: University of California Press, 2015.

Delgado Ramos, Gian Carlo, and Silvina María Romano. "Plan Colombia e iniciativa Mérida negocio y seguridad interna." *El Cotidiano* 170 (2011): 89–100.

Deloria, Philip. *Playing Indian*. New Haven, CT: Yale University Press, 1998.

Demerath, Nicholas J., and Rhys H. Williams. "Civil Religion in an Uncivil Society." *Annals of the American Academy of Political and Social Science* 480 (1985): 154–166.

Dennis, Dion. "Washington's Birthday on the Texas Border." *Ctheory* (February 1997): 1–8.

Desay, George F. "Landscape Types along the Nuevo Laredo–Mexico City Highway." *Economic Geography* 18, no. 1 (1942): 57–67.

Dewey, Alicia M. *Pesos and Dollars: Entrepreneurs in the Texas-Mexico Borderlands, 1880–1940*. College Station: Texas A&M University Press, 2014.

Díaz, George T. *Border Contraband: A History of Smuggling Across the Rio Grande*. Austin: University of Texas Press, 2015.

Dominguez, Virginia R., and Emily Metzner. "Special Section on Nativism, Nationalism, and Xenophobia: What Anthropologists Do and Have Done." *American Anthropologist* 119, no. 3 (2017): 518–519.

Donnan, Hastings, and Thomas Wilson, eds. *Borders: Frontiers of Identity, Nation and State*. Oxford, UK: Berg, 1999.

———. "Borders and Border Studies." In *A Companion to Border Studies*, edited by Hastings Donnan and Thomas Wilson, 1–25. Oxford, UK: Blackwell, 2012.

Dornbach, Márton. "Remains of a Picnic: Post-Transition Hungary and Its Austro-Hungarian Past." *Austrian History Yearbook* 44 (2013): 255–291.

Driessen, Henk. *On the Spanish-Moroccan Frontier: A Study in Ritual, Power, and Ethnicity*. Oxford, UK: Berg.

Dunn, Timothy J. *The Militarization of the US-Mexico Border, 1978–1992: Low-Intensity Conflict Comes Home*. Austin: University of Texas Press, 1996.

Durand, Jorge, and Douglas Massey. "The Costs of Contradiction: US Border Policy 1986–2000." *Latino Studies* 1 (2003): 233–252.

Eagles, Munroe. "Organizing Across the Canada-US Border: Binational Institutions in the Niagra Region." *American Review of Canadian Studies* 40, no. 3 (2010): 379–394.

Easterling, Keller. *Extrastatecraft: The Power of Infrastructure Space*. London: Verso, 2014.

Estevez, Dolia. "Wealthy Mexicans' Investment in the United States Sharply Up in 2012." *Forbes*, June 10, 2013.

Fábregas Puig, Andrés, and Jorge Ramón González Ponciano. "The Mexico-Guatemala, Guatemala-Mexico Border: 1983–2013." *Frontera Norte* 26, no. 3 (2014): 7–35.

Feldman, Ilana. "Ad Hoc Humanity: UN Peacekeeping and the Limits of International Community in Gaza." *American Anthropologist* 112, no. 3 (2014): 416–429.

Fields-Meyer, Thomas. "Who Is Stealing Laredo's Young? A Spate of Killings Just Over the Border with Mexico Has Parents Terrified." *People*, April 18, 2005.

Foley, Douglas E. *From Peones to Politicos: Class and Ethnicity in a South Texas Town, 1900 to 1977.* Austin: University of Texas Press, 1977.

Foucault, Michel. *Security, Territory, Population: Lectures at the College de France, 1977–1978.* New York: Picador, 2009.

Garcia, Mario T. *Mexican Americans: Leadership, Ideology, and Identity, 1930–1960.* New Haven, CT: Yale University Press, 1989.

García Canclini, Néstor. *Culturas híbridas: Estrategias para entrar y salir de la modernidad.* Mexico: Random House Mondadori, 2009.

García Cortés, Adrian. *Nuevo Laredo 1970: Hechos, cifras, obras y servicios públicos.* Mexico DF: Virginia S.A., 1970.

García Ortega, Roberto, and José Antonio Trujeque Díaz. *El noreste de México y Texas: Asimetrías y convergencias territoriales en las relaciones fronterizas.* Mexico: Porrúa, 2009.

Garza, James Alex. "On the Edge of a Storm: Laredo and the Mexican Revolution, 1910–1917." MA thesis, Texas A&M International University, Laredo, 1996.

Gazit, Nir, and Robert Latham. "Spatial Alternatives and Counter-Sovereignties in Israel-Palestine." *International Political Sociology* 8 (2014): 63–81.

Geertz, Clifford. *Negara: The Theatre State in Nineteenth-Century Bali.* Princeton, NJ: Princeton University Press, 1980.

Ginsberg, Allen. *Howl and Other Poems.* San Francisco: City Lights, 1956.

Gluckman, Max. "Analysis of a Social Situation in Modern Zululand." *Bantu Studies* 14, no. 1 (1940): 1–30.

Goffman, Erving. *Strategic Interaction.* Philadelphia: University of Pennsylvania Press, 1969.

Goldstein, Daniel. M. "Toward a Critical Anthropology of Security." *Current Anthropology* 51, no. 4 (2010): 487–517.

Gomberg-Muñoz, Ruth. *Becoming Legal: Immigration Law and Mixed-Status Families.* New York: Oxford University Press, 2017.

Gómez-Peña, Guillermo. "The Cruci-Fiction Project." *TDR: The Drama Review* 41, no. 1 (1997): 147–151.

———. *Dangerous Border Crossers.* New York: Routledge, 2000.

———. *The New World Border: Prophecies, Poems, and Loqueras for the End of the World.* San Francisco: City Lights, 1996.

Gorski, Philip. *American Covenant: A History of Civil Religion from the Puritans to the Present.* Princeton, NJ: Princeton University Press, 2017.

Grandin, Greg. *The End of the Myth: From the Frontier to the Border Wall in the Mind of America.* New York: Metropolitan Books, 2019.

Green, Stanley C. *Border Biographies.* Vol. 2. Laredo: Border Studies, 1993.

———. *A Celebration of Heritage.* Laredo, TX: Border Studies, 1999.

———. *Laredo, 1755–1920: An Overview.* Laredo, TX: Border Studies, 1990.

Grimes, Ronald L. "Performance Theory and the Study of Ritual." In *New Approaches to the Study of Religion*. Vol. 2, *Textual, Comparative, Sociological, and Cognitive Approaches*, edited by Peter Antes, Armin W. Geertz, and Randi R. Warne, 109–138. Berlin: Walter de Gruyter, 2004.

Gross, Ariela J. "Texas Mexicans and the Politics of Whiteness." *Law and History Review* 21, no. 1 (2003): 195–205.

Gruel Sández, Victor Manuel. "La inauguración de la Carretera Panamericana: Turismo y estereotipos entre México y Estados Unidos." *Estudios Fronterizos* 18, no. 36 (2017): 125–150.

Guss, David M. *The Festive State: Race, Ethnicity, and Nationalism as Cultural Performance*. Berkeley: University of California Press, 2000.

Gusterson, Hugh, and Catherine Besteman, eds. *The Insecure American: How We Got Here and What We Should Do About It*. Berkeley: University of California Press, 2009.

Gutiérrez, Ramón A., and Elliott Young. "Transnationalizing Border Studies." *Western Historical Quarterly* 41, no. 1 (2010): 26–53.

Hämäläinen, Pekka, and Samuel Truett. "On Borderlands." *Journal of American History* 98, no. 2 (2011): 338–361.

Harms, Victoria. "A Tale of Two Revolutions: Hungary's 1956 and the Un-doing of 1989." *East European Politics and Societies and Cultures* 31, no. 3 (2017): 479–499.

Harris, Cheryl I. "Whiteness as Property." *Harvard Law Review* 106, no. 8 (1993): 1707–1791.

Harris, Robert. "From Rhetoric to Reality: Where We Stand on Homeland Defense." Unpublished thesis, National War College of the National Defense University, Washington, DC, 2000.

Hartley, Richard D., and Rohitha Goonatilake. "An Overview of Crime Statistics and Impact of Law Enforcement Activities in US Border Cities: Laredo/Webb County." *Border Research Reports*, vol. 8. Laredo: Center for Border Economic and Enterprise Development, Texas A&M International University, 2007.

Harvey, Penny, and Hannah Knox. "The Enchantments of Infrastructure." *Mobilities* 7, no. 4 (2012): 521–536.

———. *Roads: An Anthropology of Infrastructure and Expertise*. Ithaca, NY: Cornell University Press, 2013.

Helleiner, Jane. "'As Much American as a Canadian Can Be': Cross-Border Experience and Regional Identity among Young Borderlanders in Canadian Niagara." *Anthropologica* 51, no. 1 (2009): 225–238.

Herberg, Will. "America's Civil Religion: What It Is and When It Comes." In *American Civil Religion*, edited by Russell E. Richey and Donald E. Jones, 76–88. New York: Harper and Row, 1974.

Hernández, Kelly Lytle. *Migra! A History of the US Border Patrol*. Berkeley: University of California Press, 2010.

Hernández y Hernández, Gerardo. "Análisis de la política de seguridad en México, 2006–2012." *Política y Cultura* 44 (2015): 159–187.

Herrera, Brian Eugenio. *Latin Numbers: Playing Latin in Twentieth-Century US Popular Performance*. Ann Arbor: University of Michigan Press, 2015.

Herzog, Lawrence A. "Cross-National Urban Structure in the Era of Global Cities: The US-Mexico Transfrontier Metropolis." *Urban Studies* 28 (1991): 519–533.

———. From Aztec to High Tech: Architecture and Landscape across the Mexico–United States Border. Baltimore, MD: Johns Hopkins University Press, 2001.

———. "The Political Economy of Tourism Development in the San Diego–Tijuana Trans-Frontier Metropolis." In *The Infrastructure of Play*, edited by Dennis R. Judd, 215–244. New York: Routledge, 2003.

———. *Where North Meets South: Cities, Space, and Politics on the United States–Mexico Border*. Austin: University of Texas Press, 1990.

Heyman, Josiah M. "The Border Network for Human Rights: From Community Organizing to Public Policy Action." *City and Society* 26, no. 1 (2014): 73–95.

———. "Constructing a Virtual Wall: Race and Citizenship in US-Mexico Border Policing." *Journal of the Southwest* 50, no. 3 (2008): 305–333.

———. "Culture Theory and the US-Mexico Border." In *A Companion to Border Studies*, edited by Thomas M. Wilson and H. Doonan, 48–65. London: Blackwell, 2012.

———. "US Ports of Entry on the Mexican Border." *Journal of the Southwest* 43, no. 4 (2001): 681–700.

Hinojosa, Gilberto M. *A Borderlands Town in Transition: Laredo 1755–1870*. College Station: Texas A&M University Press, 1983.

Hobsbawm, Eric. "Introduction: Inventing Traditions." In *The Invention of Tradition*, edited by Eric Hobsbawm and Terence Ranger, 1–14. Cambridge, UK: Cambridge University Press, 1983.

Hodges, Gladys A. "Building Across the Borderline: The Politics of Building the First International Rail Bridges in the Americas at the Two El Pasos, 1880–1883." *Southwestern Historical Quarterly* 116, no. 1 (2012): 26–38.

Holmes, Seth. *Fresh Fruit, Broken Bodies: Migrant Farmworkers in the United States*. Berkeley: University of California Press, 2013.

Hondagneu-Sotelo, Pierrette. *Doméstica: Immigrant Workers Cleaning and Caring in the Shadows of Affluence*. Berkeley: University of California Press, 2001.

Ibarra, Cristina, dir. *Las Marthas*. San Francisco: Independent Television Service, 2014.

Isaacson, Adam, and Maureen Meyer. *Beyond the Border Buildup: Security and Migrants along the US-Mexico Border*. Washington, DC: Washington Office on Latin America, 2013.

Isaacson, Adam, Maureen Meyer, and Gabriela Morales. *Mexico's Other Border: Security, Migration, and the Humanitarian Crisis and the Line with Central America*. Washington, DC: Washington Office on Latin America, 2014.

Jackson, Shannon. *Lines of Activity: Performance, Historiography, Hull-House Domesticity*. Ann Arbor: University of Michigan Press, 2001.

———. *Social Works: Performing Art, Supporting Publics*. New York: Routledge, 2011.

Johnson, Amanda N. "Feeling the Drive: The International Meridian Highway, Regional Boosters, and the Redefinition of Space, 1911–1930." Master's thesis, Utah State University, Logan, 2014. *All Graduate Theses and Dissertations*. 2816.

Johnson, Benjamin, and Andrew R. Graybill, eds. *Bridging National Borders in North America: Transnational and Comparative Histories*. Durham, NC: Duke University Press, 2010.

Johnson, Corey et al. "Interventions on Rethinking 'the Border' in Border Studies." *Political Geography* 30 (2011): 61–69.

Johnson, Frank W. *A History of Texas and Texans*. Vol. 4. Chicago: American Historical Society, 1914.

Jones, Reece, ed. *Border Walls: Security and the War on Terror in the United States, India, and Israel*. London: Zed Books, 2012.

———, ed. *Open Borders: In Defense of Free Movement*. Athens: University of Georgia Press, 2019.

Jusionyte, Ieva. "Called to 'Ankle Alley': Tactical Infrastructure, Migrant Injuries, and Emergency Medical Services on the US-Mexico Border." *American Anthropologist* 120, no. 1 (2018): 89–101.

———. *Savage Frontier: Making News and Security on the Argentine Border*. Berkeley: University of California Press, 2015.

Kaiser, Robert, and Elena Nikiforova. "Borderland Spaces of Identification and Dis/location: Multiscalar Narratives and Enactments of Seto Identity and Place in the Estonian-Russian Borderlands." *Ethnic and Racial Studies* 29, no. 5 (2006): 928–958.

Kallius, Annastiina, Daniel Montrescu Prem, and Kumar Rajaram. "Immobilizing Mobility: Border Ethnography, Illiberal Democracy, and the Politics of the 'Refugee Crisis' in Hungary." *American Ethnologist* 43, no. 1 (2016): 25–37.

Kan, Paul Rexton. "What We're Getting Wrong about Mexico." *Parameters* (Summer 2011): 37–48.

Kang, S. Deborah. "Crossing the Line: The INS and the Federal Regulation of the Mexican Border." In *Bridging National Borders in North America: Transnational and Comparative Histories*, edited by Benjamin H. Johnson and Andrew R. Graybill, 167–198. Durham, NC: Duke University Press, 2010.

Kapferer, Bruce. "Situations, Crisis, and the Anthropology of the Concrete: The Contribution of Max Gluckman." In *The Manchester School: Practice and Ethnographic Praxis in Anthropology*, edited by Terry Evens and Bruce Kapferer, 118–155. Oxford, UK: Berghahn, 2006.

Kearney, Milo, and Anthony Knopp. *Border* Cuates*: A History of the US-Mexican Twin Cities*. Austin: Eakind Press, 1995.

Kilburn, John, Claudia San Miguel, and Dae Hoon Kwak. "Is Fear of Crime Splitting the Sister Cities? The Case of Los Dos Laredos." *Cities* 34 (2013): 30–36.

Kim, Suk-Young. *DMZ Crossing: Performing Emotional Citizenship along the Korean Border*. New York: Columbia University Press, 2014.

Klein, Alan. *Baseball on the Border: A Tale of Two Laredos*. Princeton, NJ: Princeton University Press, 1997.

Knopp, Anthony, Manuel F. Medrano, and Priscilla Rodriguez. *Charro Days in Brownsville*. Charleston, SC: Arcadia, 2009.

Kramer, Paul A. "Power and Connection: Imperial Histories of the United States in the World." *American Historical Review* (2011): 1348–1391.

Larkin, Brian. "The Politics and Poetics of Infrastructure." *Annual Review of Anthropology* 42 (2013): 327–343.

———. *Signal and Noise: Media, Infrastructure, and Urban Culture in Nigeria*. Durham, NC: Duke University Press, 2008.

Lefebvre, Henri. *The Production of Space*. Translated by Donald Nicholson-Smith. Oxford, UK: Blackwell, 1991.

Limón, José E. *Dancing with the Devil: Society and Cultural Poetics in Mexican-American South Texas*. Madison: University of Wisconsin Press, 1994.

———. "El primer congreso mexicanista de 1911: A Precursor to Contemporary Chicanismo." *Aztlán: Journal of Contemporary Chicano Studies* 1–2 (1974): 85–117.

Lindsay, George W., Charles C. Conley, and Charles H. Litchman. *Official History of the Improved Order of Red Men*. Boston: Fraternity Publishing Co., 1893.

Löfgren, Orvar. "Concrete Transnationalism? Bridge Building in the New Economy." *Focaal: European Journal of Anthropology* 43, no. 1 (2004): 59–75.

Lomnitz, Claudio. "Chronotopes of a Dystopic Nation: Cultures of Dependency and Border Crossings in Late Porfirian Mexico." In *Globalizing American Studies*, edited by B. Edwards and D. Gaonkar, 209–239. Chicago: University of Chicago Press, 2010.

———. *Deep Mexico, Silent Mexico: An Anthropology of Nationalism*. Minneapolis: University of Minnesota Press, 2001.

Lomnitz, Larissa Adler de, Claudio Lomnitz-Adler, and Ilya Adler. *El fondo de la forma: Actos públicos de la campaña presidencial del Partido Revolucionario Institucional, Mexico, 1988*. Notre Dame, IN: Helen Kellogg Institute for International Studies, University of Notre Dame, 1990.

Lorey, David E. *United States–Mexico Border Statistics Since 1990* (1990 update). Los Angeles: UCLA Latin American Center Publications, 1993.

Low, Setha. *Behind the Gates: Life, Security, and the Pursuit of Happiness in Fortress America*. New York: Routledge, 2003.

Lugo, Alejandro. "Theorizing Border Inspections." *Cultural Dynamics* 12, no. 3 (2000): 353–373.

Lutz, Catherine. *Homefront: A Military City and the American Twentieth Century*. New York: Beacon Press, 2002.

Madrid, Alejandro L., ed. *Transnational Encounters: Music and Performance at the US-Mexico Border*. Oxford, UK: Oxford University Press, 2011.

Mahmood, Saba. "Rehearsed Spontaneity and the Conventionality of Ritual: Disciplines of Ṣalāt." *American Ethnologist* 28, no. 4 (2001): 827–853.

Margolies, Daniel S. *Spaces of Law in American Foreign Policy: Extradition and Extraterritoriality in the Borderlands and Beyond, 1877–1898*. Athens: University of Georgia Press, 2011.

Maril, Robert L. *The Fence: Human Smuggling, Terrorists, and Public Safety along the US-Mexico Border*. Lubbock: Texas Tech University Press, 2001.

Mariñez Navarro, Freddy, and Leonardo Vivas. "Violence, Governance, and Economic Development at the US-Mexico Border: The Case of Nuevo Laredo and Its Lessons." *Mexican Studies/Estudios Mexicanos* 28, no. 2 (2012): 377–416.

Marino, Angela, and Manuel Cuellar. "Fiesta Performance as Epistemology." *Performance Research* 20, no. 1 (2015): 123–135.

Marston, S. A. "The Social Construction of Scale." *Progress in Human Geography* 24, no. 2 (2000): 219–242.

Martínez, Oscar J. "Border Conflict, Border Fences, and the 'Tortilla Curtain' Incident of 1978–1979." *Journal of the Southwest* 50, no. 3 (2008): 263–278.

———, ed. *Trans-Frontier Interaction in Comparative Perspective*. El Paso: Texas Western Press, 1986.

Massey, Douglas S., and Karen A. Pren. "Origins of the New Latino Underclass." *Race and Social Problems* 4, no. 1 (2012): 5–17.

Mattingly, Doreen J. "Job Search, Social Networks, and Local Labor-Market Dynamics: The Case of Paid Household Work in San Diego, California." *Urban Geography* 20, no. 1 (1999): 46–74.

Medina, Martin. "The Cardboard Collectors of Nuevo Laredo: How Scavengers Protect the Environment and Benefit the Economy." In *Struggles for Social Rights in Latin America*, edited by Susan Eva Eckstein and Timothy P. Wickham-Crowley, 103–121. New York: Routledge, 2012.

Megoran, Nick. *Nationalism in Central Asia: A Biography of the Uzbekistan-Kyrgyzstan Boundary*. Pittsburgh, PA: University of Pittsburgh Press, 2017.

Menon, Jisha. *Performance of Nationalism: India, Pakistan, and the Memory of Partition*. Cambridge, UK: Cambridge University Press, 2013.

Miller, Tom. *On the Border: Portraits of America's Southwestern Frontier*. New York: Harper & Row, 1981.

Mitchell, T. Clyde. "Case and Situational Analysis." In *The Manchester School: Practice and Ethnographic Praxis in Anthropology*, edited by T. M. S. Evens and Don Handelman, 23–42. Oxford, UK: Berghahn, 2006.

Mize, R. L., and A. C. S. Swords. *Consuming Mexican Labor: From the Bracero Program to NAFTA*. Toronto: University of Toronto Press, 2010.

Modern, John L. *Secularism in Antebellum America*. Chicago: University of Chicago Press, 2011.

Molzahn, Cory, Viridiana Ríos Contreras, and David A. Shirk. *Drug Violence in Mexico: Data Analysis through 2011*. San Diego: Trans-Border Institute, University of California San Diego, 2012.

Momen, Mehnaaz. "Remembering Laredo: Spatial Reflections." *Space and Culture* 10, no. 1 (2007): 115–128.

Montejano, David. *Anglos and Mexicans in the Making of Texas, 1836–1986*. Austin: University of Texas Press, 1987.

Moore, David, Martha Freeman, and Tara Dudley. *The Meridian Highway in Texas*. Austin: Texas Historical Commission, 2016.

Morales, María Cristina, Oscar Morales, Angelica C. Menchaca, and Adam Sebastian. "The Mexican Drug War and the Consequent Population Exodus: Transnational Movement at the US-Mexican Border." *Societies* 3 (2013): 80–103.

Mora-Torres, Juan. *The Making of the US-Mexico Border*. Austin: University of Texas Press, 2001.

Morgan, Lewis Henry. *The League of the Ho-de-no-sau-nee or Iroquois*. Rochester, NY: Sage and Brothers, 1851.

Nevins, Joseph. *Operation Gatekeeper*. New York: Routledge, 2001.

Newman, David. "The Lines that Continue to Separate Us: Borders in a 'Borderless' World." *Progress in Human Geography* 30, no. 2 (2006): 143–161.

Newman, David, and Anssi Paasi. "Fences and Neighbours in the Postmodern World: Boundary Narratives in Political Geography." *Progress in Human Geography* 22, no. 2 (1998): 186–207.

Ngai, Mae M. *Impossible Subjects: Illegal Aliens and the Making of Modern America*. Princeton, NJ: Princeton University Press, 2005.

Nicol, Heather. *The Fence and the Bridge: Geopolitics and Identity along the Canada-US Border.* Waterloo, Ont., Can.: Wilfrid Laurier University Press, 2015.

Nugent, Paul. "Border Towns and Cities in Comparative Perspective." In *A Companion to Border Studies*, edited by Thomas M. Wilson and Hastings Doonan, 557–572. Oxford, UK: Blackwell, 2012.

———. *Boundaries, Communities, and State-Making in West Africa: The Centrality of the Margins.* Cambridge, UK: Cambridge University Press, 2019.

———. "Cyclical History in the Gambia/Casamance Borderlands: Refuge Settlement and Islam from c. 1880 to the Present." *Journal of African History* 48 (2007): 221–243.

Oliveras-González, Xavier. "Fiestas transfronterizas y representaciones espaciales en la frontera México-Texas." *Economía, Sociedad, y Territorio* 16, no. 50 (2016): 133–169.

O'Neil, Shannon. *Two Nations Indivisible: Mexico, the United States, and the Road Ahead.* New York: Oxford University Press, 2013.

O'Neill, Bruce, and Dennis Rodgers. "Infrastructural Violence: Introduction to the Special Issue." *Ethnography* 13, no. 4 (2012): 401–412.

O'Neill, Kevin Lewis. "Left Behind: Security, Salvation, and the Subject of Prevention." *Cultural Anthropology* 28, no. 2 (2013): 204–226.

Orozco, Cynthia. "The Origins of the League of United Latin American Citizens (LULAC) and the Mexican-American Civil Rights Movement in Texas with an Analysis of Women's Political Participation in a Gendered Context, 1910–1920." PhD diss., University of California, Los Angeles, 1992.

Palafox, José. "Open Up Border Studies: A Review of US-Mexico Militarization Discourse." *Social Justice* 27, no. 3 (2000): 56–72.

Pallitto, Robert, and Josiah McC. Heyman. "Theorizing Cross-Border Mobility: Surveillance, Security, and Identity." *Surveillance and Society* 5, no. 3 (2008): 315–333.

Paredes, Américo. *Folklore and Culture on the Texas-Mexican Border.* Austin: Center for Mexican American Studies, University of Texas, 1993.

———. *George Washington Gómez.* Houston: Arte Publico Press, 1990.

———. *"With His Pistol in His Hand": A Border Ballad and Its Hero.* Austin: University of Texas Press, 1970.

Paris, Jerry, dir. *Viva Max!* California: Commonwealth United Entertainment, 1969.

Paton, Andrew H. *Ceremonies for Celebration of 'Washington's Birthday' and 'Tamina's Day.'* Camden, MA: Stevens, 1901.

Payan, Tony. "Crossborder Governance in a Tristate, Binational Region." In *Cities and Citizenship at the US-Mexico Border*, edited by Kathleen Staudt, César M Fuentes, and Julia Monárrez-Fragaso, 217–244. New York: Palgrave MacMillan, 2010.

———. *The Three US-Mexico Border Wars: Drugs, Immigration, and Homeland Security.* Westport, CT: Praeger, 2006.

Payan, Tony, Kathleen A. Staudt, and Z. Anthony Kruszewski, eds. *A War That Can't Be Won: Binational Perspectives on the War of Drugs.* Tucson: University of Arizona Press, 2013.

Peña, Elaine A. "De-Politicizing Border Space." *e-misférica* 3, no. 2 (2006). Online.

———. "More Than a Dead American Hero: Washington, the Improved Order of Red Men, and the Limits of Civil Religion." *American Literary History* 26, no. 1 (2014): 61–82.

———. "Paso Libre (Open Border): Border Enactment, Infrastructure, and Crisis Resolution at the Port of Laredo (1954–1957)." *Drama Review* 61, no. 2 (2017): 11–31.

———. *Performing Piety: Making Space Sacred with the Virgin of Guadalupe*. Berkeley: University of California Press, 2011.

———. "Reveling in Patriotism: Celebrating America on the US-Mexico Border during the Mexican Revolution." In *Open Borders to a Revolution: Culture, Politics, and Migration*, edited by Jamie Marroquín, Adela Pineda, and Magdalena Mieri, 191–212. Washington, DC: Smithsonian Scholarly Press, 2013.

———. Review of *The US-Mexico Transborder Region: Cultural Dynamics and Historical Interactions*, by Carlos G. Vélez-Ibáñez and Josiah Heyman. In *American Ethnologist* 45, no. 3 (2018): 426–427.

———. "Time to Pray: Devotional Rhythms and Space Sacralization Processes at the Mexico-US Border." *Material Religion: Journal of Objects, Art, and Belief* 13, no. 4 (2017): 461–481.

Perales, Alonso S. *En defense de mi raza*. San Antonio, TX: Artes Gráficas, 1936.

Piñon, Fernando. *Patron Democracy*. Mexico, DF: Contraste, 1985.

———. *Searching for America in the Streets of Laredo*. Mexico, DF: Centro de Estudios Sociales Antonio Gramsci A.C., 2015.

Pisani, Michael J., and David W. Yoskowitz. "The Maid Trade: Cross-Border Work in South Texas." *Social Science Quarterly* 83, no. 2 (2002): 568–579.

Pratt, Mary Louise. *Imperial Eyes: Travel Writing and Transculturation*. New York: Routledge, 1992.

Rael, Ronald. *Borderwall as Architecture: A Manifesto for the U.S.-Mexico Boundary*. Berkeley: University of California Press, 2017.

———. "Boundary Line Infrastructure." *Thresholds* 40 (2012): 75–82.

Rappaport, Roy. *Ritual and Religion in the Making of Humanity*. Cambridge, UK: Cambridge University Press, 1999.

Reséndez, Andrés. *Changing National Identities at the Frontier: Texas and New Mexico, 1800–1850*. Cambridge, UK: Cambridge University Press, 2004.

Revista Mensual Nuevo Laredo: Primer Puerto Fronterizo de México 1, no. 5 (1948). Nuevo Laredo, Tamaulipas.

Revista Mensual Nuevo Laredo: Primer Puerto Fronterizo de México 4, no. 46 (1952). Nuevo Laredo, Tamaulipas.

Ribando Seelke, Clare, and Kristin Finklea. *US-Mexican Security Cooperation: The Mérida Initiative and Beyond*. Washington, DC: Congressional Research Service, 2014.

Richardson, Chad, and Michael J. Pisani. *The Informal and Underground Economy of the South Texas Border*. Austin: University of Texas Press, 2012.

Richer, Juan E. *Reseña histórica de Nuevo Laredo*. 2nd ed. Nuevo Laredo, Tamaulipas, Mexico: Impresores del Norte, 1958.

Ríos, Contreras Viridiana. "The Role of Drug-Related Violence and Extortion in Promoting Mexican Migration: Unexpected Consequences of a Drug War." *Latin American Research Review* 49, no. 3 (2014): 199–217.

Rippberger, Susan J., and Kathleen Staudt. *Pledging Allegiance: Learning Nationalism at the El Paso–Juárez Border*. New York: Routledge, 2003.

Rivera-Servera, Ramón, and Harvey Young. *Performance in the Borderlands*. New York: Palgrave MacMillan, 2011.

Roach, Joseph. *Cities of the Dead: Circum-Atlantic Performance*. New York: Columbia University Press, 1996.

Roper, Danielle. "Blackface at the Andean Fiesta: Performing Blackness in the Danza de Corporales." *Latin American Research Review* 54, no. 2 (2019): 381–397.

Rosaldo, Renato. *Culture and Truth: The Remaking of Social Analysis*. Boston: Beacon, 1993.

Rosas, Gilberto. *Barrio Libre: Criminalizing States and Delinquent Refusals of the New Frontier*. Durham, NC: Duke University Press, 2012.

Roseberry, William. "Social Fields and Cultural Encounters." In *Close Encounters of Empire: Writing the Cultural History of U.S.–Latin American Relations*, edited by Gilbert M. Joseph, Catherine C. LeGrand, and Ricardo D. Salvatore, 515–524. Durham, NC: Duke University Press, 1998.

Ruiz, Vicki L. "By the Day or the Week: Mexicana Domestic Workers in El Paso." In *Women on the U.S.-Mexico Border: Responses to Change*, edited by Vicki L. Ruiz and Susan Tiano, 61–76. Boston: Allen Unwin, 1987.

Rutherford, Danilyn. *Laughing at Leviathan: Sovereignty and Audience in West Papua*. Chicago: University of Chicago Press, 2012.

Saldaña-Portillo, Josefina María. *Indian Given: Racial Geographies across Mexico and the United States*. Durham, NC: Duke University Press, 2016.

Salinas Domínguez, Manuel I. *Orígenes de Nuevo Laredo*. Victoria, Tamaulipas: Universidad Autónoma de Tamaulipas, 1981.

Salter, Mark. "Places Everyone! Studying the Performativity of the Border." *Political Geography* 30 (2011): 66–67.

Sánchez Munguía, V. "La actual lucha del gobierno mexicano contra la delincuencia en la frontera con Estados Unidos." *Frontera Norte* 23, no. 45 (2011): 97–129.

Sassen, Saskia. "Spatialities and Temporalities of the Global: Elements for a Theorization." *Public Culture* 12, no. 1 (2000): 215–232.

Schechner, Richard. *Between Theater and Anthropology*. Philadelphia: University of Pennsylvania Press, 1985.

———. *Environmental Theater*. New York: Hawthorne, 1973.

———. *Performance Studies: An Introduction*. 3rd ed. New York: Routledge, 2013.

Schwenkel, Christina. "Spectacular Infrastructure and Its Breakdown in Socialist Vietnam." *American Ethnologist* 42, no. 3 (2015): 520–534.

Shanks, Ann. *Laredo: Reflections*. Laredo, TX: Velia E. Uribe, 1985.

Shapira, Harel. "The Border: Infrastructure of the Global." *Public Culture* 25, no. 2 (2013): 249–260.

Simone, AbdouMaliq. "People as Infrastructure: Intersecting Fragments in Johannesburg." *Public Culture* 16, no. 3 (2004): 407–429.

Simpson, Audra. *Mohawk Interruptus: Political Life across the Borders of Settler States*. Durham, NC: Duke University Press, 2014.

Singer, Milton. *When a Great Tradition Modernizes: An Anthropological Approach to Modern Civilization*. New York: Praeger, 1972.

Sloan, John W., and Jonathon P. West. "Community Integration and Policies among Elites in Two Border Cities: Los dos Laredos." *Journal of Interamerican Studies and World Affairs* 18, no. 4 (1976): 451–474.

Slotkin, Richard. *Regeneration through Violence: The Mythology of the American Frontier, 1600–1860.* Norman: University of Oklahoma Press, 2000.

Spener, David. *Clandestine Crossings: Migrants and Coyotes on the Texas-Mexico Border.* Ithaca, NY: Cornell University Press, 2009.

Squint, Dale. *My Border Patrol Diary.* Bloomington, IN: AuthorHouse, 2007.

Stamp, R. M. *Bridging the Border: The Structures of Canadian-American Relations.* Toronto: Dundurn Press, 1992.

Stoss, Matthew. "The Border Ball." *GW Magazine* (2019): 2–10.

Swartz, Mimi. "Once Upon a Time in Laredo." *National Geographic* (November/December 2006): 94–109.

Tambiah, Stanley J. "A Performative Approach to Ritual." *Proceedings of the British Academy* 65 (1980): 113–169.

Tarver, E. R. *Laredo, the Gate Way between the United States and Mexico: An Illustrated Description of the Future City of the Great Southwest.* Laredo, TX: Laredo Daily Times, 1889.

Taylor, Diana. *The Archive and the Repertoire: Performing Cultural Memory in the Americas.* Durham, NC: Duke University Press, 2003.

———. *Disappearing Acts: Spectacles of Gender and Nationalism in Argentina's "Dirty War."* Durham, NC: Duke University Press, 1997.

———. "Performance and/as History." *TDR: The Drama Review* 50, no. 1 (2006): 67–86.

Tenorio-Trillo, Mauricio. *Mexico at the World's Fairs: Crafting a Modern Nation.* Berkeley: University of California Press, 1996.

Texas Highway Department. *Laredo Urban Transportation Study.* Origin Destination Survey, vol. 1. Laredo, TX: Department of Transportation, 1964.

Thompson, Jerry. *Warm Weather and Bad Whiskey: The 1886 Laredo Election Riot.* El Paso: Texas Western Press, 1991.

Truett, Samuel, Elliott Young, Karl Jacoby, and Raúl Ramos, eds. *Continental Crossroads: Remapping US-Mexico Borderlands History.* Durham, NC: Duke University Press, 2004.

Turner, Frederick Jackson. *Frontier and Section: Selected Essays of Frederick Jackson Turner,* edited by Ray Allen Billington. Englewood Cliffs, NJ: Prentice-Hall, 1961.

Turner, John Kenneth. *Barbarous Mexico.* Austin: University of Texas Press, 1969.

Turner, Victor. *The Anthropology of Performance.* New York: Performing Arts Journal Publications, 1986.

———. Dramas, Fields, and Metaphors: Symbolic Action in Human Societies. Ithaca, NY: Cornell University Press, 1974.

———. *The Ritual Process: Structure and Anti-Structure.* Ithaca, NY: Cornell University Press, 1969.

Valenzuela Arce, José Manuel, ed. *Por las fronteras del norte: Una aproximación cultural a la frontera México-Estados Unidos.* Mexico, DF: Fondo de Cultura Económica, 2003.

Valerio-Jiménez, Omar S. *River of Hope: Forging Identity and Nation in the Rio Grande Borderlands.* Durham, NC: Duke University Press, 2013.

Vélez-Ibáñez, Carlos. *Hegemonies of Language and Their Discontents: The Southwest North American Region since 1540.* Tucson: University of Arizona Press, 2017.

Vélez-Ibáñez, Carlos, and Josiah Heyman, eds. *The US-Mexico Transborder Region:*

Cultural Dynamics and Historical Interactions. Tucson: University of Arizona Press, 2017.

Venkatesan, Soumhya, Laura Bear, Penny Harvey, Sian Lazar, Laura Rival, and AbdouMaliq Simone. "Attention to Infrastructure Offers a Welcome Reconfiguration of Anthropological Approaches to the Political." *Critique of Anthropology* 38, no. 1 (2018): 3–52.

Venken, Machteld. *Borderland Studies Meets Child Studies: A European Encounter*. New York: Peter Lang, 2017.

Vila, Pablo. *Crossing Borders, Reinforcing Borders: Social Categories, Metaphors, and Narrative Identities on the US-Mexico Frontier*. Austin: University of Texas Press, 2000.

Walsh, Casey. *Building the Borderlands: A Transnational History of Irrigated Cotton along the Mexico-Texas Border*. College Station: Texas A&M University Press, 2008.

Ward, Peter M. *Colonias and Public Policy in Texas and Mexico*. Austin: University of Texas Press, 1999.

Weber, David J. "Conflicts and Accommodations: Hispanic and Anglo-American Borders in Historical Perspective, 1670–1853." *Journal of the Southwest* 39, no. 1 (1997): 1–32.

Weeks, O. Douglas. "The League of United Latin-American Citizens." *Southwestern Political and Social Science Quarterly* 10, no. 3 (1929): 257–278.

Wimmer, Andreas, and Nina Glick Schiller. "Methodological Nationalism, the Social Sciences, and the Study of Migration." *International Migration Review* 37, no. 2 (2003): 576–610.

Wooldridge, Ruby, and Robert B. Vezzetti. "The Founding of Charro Days." In *More Studies in Brownsville History*, edited by Milo Kearney, 390–391. Brownsville: University of Texas at Brownsville, 1989.

Yang, Chun. "The Geopolitics of Cross-Boundary Governance in the Greater Pearl River Delta, China: A Case Study of the Proposed Hong Kong-Zhuhai-Macao Bridge." *Political Geography* 25, no. 7 (2006): 817–835.

Yoder, Michael. "La infraestructura del transporte y la planeación urbana en la zona fronteriza México y Texas: El caso del desarrollo de tres puentes internacionales." In *El noreste de México y Texas: Asimetrías y convergencias territoriales en la relaciones transfronterizas*, edited by Roberto García Ortega and José Antonio Trujeque Díaz, 89–119. Mexico, DF: El Colegio de la Frontera Norte y Porrúa, 2009.

Yokota, Kariann Akemi. *Unbecoming British: How Revolutionary America Became a Postcolonial Nation*. New York: Oxford University Press, 2011.

Young, Elliott. "Deconstructing 'la Raza': Identifying the 'Gente Decente' of Laredo, 1904–1911." *Southwestern Historical Quarterly* 98, no. 2 (1994): 227–259.

———. "Red Men, Princess Pocahontas, and George Washington: Harmonizing Race Relations in Laredo at the Turn of the Century." *Western Historical Quarterly* 29, no. 1 (1998): 48–85.

Index

Page numbers in *italics* indicate information contained in images or image captions.